D1395386

£60.05
D
KD

The Russian Civil War
Primary Sources

A. B. Murphy
Professor Emeritus
University of Ulster

with the assistance of

F. Patrikeeff
Lecturer in Politics
University of Adelaide

First published in Great Britain 2000 by
MACMILLAN PRESS LTD
Houndmills, Basingstoke, Hampshire RG21 6XS and London
Companies and representatives throughout the world

A catalogue record for this book is available from the British Library.

ISBN 0–333–77013–7

 First published in the United States of America 2000 by
ST. MARTIN'S PRESS, LLC,
Scholarly and Reference Division,
175 Fifth Avenue, New York, N.Y. 10010

ISBN 0–312–23232–2

Library of Congress Cataloging-in-Publication Data
Murphy, Brian, 1923–
The Russian Civil War : primary sources / A.B. Murphy.
p.   cm.
Includes bibliographical references and index.
ISBN 0–312–23232–2
1. Soviet Union—History—Revolution, 1917–1921—Sources. I. Title.

DK265 .A5255   2000
947.084'1—dc21
                                                                99–059567

This book is printed on paper suitable for recycling and made from fully managed and sustained forest sources.

10   9   8   7   6   5   4   3   2   1
09   08   07   06   05   04   03   02   01   00

Printed and bound in Great Britain by
Antony Rowe Ltd, Chippenham, Wiltshire

To John Simmons

Contents

Preface

Every history book comes to us ready packaged with the views of its author, charged with the prejudices and assumptions of our time. Memoirs can be notoriously unreliable. The recollections of those who shaped events are often exercises in self-justification, deceiving both the reader – and sometimes the author himself. To get at the raw material of history we must go to direct evidence from the period. Documents are incontrovertible truth that so-and-so set these words down at the time history was being made. Readers can at least use their own intelligence to suggest what motivated the speaker to say this at the time. We also gain the ability to judge more clearly how historians have interpreted their sources in the light of subsequent events.

Documents are the stuff from which a historical overview must be constructed. Some of the more public files show the grand designs of the leaders who were making large scale decisions. Others 'from below' transmit clearly the reactions of those who were making history at the time. There is no better way to capture the 'feel' of the Russian Revolution and civil war than by passing through our hands the rough scraps of paper on which those at the front recorded the triumphs or disasters of the days they were living through, their appeals for more men, for more food and clothing – to forestall those at the front from running back to their homes where so much lay neglected in their absence. The commander who orders the grand strategy must always remember that he is relying on the steadfastness of his men to risk death, mutilation or disease for what may seem to many to be remote and unattainable ideals.

Both sides in the civil war perpetrated unspeakable outrages; both sides suffered immense hardships. The Reds, particularly, went short of the most elementary supplies, and their forces were subject to what must seem absurdly high rates of desertion. It is only natural that documents record mostly what has gone wrong, and what must be put right. There is much less need to expand in reports if everything is going according to plan. When we read the pieces in this selection we may be led to wonder how the Communists managed to achieve victory. We have to offset the negative factors revealed in these pages by remembering that the Red Army cannot have been made up completely of careerists, time-servers, or potential deserters, that there were many commanders and men who believed fiercely in the ideals of the Revolution.

I collected the documents for this book on visits to Russia when the archives became accessible for non-Soviet citizens. Vaughan James has made excellent translations of the pieces relating to Budyonny, and I translated the rest. I am most grateful to the staff in the archives at RTsKhIDNI (Rossiysky Tsentr Khraneniya i Izucheniya Dokumentov Noveyshey Istorii, formerly Tsentralny Partiyny Arkhiv Instituta Marksizma–Leninizma, pri TsK KPSS, Moscow), and also GARO (Gosudarstenny arkhiv Rostovskoy oblasti)...

I wish to thank the British Academy for facilitating the research visits to Russian archives on which this book is based. I am most grateful to A. V. Venkov, who gave invaluable help on the historical background to several documents. I would also like to thank Harry Shukman, Herman Ermolaev, Geoffrey and Diana Swain for useful advice on editing the texts. I am indebted to my wife, Joan, and to John Simmons for their careful reading of the proofs. Finally, I must pay tribute to my editor, Keith Povey, sharp-eyed, wise and most helpful in finalizing the work to be printed. I am of course responsible for any errors remaining.

To enable readers to trace the Russian versions items are headed where possible: *fond, opis', delo yedineniye sokhraneniya* has also been abbreviated to *d., list* (page). To the best of my knowledge, only one of these pieces has been previously translated into English, and few of them have appeared in Russian printed sources.

As far as possible I have tried to present documents as a whole and kept my commentary separate, generally preceding the document to which it relates. Many letters and reports were compiled in the turbulence of the civil war by men whose grasp of syntax was less than perfect. I have not attempted to reproduce this feature in my English translation. Some pieces are rich in the period's repetitious clichés, and in a few cases I have pruned out a little verbiage. Most documents are signed at the end, often with the signature attested by a junior officer. Where possible I have tried to place at the start: addressee, originator and date. I have transliteratd Cyrillic into Roman letters on the basis of the former SEER system, though I have not always marked soft signs with an apostrophe.

A. B. Murphy

Introduction

Conflicting views of the post-revolutionary struggle

Russia's civil war of 1917–20 cast a long shadow on the entire history of the twentieth century. Open conflict started after the October Revolution, and is conventionally regarded as ending when the main White forces were evacuated from the Crimea three years later. It would be simplistic to see the struggle as purely between the Bolsheviks and 'the others'. Both sides had diverse strands of 'left' or 'right' opinion, and the interests of both sides cut across nationalist aspirations in outlying regions of the former Tsarist Empire. John Bradley rightly observed that there is an innate problem for historians describing any civil war from the 'outside'. He argued that the Russian civil war was a conflict that 'remains so topical and politically controversial that not only politicians and ideologues but also historians tend to take up philosophic positions and quarrel among themselves' (Bradley, 1975, p. 9).

With the collapse of the Soviet Union in 1991, one might expect the topicality of the conflict would lose its edge – notwithstanding the opening of Soviet archives which provide so much grist to the historians' mill. However, a problem arose when the political side of the equation was diminished. With the eclipse of the political positions taken up by historians accusing their peers of 'bourgeois falsification' (or, from the other side, 'political time-serving', as Bradley puts it), the exercise of looking at the civil war became remote and 'academic'. In the former Soviet Union the desire to know about its past was quickly replaced by the pressures of how to deal with a bleak present and a troubled future. Russian scholars have been hampered in their ability to contribute to the debate by the disappearance of any extensive market or public forum for their ideas. The policy of 'glasnost' opened up access to memoirs and archives which had previously not been available to them, but Russians of the older generation were often unable to exploit these new sources because they had been trained in rather pedantic methods of historical analysis.

Much of the work that has appeared since previous taboos were lifted has been shaped by non-Russians, who have striven to produce new interpretations of the civil war period. In 'the West' some scholars are now querying whether the civil war can properly be said to have finished in 1920. They suggest that conventional Russian historians may have underplayed the importance of later resistance to the Soviets, which continued after 1920 in Central Asia, eastern Siberia and the Russian Far East. A striking example is provided by General Diterikhs who led his men against the Red Army through to the autumn of 1922, when he was eventually forced to retreat into China (see Butt *et al.*, 1996, ch. 5 'The Final Curtain').

The civil war gave rise to a long debate on the importance of individuals in the conflict. Stalin must be given some credit for his part in the defence of Tsaritsyn, but, as he became all-powerful in the 1930s time-serving scribes were busy fabricating a hagiography for him, as if his contribution had been the decisive factor in the Red Army's victory. In reality it was Trotsky who played an omnipresent role, his image enhanced by his untiring activity as strategist, activist, combatant and – it must be said – the most forceful commentator on the events he had helped to shape.

Core and periphery: the conduct of the war

The new Soviet system quickly took shape in European Russia. Major exceptions to this transformation were Ukraine, the Cossack lands of the Don, the Volga, coastal areas round the Caspian, the Black Sea and the Sea of Azov. After the October Revolution Ukrainians held an election in which the Bolsheviks gained only 10 per cent of the seats in the Assembly, the majority wishing to establish the Ukrainian People's Republic. Only in one small area, Kharkov, were the Bolsheviks victorious.

The White officers in the south named themselves the 'Volunteer Army', and allied with them were many Cossacks in the Don Army (Donskoye Voysko). It was mainly the better-off Cossacks who were set against the Bolsheviks. On the Don, Ataman Kaledin declared a state of war on 9 December, threatening Kharkov and Yekaterinoslav.

Novocherkassk, the Don Cossack capital, became the cradle of the White Volunteer Army which came together rapidly under General Alekseyev, the former Tsar's Chief of Staff.

Supporting Alekseyev and Kaledin, Ataman Dutov opened up a line of resistance taking in Chelyabinsk, Ufa and Orenburg in the Urals. In defiance of the Soviet government's ultimatum the Ukrainian People's Republic aligned itself with Kaledin. Soviet forces under Antonov-Ovseyenko quickly defeated Ukrainian troops at Kharkov in January 1918, occupying Kiev on 29 January. Antonov-Ovseyenko's forces completed the conquest of Ukraine, but the line of resistance to Soviet power had been set into place.

On 10 January 1918 Soviet forces began an offensive on the lower Don against Kaledin's Cossacks and General Kornilov's Volunteer Army, which was based in Taganrog, Rostov and Novocherkassk. Facing the loss of the Don, Kaledin committed suicide in Novocherkassk. Kornilov took command of the Whites. He abandoned Rostov and entered the Kuban, but was killed in a vain attempt to take the Kuban capital, Yekaterinodar. Denikin then assumed command of the Volunteer Army, moving it from the Kuban to the Don.

The Red Army: dilemmas of recruitment

There were two levels on which the Bolsheviks had to fight for victory. One was to deal with a conflict which was fragmented over huge distances in European and Asiatic Russia. The other was the question of the Bolshevik self-image.

To cope with the great task of dealing with the conflict, expansive strategies were adopted. On 29 May 1918 conscription was introduced, and the first steps were taken to create a uniform force on a country-wide basis. The task of organizing this force was entrusted to Trotsky as Commissar for War. The purpose of the Red Army was to conduct operations against any counter-revolutionary armies confronting Soviet Russia. In addition to this, Revolutionary Military Councils were to control each front, with Trotsky as Chairman of the supreme RVS, responsible for the overall conduct of the war.

The centralization of forces was a wise action for a number of reasons. One advantage was that the Communists could deal more easily with internally dissonant groups within the White movement. Centralization also provided the Soviet war effort with an image, around which separate actions could be rallied. Such promotional efforts were quite slow to give results. For example, the image of a Red

Army did not dramatically increase the response to conscription notices. The Kremlin remained disappointed for some time because it had raised only half the number of recruits it felt it needed. By the autumn of 1918, thanks to harsh conscription policies, the Red Army had risen to 400 000. By the end of 1920 the numbers reached the astonishing total of five million.

Partly due to this rise in numbers, the questions of image and ideological commitment remained, and indeed were to become more pressing. The loyalty of ordinary soldiers could often be relied on from a combination of their simple patriotism and by providing them with essentials, such as suitable clothing, footwear and food. It remains a remarkable aside to the conflict in Siberia that White forces were unable to capitalize on their Western Front. Thousands of men swarmed across the Urals, only to find that the White leaders would not meet their most basic needs – for food, warm clothing and boots. The Bolsheviks, on the other hand, quickly realized that this was a fundamental way to win over recruits, and therefore ensured that these needs were dealt with at railway stations while the men were in transit. Despite the initial success of this strategy, Bolshevik supply lines began to shrivel as the conflict wore on. The present set of documents shows all too clearly how failure of supplies could affect the fighting spirit of the troops. If supplies ran short, morale and ideological commitment were plagued by a degree of uncertainty that resulted in very high rates of desertion.

In such a tangled struggle talented and imaginative commanders were essential. The Soviet government had to recruit former Tsarist officers into its new Red Army. How could they be relied on to serve the new State loyally? The issue became all the more pressing, given the vagaries of conscription. If the political reliability of enlisted men could not be trusted, all the more important became the need to have solid, politically correct leadership in the field. This was even more essential for filling the highest strategy-making posts. To some extent the dilemma had been resolved by natural selection: Tsarist officers opposed to the Soviet regime had already joined the White forces. Others had been killed off by their own men in the early stages of revolution.

The Red Army's high command was staffed almost entirely by former Tsarist officers, including Colonel S. S. Kamenev, who had served on the Tsar's general staff. Trotsky maintained a remarkably mobile control of the new army and covered enormous distances to command its operations. His armoured train moved from one front to another, carrying him as supreme commander, his staff officers, technicians and teachers of Soviet ideology, thereby developing not only central control over the forces, but generating important *élan*. His mobile headquarters, which came to be known simply as 'Trotsky's train', became a legend, reportedly covering a hundred thousand miles in its two and a half years of existence. More pragmatic forms of control were also in place: Bolshevik commissars at the front kept their revolvers at the ready, and the families of officers suspected of ideological weakness were held as hostages to ensure the officers' political reliability.

The new army was a successful concept, brought into being despite formidable difficulties. Trotsky's ideas appeared to have been proven correct. Despite this, critics of his strategy – as a group these were known as 'The Military Opposition' – remained implacable, notably Stalin, who had been despatched to Tsaritsyn as Food Controller to oversee the flow of grain from the northern Caucasus and the lower Volga. Stalin used this posting to create a quasi-independent centre of military authority for himself in that town, and persistently defied Trotsky's orders in defending it. A central argument in the criticism that Stalin levelled against Trotsky was precisely the use of Tsarist ex-officers in the Red Army. On 4 October 1918 Trotsky forced Stalin's recall, thereby fuelling what was to become a long and bitter struggle between two of Lenin's most powerful aides. The significance of Tsaritsyn as an alternative centre of power and political intrigue is demonstrated by documents in this collection.

Reasons for success: the hand of historical inevitability

From the account given above, it seems clear that Bolshevik victory was due to a combination of factors. In addition to those already discussed there was the element of chance: the Whites were ranged around an extended periphery, giving the Communists the strategic advantage of inner communications. Coupled with this was the overriding impression that the White armies and their governments had no concerted plan of action. It could be argued that the outcome might have been very different, if there had been greater coordination. With the exception of a brief moment in the summer of 1919, at no point was there a concerted drive on a number of fronts, which might have squeezed an over-extended Bolshevik war effort into weakness and disarray.

We may also look at the positive steps taken by the Communists and their Red Army in defending the young Soviet State. Here we must

note the revolutionary fervour and strength of purpose that characterized Bolshevik warfare. Of equal importance were the inspirational
qualities and daring of Trotsky's leadership. And, finally, the so-called
'White Terror' perpetrated by the White forces, bent on expunging left-
wing influence in territory held by them, was repellent to an otherwise
conservative peasantry.

The more frayed the White war effort appeared, the more pronounced was the sense of the Red Army's increasing might, reinforced
by Trotsky's steely leadership and growing popular appeal, with his
larger-than-life image and presence on every front. This was aided by
the Communist hierarchy's concerted effort to generate the image of a
'hero army' for its forces.

The year 1919 must be seen as the vital turning point when the
history of the twentieth century was shaped for good or ill. Most
people would now regard the Soviet Union with a mixture of horror
and ridicule. Its claims to superiority seem derisory when viewed in the
light of collectivization, Stalinism and economic stagnation. We have
to make an imaginative leap to comprehend how the ideals of the
Russian Revolution could inspire men to risk their all – how its objectives seemed so desirable and their attainment easy to grasp. Some of
the documents which follow can help us to feel the zeal and single-
mindedness which were the bread of life for so many Communists at
that time.

1
1918: Germans Rout Reds

Yield nothing to the Germans

Soviet policy after revolution was led by the expectation that other nations would shake off the capitalists who were exploiting them, and join Russia in a peaceful Socialist world. As the Russian army streamed back from the front the Bolsheviks were forced to accept the humiliating terms of the Treaty of Brest-Litovsk, which they eventually signed on 3 March 1918. However, the Germans had by far the most powerful force in Russia, and soon showed they would serve their own interests without any nicety of scruple. The following General Order comes from the period after 18 February, when the Communist government was still trying to gain time by refusing to sign the Treaty.

GARO f. 3440, op. 1, d. 13, l.1

To: Vladikavkaz, 23/10/2 Circular to all Soviets for People's Deputies.
From: Latsis, People's Commissar for Internal Affairs, Petrograd.

The Department of Local Administration of the Commissariat of Internal Affairs is communicating to you resolutions of the Soviet of People's Commissars of 21 February. We agreed to a huge sacrifice, and declared to the Germans our readiness to sign their conditions of peace. In the evening of 27 February our envoys left Rezhitse (Rezekne) Dvinsk, and there still is no reply. The German Government is evidently delaying its answer. We are in danger till the German proletariat rise. The Soviet of People's Commissars decrees:

(1) All forces must go into the cause of the revolutionary struggle.
(2) Defend every position to the last drop of blood.
(3) It must be a cast-iron principle that organizations controlling ways of communication, and the Soviets connected to them, must make every endeavour to prevent the enemy using the road and rail network. When retreating they must destroy roads and burn railway buildings. All rolling stock, carriages and locomotives must be immediately sent east into the depths of our country.
(4) All stocks of grain and all foodstocks in general, as also any valuable property in danger of falling into enemy hands, must be completely destroyed.
(5) Mobilize battalions to dig trenches.
(6) These battalions must contain members of the bourgeois class. Anyone who resists is to be shot.
(7) All publications against the idea of revolutionary defence are to be shut down. Mobilize for trench digging editors and staff of these journals who are fit for work.
(8) Counter-revolutionary propagandists and German spies are to be shot at the scene of their crime.

Don Soviet Republic

The civil war started in the Urals, Siberia, and on the Don shortly after the Bolsheviks took power in Petrograd in October 1917. The armed forces on the Bolshevik side were originally known as Red Guards. The more formal term 'Red Army' was not introduced till February 1918, and the designation Red Guards continued to be widely used throughout the war.

During its later years the Tsarist government relied largely on the Cossacks to put down disturbances. They were regarded as being hostile to any sort of liberal reform, hated for their anti-Semitism and the brutality with which they repressed any manifestation of dissent.

At the end of the nineteenth century the population of the Cossack territories was becoming diluted by non-Cossacks, who came in from the central Russian homeland. By 1914 Cossacks made up only half the population on the Don. In areas where Cossacks predominated, their system of land tenure attempted a crude sort of justice: for each male child a family was given an allotment of land, and if the household did not farm this land well the village could take it back, to be reassigned. Increased population density had made it difficult to provide each family with a holding which could meet their needs. In the latter half of 1917, in areas where the Cossacks were in a minority, the non-Cossack population put into practice a form of 'de-Cossackification', aimed at destroying the structure of Cossack society, and making it easier for non-Cossacks to acquire land.

In 1917, as the Imperial Army disintegrated, Cossack units eventually deserted from the front. Many found their way back to the Don and the Kuban, getting rid of former officers on the way, and electing their own commanders. Under the Provisional Government an All-Russian Peasant Congress noted in May 1917 that Cossacks had larger farms than the non-Cossack peasants, and decreed that they should give up some of their land to make a fairer apportionment throughout Russia. In June, an All-Russian Cossack Congress declared in favour of leaving each Voysko its own land. Trying to be all things to all men the Provisional Government took no steps to resolve this conflict of views.

On 26 November 1917, Rostov came for several days into the hands of the Soviet, which was dominated by the Bolsheviks. Their comparatively weak forces were driven out on 2 December, and they vied with General Kaledin for the loyalty of the Cossack regiments which were returning from the front. In January 1918 the Reds summoned a conference in Kamenskaya, which elected Podtyolkov and Krivoshlykov as their leaders. They made a show of negotiating with Kaledin in Novocherkassk, but not surprisingly, reconciliation could not be achieved. On 11 February 1918 Kaledin declared himself unable to withstand the Bolsheviks, and committed suicide.

The Don Cossack Military Revolutionary Committee sought support from Moscow. Antonov-Ovseyenko, commanding the Communists' Southern Front, made it clear that they must recognize the authority of the Council of People's Commissars, which they agreed to. Lenin welcomed the establishment of Soviet power on the Don, and on 23 March the Don Soviet Republic was proclaimed, retaining Podtyolkov and Krivoshlykov as its leaders. Podtyolkov's Revolutionary Committee refused to pass on arms to miners' representatives or to countenance any ceding of land holdings to non-Cossacks. Podtyolkov favoured the Reds, but he was not formally enrolled as a Bolshevik. His regime came close to enjoying independence as a separate Cossack Republic.

Thinking in Marxist terms Lenin could only consider Cossack society as a hostile class. With his usual pragmatism, he nonetheless welcomed the establishment of the Don Soviet Republic. Throughout the civil war the Soviet Government gained much from their flexible attitude towards meeting aspirations for some form of local autonomy in outlying areas of the former Russian Empire. From the outset there were bound to be tensions between Podtyolkov, as a true-born Cossack, and Syrtsov, who had been schooled in Communist doctrine in Petrograd. Formally, however, Podtyolkov agreed to place himself under the military direction of Antonov-Ovesyenko.

The documents in this section may be accounted something of a rarity. Collected as they were from an area which was a veritable cockpit of the civil war, we may be surprised that so many have survived in the archives, even if they are not always in a perfectly ordered state. The following pieces were filed in the State Archive of Rostov Oblast (GARO). This selection should be a useful source for studying the events of 1918.

Nominal roll

GARO f. 3440, op. 1, d. 2, l.87

To: Persons in authority in the Military Revolutionary Council of the
Don Oblast.
List
Composed March 1918

(I) Administration Section
Presidium of Oblast Military Revolutionary Committee

Podyolkov F. G.	Chairman	Palace Hotel No. 30 [*first two sections all in Palace Hotel + Bocharnikov and Dement' ev*]
Krivoshlykov M. V.	Secretary	"
Doroshev I. A.	Second secretary	
Yermilov I. A.	Deputy	
Syrtsov S. I.		Palace Hotel 35/ Lermontovskaya 75
Chentsov		
Vlasov		

Secretariat of Administration

Polyakov L. F.	Personal Secretary
Sudarkin P. E.	Chief Clerk
Sinebryvkhov I. I.	Clerk
Dukmasov	"
Sutormin I. I.	"
Minodayev Ya. V.	"
Boldyrev N. I.	"

(II) National Economy Section

Syrtsov S. I.	Chairman	Lermontovskaya ul. 75
Popova A. Ye.	Secretary	Dmitriyevskaya 122
Bocharnikov I. V.	Official	
Kirsta K. A.	"	Lermontovskaya 75
Tatarinov A. P.	"	Bratsk 72, apartment 5
Shchepkin M. I	"	
Mosolov A. K.	"	
Zubov S. M.	"	
Dementev A. Ya.	"	N. Bushv 4
Zak S. Ye.	"	

(III) Finance Section

Strelyanov P. P.	Superintendent of section	Palace Hotel 53
Bolotin Ye. A.	Official	"
Parfanyak P. A.	"	"
Dell	Clerk	
Mashenistka	"	

(IV) Communications Section

Bezrukikh P. Ye.	Commissar	Rail station, South-east railways
Ivanov Z. D.	Assistant	
Khmel′ nitsky N. Ye.	″	

(V) Political Education Section

Yermilov N. A.			
Doroshev I. A.			
Frenkel′			
Kovalyov I. I.	Official	Bratsky 79	
Simonov I. I.	″	Palace Hotel 32	
Zakharov	″	″	
Chernikov S.	″	″	31
Shkrudev A. G.	″	″	54

(VI) Troop Movement Section

Gavrilov V. I.	Superintendent	Palace Hotel
Gusev D. I.	Official	″

(VII) Food Supply Section

Vasil′ev S. K.	Superintendent	″

(VIII) Prisoner of War Section

Vasil′ chenko		″	
Kriushov	Committee member	″	35
Koptarov			
Sukhorevksy	″	″	98

(IX) Labour Section

Babkin Iv. Petr.	Ul. [itsa] Star[oy] – Pochtovoy and Bol[′shoy] prosp[ekt] d.[om] professoyuzov

Individual appointments

In the weeks before the Don Soviet Republic was set up in March, there was a confused time during which the Communists were trying to set up some primitive basis of rule on the Don. Among a population which was still largely illiterate one can understand all too well the many misspellings in the following attestation.

On 1 February 1918 the Soviets had gone over to the Western (Gregorian) calendar, redating 1 February Old Style as 14 February New Style. Shchetovsky's 'application' was written shortly after the change had taken place, hence his reference to 20/7 February.

The following documents refer to the 1st Don Cossack Independent Battalion.

f. 3440, op. 1, d. 25, l.2

Certificate
10 February 1918

This document has been issued by the village administration of V. Bubnovsky, coming from the Military Revolutionary Committee for comrades Klimov and Yushkin, to certify that today they were at a meeting in the village. They were speaking in favour of organizing the administration of the rights of the working class people. This is attested by the village administration of V. Bubnovsky.

Signed and sealed 10 February

f. 3440, op. 1, d. 25, l.6

To: Don Oblast Military Revolutionary Committee.
From: Commander of 2nd Squadron of 20th Don Cossack Regiment, Vasiliy
Shchetkovsky.
Application
13 March 1918

On 20/7 February I sent an application to the Oblast Military Revolutionary Committee requesting leave of absence from 20th Don Cossack Regiment, to visit the house of my father who is a priest at the Voysko Horse Stud, and in the application I asked the Committee to issue instructions concerning my request. But up to now I have received no instructions or orders from the Committee. I most humbly beg the Committee to give me some indication of how I am to proceed. My postal and telegraphic address is as follows: Proval' station, Yekaterinodar Railway, Voysko Stud Farm, Vasily Shchetkovsky.

Commander of 2 Squadron Shchetkovsky

f. 3440, op. 1, d. 25, l.9

To: Committee of Internal Management of the main workshops in Rostov on Don.
From: Skilled workers and workers of the main Rostov workshops.
Warrant
13 March 1918

Acting on a proposal of the Military Revolutionary Committee, as expressed at a general meeting of skilled workers and workers in the Main Railway workshops on 13 March 1918 –

The General Meeting of Railwaymen welcomes the proposal of the Oblast Military Revolutionary Committee to elect a representative from its ranks, on whom they will place the duty to render assistance to the Military Revolutionary Committee, contributing his experience and knowledge of railwayman's business.

Comrade KORPENKO has been elected as this type of representative, and he is hereby empowered to act as the representative of the railwaymen.

Chairman   signatures
Secretary

f. 3440, op. 1, d. 25, l.8

Main Railways Committee of Railwaymen's Union of Vladikavkaz line 1404,
Rostov on Don.
Warrant
14 March 1918

The bearer of this document, being a Member of Railwaymen's Union of Vladikavkaz line, KORPENKO, has been elected by the Main Railwaymen's Committee to attend in a permanent capacity the Oblast Military Revolutionary Committee, which is hereby affirmed by my signature and the application of the official seal.

To be presented

Secretary   signature

f. 3440, op. 1, d. 25, l.14

To: Rostov Oblast Military Revolutionary Committee.
Form: Executive Committee of Donets District Soviet.
Telegram   *Urgent*

Executive Committee of Donets District Soviet asks permission to keep in post for the time being the member of Oblast Military Revolutionary Committee, comrade Shurupov, until the conflict of the Kamenskaya garrison has been settled.

signed for the Chairman Bondarev

f. 3440, op 1, d. 25, l.15

To: ? Rostov on Don Oblast Committee.
From: Army Commander, Smirnov, ?R Novocherkassk.

A general meeting of workers asks that Zaporozhtsev should be confirmed in his post as stationmaster at Novocherkassk, instead of Tolstoglazov who has been appointed. I request instructions.

Army Commander, Smirnov

During the struggle to establish Soviet power in 1918, Kovalyov made his name as a Cossack devoted to the Soviets. It is significant that in this early stage of the civil war the Bolsheviks appointed another Cossack, Trifonov, as his second-in-command. This would contrast with their anti-Cossack feeling in 1919, when they obviously distrusted even Kovalyov.

f. 3440, op. 1, d. 4, l.127

Order No. 140
22 April 1918

Comrade Kovalyov is appointed to command our forces operating against the counter-revolutionary troops, with comrade Trifonov as his second in command. Comrade Degtyarev is appointed as Chief of Staff, comrade Zolotov as Quartermaster, comrade Pushkarev as Head of the engineer unit, Comrade Antonov Head of Column 1, comrade Sulimenko of Column 2.

It is proposed that the Executive Committee of Novocherkassk Soviet should immediately take over the government of Novocherkassk and set right the Military Section without delay.

Alek

Central Committee member VVA

f. 3440, op. 1, d. 13, I.46

Urgent
To: comrade Podtyolkov

You promised to give me a reply to my enquiry as to who is in charge of the troops that have occupied Chir stanitsa. Trutovsky and Goloboyunsky are asking: 'Is there not someone from the Left Socialist Revolutionaries?'

I am asking on the instructions of Muralov, who commands Moscow Military District.

On the question of who commands the troops who took Chir stanitsa I do not know. Be so kind as to reply.

Disorders in Don territory

Antonov-Ovseyenko appointed Voytsekhovsky as Commissar, and he became the effective ruler of the area. In March a Party official such as Voytsekhovsky might well have found the chain of command confusing. He managed to work in conjunction with Sivers in charge of the Red forces round Tikhoretsyaka. The Soviet commander had ordered that all ex-Whites should be shot, and this threatened many people in Rostov who up to then had not been active against the Bolsheviks.

On the other hand Voytsekhovsky was confronted with Podtyolkov and his semi-independent Don Soviet Republic. Smirnov had been appointed as commander of the Red Cossacks who were supporting Podtyolkov. On several occasions, Voytsekhovsky found himself in dispute with Podtyolkov when he tried to overrule his authority.

The documents which follow relate to military dispositions which were intented to deal with sporadic disorders in the Don territory.

f. 3440, op. 1, d. 13, 1. 9

To: Voytsekhovsky, Rostov on Don; copies to Don Oblast Revolutionary
Committee; Smirnov, Commander of Don Revolutionary forces.
From: People's Commissar of Soviet Authorities of Donets Republic,
Vasilchenko, Kharkov.
Received by Ye. Semyonova 14 March 1918

Comrade Antonov is no longer here today. He has left for Kursk. I was therefore unable to speak to him about leaving part of the military equipment in Rostov, but on my own initiative I suggest to citizen Voytsekhovsky that he should meet the demands of Smirnov as commander of the forces, if that was not expressly forbidden by Comrade Antonov. You must remember that only by you and citizen Voytsekhovsky acting in line with demands made by the legal Soviet authorities can you avoid dire consequences, which otherwise must break over your head as a most grievous blow.

f. 3440, op. 1, d. 13, 1.10

To : Military Commissar, Voytsekhovsky, Rostov; copy to Military
Revolutionary Committee, Novocherkassk.
From: Commander Smirnov.
Telegram
15 March

In accordance with telegram 224 from Main Commander-in-Chief Antonov send immediately two armoured cars to be at my disposal in Novocherkassk. Pass the other two and machine-guns to be at the disposal for the time being of the Don Oblast Military Revolutionary Committee.

Commander Smirnov 59

f. 3440, op. 1, d. 4, 1. 138

To: Chairman of Central Executive Committee, Arktenitid.
From: Shabminsk.

2 armoured cars were sent with Petrenko's detachment at 8 o'clock yesterday.

To solve difficulties on the Don, some hardline Bolsheviks proposed to expel the Cossacks from the area where they had lived for centuries and to give their holdings to peasants from the poor lands further to the north. From 1917 to 1921, most Party men believed that Russian Communism would soon be helped by successful revolutions in Europe. There was a widespread feeling that the Red Army could not go to support Communists in other countries if it left a potentially hostile society behind. Those Communists, such as Trifonov, who understood Cossack pride and love for their homeland realized that driving the Cossacks from the Don could only inflame the whole population to fierce resistance against the Soviet regime.

In the following document resettlement can only be carried out after a thorough survey of the land to be redistributed and the numbers of people involved in the transfer. Koletayev uses the term *khodoki* for the men he would send in to establish how many people would involved and how much land could be given to each family. *Khodoki* was a word used to denote individuals appointed by a stanitsa to establish such details. Presumably, when Koletayev mentions 'privileged rates' he envisages that poorer families will be compensated by a more generous allocation of land.

f.3440, op. 1, d. 25, 1. 36

To: Rostov on Don (only), for distribution to all Committees of Provinces.
From: People's Commissar for Lands.

I shall explain the addendum to telegram 2375 from People's Commissar for Internal Affairs *re* ceasing the transfer of population by the necessity to restrain the people in every way possible from hasty decisions on resettlement, witness the fatal effect of selling off farming and food-producing equipment and the ruinous cost of journeys without properly appointed representatives making a preliminary survey to count what land could be transferred. A conference is being speedily convened to restart the movement of those who are being resettled. Until that conference has come to a decision it is of course impermissible that any privileged rates should be introduced. Rules for notifying migrants, and also the necessary materials, will shortly be announced.

A. Koletayev

As Cossack soldiers dispersed to their homes they were no longer influenced by Red propaganda from their units' Revolutionary Committees. In the countryside the older Cossacks continued to oppose the Reds. Even when the Soviets held elections it was the older men who were returned to rule as village atamans, so that the Don was constantly troubled by unrest against Communist rule. In the eighteenth century Catherine the Great had brought Armenians to the right bank of the Don from Nakhichevan on the Caspian. Their settlement was still referred to as a separate entity, though it had already become part of Rostov.

Torgovaya was the name of one rail station in the town of Salsk. Some documents, such as the following report from there, were composed by officials who had only a rudimentary grasp of orthography and punctuation. The Soviet Government introduced the Gregorian calendar in this month of February 1918. Hence 17 February as the date of the Congress might be adjusted to 2 March New Style. Velikoknyazheskaya was the administrative centre of Salsk District (misspelt as Sokolsky in Torgovaga's haste to compose the telegram).

GARO f. 3440, op. 1, d. 13, l.3

To: Oblast Military Revolutionary Committee, Novocherkassk; copy to Council of Commissars, Rostov.
From: Torgovaga Telegraph Office of Vladikavkaz Railway, 12 March 1918.

Following the Committee of separate revolutionary units of Cossack population of Velikoknyazheskaya stanitsa we face a threat that there may be an attempt to settle scores, with those elements of the population receiving support from other stanitas in the area. The Executive Committee of Salsk District, elected by the Congress of Soviets of District on 17 February, was forced by White partisan detachments to leave the stanitsa. On 22 February the stanitsa was occupied by partisan detachments. Arrests are being carried out and acts of violence against those who support Soviet power. We must have the backing of some military strength in order to stand up to these detachments. Seeing that the population of Salsk District have not much political consciousnesss, we run the risk of a White partisan movement growing up. To get exact information on events in the District the delegation are instructed to believe only personal identification documents.

Nizhne–Chirskaya uprising (led by Rastegayev)

At the beginning of March 1918, Colonel Rastegayev headed an anti–Soviet movement in the 2nd Don District (of which the centre was Nizhne-Chirskaya). The uprising was crushed and the rebels forced to flee to their villages. Ataman Popov sent Mamontov to help them and further trouble broke out.

Morozovskaya is situated on the River Tikhaya which flows into the Don to the west of Vyoshenskaya. The Chir was also a right-bank tributary of the Don, but flowing south from the Upper Don Ridge.

GARO f. 3440, op. 1, d. 13, l.17

To : Podtyolkov, Oblast Military Revolutionary Committee, Rostov on Don.
From: Head of Morozovsky garrison.
12 March 1918

Order has been restored in Nizhne-Chirsky. Counter-revolutionaries arrested and will be delivered to Novocherkassk.

Andreyev

Anti-Soviet rebellion, Salsk

South of the River Manych in the centre of Salsk District lay the town of Torgovy, renamed Salsk in 1926. To the north of the Manych was Velikoknyazheskaya (Proletarsk from 1920). The stanitsa Remontnaya was a local centre on the upper course of the River Sal renamed as a town, Remontnoye). The River Tsymla was a west-bank tributary entering the Don south of the River Chir (which now flows into the Tsymlyansky Reservoir at Nizhnegutov).

In 1915 Golubov commanded the 27th Cossack Regiment, as a lieutenant colonel (*voyskovoy starshina*). He had ambitions to make himself a 'Red Ataman'. He stood against Kaledin for election in December 1917, but received only 10 per cent of the votes. On 12/25 February 1918 he burst in on the last meeting of the Krug. He had leanings towards Cossack separatism and was disappointed that the command of Red forces was given to Smirnov rather than himself. He tried to hold the deposed Ataman Mitrofan Bogayevsky (brother of Afrikan) as a bargaining counter. Golubov was driven out of Novocherkassk and eventually killed at Zaplavskaya by a student, Pukhlyakov (who is thought to have been motivated by a personal feud with Golubov).

f. 3440, op. 1, d. 13, I.19

To: Oblast Military Revolutionary Committee, Novocherkassk, Note to
Commander Smirnov.
From: Puchkov, Temporary Commander of Salsk District, Velikoknyazheskaya.
29 March 1918

We are cut off from Tsaritsyn. A shell fell on Remontnaya from the direction of Tsymla. We have not yet received arms and money from Minin. Lopato, Chief of Staff of Salsk District, went off towards Remontnaya the day before yesterday. There is no news about the front along the line of Tsaritsyn. We have sent north-east to Zimovniki station a detachment of 760 men from Torgovaya, three machine-guns and two field guns. The Whites are from 60 to 70 Versts from Velikoknyazheska. Watch out for a new front – the stanitsas of Tsymlyanskaya, Romanovskaya, Ternovskaya, Yefremovskaya, Filonovskaya and Baklanovskaya have been caught up by a rebellion, which has gone as far as the hills along the Sal. The moving spirit in this is some Ataman of District 2, ' Rastegayev, elected by the people'. I telegraphed to you and Golubov about the situation which has built up. There has been no reply. If Golubov does not arrive by twelve o'clock on the eleventh [? of April] I am leaving for Novocherkassk for face-to-face talks, having first made preliminary plans to retreat in the direction of Stavropol Province and to Torgovaya.

Paromonov miners

f. 3440, op. 1, d. 13, I.40

To: Commander of Don Oblast, Antonov, Rostov-on-Don.
From: Andreyev, Military Commissar at Morozovskaya.
April 1918

Lower Chir front has been abandoned by Military Revolutionary soliders. Chir stanitsa has been occupied by Whites. The garrison is too weak to face the Whites on its own. It cannot hold out. This threatens the whole line of the Donets and the railway, and Soviet power in the area. Take steps to prepare defence. The telegraph is not working, there is no way of repairing it.

The Russian of the following telegram (1. 28), composed evidently under stress, contained virtually no punctuation. Paromonov was a Cossack merchant, who owned the so-called 'Paromonov Mines',

80 kilometres north of Rostov. The centre of the district was the town of Aleksandrov-Grushevsky, later renamed Shakhty ('mines') In 1918 some Communist policy was still aimed at winning Cossacks to their cause, and in pursuit of this they tended to fill many official posts with Cossacks. This led to considerable resentment among the miners, hence this outburst against Podtyolkov's rule.

f. 3440, op. 1, d. 13, I.28

To : (Priority) Comrade Podtyolkov, Palace Hotel, Taganrogsky prospekt,
Rostov on Don.
From: Zhuzhnev, from Shakhty, Aksayskaya, No. 288.
Telegrams

I, Zhuzhnev, town major of Aksayskaya stanitsa, am reporting about a written communication, received from comrade Andreyev, that the Paromonov Miners' Committee is gathering Red Guards together, and they want to send them to arrest you. They are making propaganda that comrade Podtyolkov was not elected by the people, but became Chariman of the Committee on his own accord, gathered a gang, who want, as they say, to destroy the whole working class. But I am telling you, as our hero and leader of the whole Don Oblast, you must take the most forceful measures against the Red gang of Paromonov miners, who want to undermine the whole Don Oblast and want to arrest you, comrade Podtyolkov, and comrade Gavrilov and comrade Smirnov, and want to seize power over the whole Don Oblast. I am telling you this and ask you to take the most forceful measures against that gang.

Organizer of Soviets Pustovoytov
Town Major Zhuzhnev, signature attested
(circular stamp Upper Don Oblast)

Reds retreat in Ukraine

The following documents relate to the period when the Whites were rallying and Sivers was losing control of the Don. The morale of the Volunteer Army had been strengthened by their battles in the Kuban, the so-called Ice Campaign. Not only did they survive appalling conditions of hardship, on several occasions they defeated much larger Red forces. In April White forces were still numerically less strong than the Reds, but this was more than outweighted by the Whites' *élan* and better discipline. One of their first objectives was to conquer the Donets Basin with its valuable reserves of coal.

By April 1918 the Volunteer Army already numbered several thousand combatants. Denikin recruited many Kuban Cossacks, and in September he had some 40 000 men. Mawdsley is correct in emphasizing that the Volunteer Army eventually became the main threat to the survival of the whole Soviet regime.

Yekaterinoslav was renamed Dnepropetrovsk from 1926. Samara River here refers to the left-bank tributary of the Dnieper. Slavyansk is on the railway north from Yuzovka.

f. 3440, op. 1, d. 13, l.23

From: Baranov,Commander of Donets Army.
Summary of operations
7 April 1918

We have given up Yekaterinoslav. Now our positions are on left bank of the Samara River at the station Ugren. The situation in Kharkov is not clear. We are continuing to assemble detachments in the Donets Red Army. Order No. 117 has been given to construct a defence line. The general position remains tense. We must strain all our efforts to see our task through.

f. 3440, op. 1, d. 13, l.26

From: Baranov, Commander of Donets Army.
Summary of operations
8 April

The position at Kharkov is still unclear. We have not managed to restore communications with them. Levitsky's Army has suffered a defeat and is retreating under pressure from superior enemy forces. Lazarev's Army is deploying troops at Lozovaya for defence along the River Oryol. The position there is stable. Morale good. Venediktov's Army is on the Samara River. Enemy beaten back from Sinelnikovo and now our line lies along the bank of the Samara River. No information has come in from fronts south of Ugren station. In our sector we are continuing to assemble detachments and fortification of our position has begun as per order 52.

Nikitovka field Headquarters of Donets Army.

f. 3440, op. 1, d. 13, l.47

To: Yuzovka, Central Headquarters, Clearance Section Priority.
From: Lebedev, Slavyansk.
[after 7 April]

We have received a telegram from Lozovaya from Commander in charge, Lazarev, to send 4 field pieces and 3 inch gun. Steps have been taken. I have no communication with other comrades. With Kharkov I am in touch only with the railway station, not with Headquarters nor in general. Communications are fading. Medvedev's detachment left Slavyansk on 7 April going towards Taganrog. On 6 April the Independent Degon Division left for Kharkov on reconnaissance. As yet there is no information from them. Urgent measures have been put in hand for evacuating Slavyansk.

Why are there no communications from you? Work in the military section is getting organized.

f. 3440, op. 1, d. 13, l.34

To: Central Headquarters, Yuzovo, copies to district Soviets of the Donets Krivoy Rog Basin, town of Slavyansk, transmits to all addresses.
From: Antonov-Ovseyenko, Supreme Commander, Oblast Military Revolutionary Committee, Rostov Don.
Telegram
13 April 1918 (Received 19 April Nikitovka)

Even at the time when revolutionary soldiers are holding back the enemy's pressure, news is coming through that Soviets are evacuating, or rather voluntarily abandoning, their districts. Over the whole area Soviet power is leaving districts which are under no threat from the enemy, even though the fact that the enemy is near cannot serve as a pretext for organs of government to leave. Anarchy is created by the Soviets leaving. It causes panic and a bad reaction among the mass of the people. It compromises the cause of the revolution and of socialism, to say nothing about increasing utter anarchy and collapse in every aspect of life. Soviets have no right to desert their posts at this most critical moment. This cannot be allowed; it means desertion and betrayal of the revolution. I propose to Central Headquarters and other oblast bodies to take energetic measures to make all deserters and self-evacuees face up to their responsibilities.

Food shortage

Tsaritsyn (later Stalingrad, Volgograd) is a large town on the Volga. Its defence assumed a symbolic importance for the Reds and, under Stalin, it became a centre of opposition to Trotsky.

Given proper distribution, the southern parts of Russia produced a surplus of grain. The more northerly areas of the Don, along the Rivers Khopyor and Medveditsa had poorer soils, hence the desire to bring some food from Bataysk and the villages of the lower Don. At the time when Red Cossacks were summoning their Congress in Kamenskaya, the following newspaper report shows famine in Vyoshenskaya on the middle course of the Don:

Starvation in the Don Oblast
The Voysko Government has received telegrams from the Oblast Food Administration. In Serebryakov there is absolutely no grain, and they have ceased bringing any in. The people in Vyoshenskaya stanitsa are eating the grain they had put by for sowing. For lack of bread many families are keeping themselves alive with sunflower husks and other substitutes. They are starting to fall ill. Just at this very moment the Revolutionary Military Committee in Tsaritsyn has requisitioned consignments of food sent by the Food Administration to the hungry northern districts.

Rostovskaya Rech, 10 January 1918

In March 1918 the Rostov area was theoretically under the authority of the Don Soviet Republic. The Volunteer Army were struggling to survive the rigours of the Ice Campaign, while almost all the Kuban remained, at least nominally, under the control of local Soviets.

f. 3440, op. 1, d. 25, l.13

To: Avtonostov, Rostov on Don.
From: Chairman of Revolutionary Committee, Tikhoretskaya.
Telegram
15 March

Oblast Revolutionary Committee is appealing to Soviets in Kuban Oblast to send grain for sowings in the fields and for workers in the mines, where men are condemned to starve to death. In the city of Rostov there are only supplies for two days. In order to strengthen and secure the rights of the working people we beg you not to refuse. We wait your reply.

Chairman

We can give ten million square metres.

f. 3440, op. 1, d. 25, l.10

[*4 typescript telegrams, not on telegraph forms. Old orthography*]
Telegram
March 1918
To: Tsaritsyn Soviet of Soldiers, Cossack and Peasant Deputies.

Telegraph immediately where have been despatched <u>one hundred and nine</u> **wagons of grain** intended for the Ust-Medveditskaya and Khopyor Districts of the former Don Oblast Food Supply Management.

Telegram
To: Stationmaster, Bataysk.

Send off immediately twenty-nine wagons of wheat, seventeen wagons of barley and three wagons of oats to be placed at the disposition of the Don Oblast Military Revolutionary Committee. If these loads have been redirected and sent off somewhere else, then telegraph on whose authority and when that was done.

Telegram
To: Stationmaster, Khopry.
15 March 1918

At Khopry station there were forty-six wagons of grain, belonging to Don Oblast Food Supply Management. Despatch them immediately to Rostov to be placed at the disposal of Don Oblast Military Revolutionary Committee. If these loads have been redirected and sent off somewhere else, then telegraph on whose authority and when that was done.

Telegram
To: Donets District Soviet of Soldiers and Peasant Deputies.
15 March 1918

Telegraph immediately to the Oblast Military Revolutionary Committee what instructions were given for the purchase of grain in other Districts and at what prices.

f. 3440, op. 1, d. 25, I.10

To: Podtyolkov, Chairman of Oblast Military Revolutionary Committee.
From: Telegraph Commissar.
17 March 1918

At the request of a member of Aksayskaya stanitsa Executive Military Revolutionary Committee I must ask you to come to the telegraph office immediately for talks.

f. 3440, op. 1, d. 4, I.28

To: Council of People's Commissars.
From: Staff of Don Soviet Republic.
Telegram
?February 1918

Counter-revolutionary gangs, trying to approach the town of Nakhichevan have been defeated by the combined efforts of Soviet forces and driven back to the village of Mishkinsky, which is seven versts from the town of Novocherkassk. We have taken machine-guns, weapons, many cartridges and shells.

Chairman of Special Staff	V. Kovalyov
Commander of the Forces	Podtyolkov
Chief of Staff	Degtyarov

Kornilov killed: Denikin heads Volunteer Army

On 10 April 1918 the Volunteer Army attacked Yekaterinodar. Their leader, General Kornilov, was killed on 13 April. Denikin took over command, abandoned the attempt to take Yekaterinodar, and led his force back towards Novocherkassk.

Soviet power on the Don was under increasing threat. The Volunteer Army was pushing in from the south. Colonel Drozdovsky had brought a well-disciplined unit of 1000 soldiers across the turbulent Ukraine and on 6 May he led them into Rostov and then on towards Novocherkassk.

f. 3440, op. 1, d. 13, l.43

To: All from Yekaterinodar to Armavir, Tikhoretskaya, Rostov, Maykop.
From: Commander-in-Chief Antonov.
Operational priority

There is a great battle at Yekaterinodar. Comrades, your support is needed. Send all the forces that you have, and also cartridges and shells. Do not delay a single minute.

f. 3440, op. 1, d. 4, l.30

To: Zagitayko, Assistant to Commissar of Military Section.
Military report
17 April 1918

The remains of Kornilov's forces have broken through from the battle at Yekaterinodar and after their breakthrough have set off along a dirt road towards the Don Oblast. At the present moment Kornilov's force is between the stations of Tikhoretskaya and Pavlovskaya. At the Yeysk railway we suppose that they will make for Rostov, pushing their way through to Ukraine. If you have armed forces, and if the opportunity presents itself, then send them to Kushchevskaya station, and from Kushchevskaya send part along the way to Vladikavkaz and part along the Black Sea route, to strengthen our detachments, so that we can finish them off here – but if he breaks through our front, then there will be something to hold him up before he gets to Rostov. We have not ascertained the exact numbers of Kornilov's gang. At four o'clock this afternoon we got a telegram that he has 3000 cavalry – the number of infantry was not established. On the same date (17 April) a message was received at 11 o'clock at night that he has 1500 cavalry, but the number of infantry was still not clear. Not all the troops who fought at Yekaterinodar are managing to keep up with him. He is making off at a great speed.

The next telegram would seem to indicate that by 19 April the Reds were still not aware of Kornilov's death on 13 April. Throughout the civil war it was common practice for the Reds to refer to any forces opposing them as a 'band' or a 'gang'. This persisted even when they were fighting against large regular armies with many thousands of men, cf. the Central Committee's circular letter of 20 September 1919: 'The whole of our State apparatus must be brought to bear on a single task, namely victory over Denikin, by destroying those who make up the strength of his White Guard gangs.'

f. 3440, op. 1, d. 4, l.14

> *To: Emergency HQ, Hotel Palace, Rostov on Don.*
> *From: Chief of Emergency General Staff.*
> *Telegram*
> *Received 19 April*

Yesterday 18 April 9 a.m. we were in action to the east of Novocherkassk and took Krivyanskaya stanitsa. The fighting lasted from 8 a.m. till 10 o'clock in the evening, after which Kornilov's detachments fled, leaving much military material in our hands. The stanitsa suffered severely from artillery fire. Details are being clarified. West of Novocherkassk we have occupied without resistance Grushevskaya stanitsa. Gangs of Kornilov's men hiding in the stanitsa have been disarmed. We have taken a mass of machine-guns, cartridges and rifles. We have freed one nurse and twenty soldiers who had been taken prisoner.

Chief of Staff Degtyarov

Deceiving the Germans

Three days later Alekhin knew that the Whites had given up their attacks, though he possibly did not know of Kornilov's death.

The Germans were suffering from the Allied blockade. They were anxious to establish settled conditions, enabling them to take grain from Russia and Ukraine to feed their own people, besides coal from the Donets Basin. They had far and away the most powerful force in Russia: their troops had advanced across Ukraine, and entered Rostov on 8 May 1918.

Formally the Soviet Government had made an agreement with the Germans that they would disarm all units which entered Russia and

Ukraine. In practice, instead of disarming them, the Communists simply regrouped these forces and placed them under fresh commanders, hence their anxiety to conceal the names of those who had formerly been in charge.

From April 1918 Moscow granted Ordzhonokidze exceptional powers as Extraordinary Commissar of South Russia. He was also a member of the Central Executive Committee of the Don Soviet Republic.

f. 3440, op. 1, d. 4, l.159

To: Ordzhonokidze.
From: Yermilov.
25 April 1918

This is Ordzhonokidze on the phone.
Yermilov speaking: Comrade Goroshov asked me over the phone today to tell whether Bekenkovich, commanding the forces of Taganrog District had given up his command. Bekenkovich informs me that from 24 April he has been removed by the District Soviet from his post as commander, of which he has been officially informed. The 200 000 roubles seized by him from the commander of the special striking force, comrade Nikolayenko, will be immediately taken away to organize the military forces of the Taganrog District, for the strengthening of Soviet power in its struggle against anarchy and bandits. It is essential to pass the post of commandant of the town to Taganrog, as also the post of commander of the Taganrog Military District, to the commander of the Executive Committee. The District Committee wants to appoint comrade Nikolayenko.

The candidature of that same man is supported by military commissar Rodyonov. I personally regard his candidacy as completely acceptable. I do beg you to speak out on that same subject. The local Soviet will also put forward a candidate – we do not know who. Is it that Nikolayenko who was appointed by Antonov to command the Mariupol and Taganrog fronts and who told us about himself by telegram? If that is the case, so as not to give ourselves away we shall have to rename Nikolayenko as Mikhaylenko, or appoint someone else. After all you know perfectly well that the Germans may say tomorrow that Nikolayenko was the same man who commanded Soviet units of the Ukrainian Soviet Republic. Dear comrade, never lose sight of that for a moment. So of course I should not object in the slightest. Today Stepanov and Doroshev set off to go to you, have they arrived? Not yet. Do tell me please – is it not possible to prepare tomorrow's press for a very special colleague of ours who commands the armed forces of Taganrog District and is commandant of the town of Taganrog? I have in mind tomorrow evening, because tomorrow morning the Chairman is going to Rostov …

The following *list* 11 refers to transferring the 3rd Ukrainian Socialist Army to come under the command of Grigory Petrov. Petrov was at that time in charge of the 1st Special Revolutionary Army, which was operating in the north of the Don territory on the border with Voronezh Province. The Revolutionary Military Council felt they had to deal firmly with Dyogot's uncompromising attitude. They feared that his reluctance to give up command of the 3rd Army might provoke an even more serious breach with the Germans.

f. 3440, op. 1, d. 25, I.11

To: Revolutionary Military Council, Rostov station, Telegraph Office of Vladikavkaz Railway, copy to Revolutionary Military Council Voronezh District. From: Chairman Military Revolutionary Committee, Glashko.
3 May 1918

I am proposing that comrade Dyogot should hand over his post as commander of 3rd Army to comrade Petrov, and leave for Taganrog. If he does not do so decisive measures will be taken, and he will be brought to trial by the Military Revolutionary Court.

On 8 May the Bolsheviks were forced to leave Rostov. The Don Soviet Republic was overthrown by the Cossacks who had turned against it, and by the Volunteer Army which had now regained strength.

Podtyolkov, Krivoshlykov and about a hundred followers attempted to travel to the north of the Don area, where they hoped they might rouse more support for the Reds. They were cornered by hostile Cossacks in the steppelands and executed – as described in Sholokhov's novel *Quiet flows the Don*.

2
1919: Whites

White agents' instructions

No explanation is given of how the Reds acquired the following instructions to White agents, of which we have printed only the more interesting sections.

In point 2 Denikin's insistence on a single united Russia ran against separatist ambitions in many outlying areas of the former Tsarist empire. This rigid policy prevented him from seeking any sort of deal even with moderate nationalists in important countries such as Ukraine or Georgia, where the Whites might well have expected support for their anti-Bolshevik crusade. His dogmatic refusal to consider any concessions to local autonomy was very damaging to the Whites. Denikin's slogan of 'Russia One and Indivisible' proved a mill-stone round his neck, provoking a bitter feud with the Kuban Rada – this latter being a particular folly, since they represented the chief area from which the Volunteer Army drew its Cossack cavalry.

Trying to sap the Volunteer Army's sources for recruitment, the Germans supported the so-called Right Centre, and encouraged rival White military formations, the Southern Army and the Astrakhan Army. These were formed only in the closing months of the First World War, when Germany could ill afford to commit military resources to southern Russia. As Germany approached defeat these puppet organizations were starved of finance and failed to build up to any significant numbers.

Point 9 enquires whether officers are treating their men 'normally' – a warning which may have seemed superfluous after so many units in the old Tsarist army had rid themselves of unpopular officers.

GARO f. 17, op. 65, d. 35, I.151(extracts)

INSTRUCTION
To: *Front line Agents of the Don Section of Secret Propaganda*
Copy received by Central Committee 15 October 1919

(1) The work of local agents consists of instruction on questions of:
  (a) The war.
  (b) Latest news.
(2) Campaigning, which should reinforce and instil the following ideas:
  (a) Russia One and Indivisible.
  (b) Slogans of the Volunteer Army.
  (c) Government by the people.

AN AGENT'S DUTIES
(2) To carry on the fight against the Bolsheviks, exposing all the disastrous consequences of Bolshevism in Russia, and for the Cossacks in particular. For this one must point to the origin of Bolshevism, and to the way it is aiming to destroy Cossack society, to demoralize it, and to undermine its economy – by robbing not only the well-to-do Cossacks, but also the small-scale proprietors.
(7) If an agent provides any false information he may be dismissed and handed over to a field court-martial.
(8) An agent must study the unit he is working in, both to sound out its members' political orientation and their economic status.
(9) In units on active service, political meetings sometimes take place, and men refuse to carry out military orders. The agent must clarify what has been at the root of these undesirable events, whether they arise from dissatisfaction with the command staff because the officers do not treat the Cossacks normally.

Dates in White archives are normally Old Style, in 1918 13 days behind the Gregorian calendar, which the Reds had gone over to in February, when they renumbered the first day as 14 February. 26 May Old Style should therefore be adjusted to New Style 8 June, and so on.

As the Reds were driven out of their country the Don Cossacks elected delegates to a special meeting to be held in their capital, Novocherkassk. This 'parliament' was given the title of 'Assembly for the Salvation of the Don' (*Krug Spaseniya Dona*). General Krasnov was elected Ataman on 3/16 May by a large majority of those present.

Hoping to revive proud Cossack traditions he gave his army the ancient name of 'Almighty Voysko of the Don'. His forces were growing rapidly, and in the summer of 1918 the Voysko far outnumbered Denikin's Volunteer Army.

Krasnov was not over-scrupulous in seeking allies to help him form an independent Cossack State. He wrote to the Kaiser, supporting the German idea of creating a South Russian Federation. When Germany fell in November 1918 Krasnov's pro-German stance became an embarrassment, and in February 1919 the Krug elected Afrikan Bogayevsky to succeed him as Ataman.

Up to May 1918, Cossack forces had largely followed individual officers, and owed their first loyalty to them. The following tables outline Krasnov's attempts to regularize the disparate units which hitherto had been more loosely organized. The Instructions for White agents fell into the hands of the Reds and are quoted from RTsKhDNI. All further documents in this chapter have been drawn from the State Archive at Rostov on Don (GARO).

Establishments for artillery, medical, communications, armoured cars

f. 865, op. 1, d. 237, l.110

Provisional establishment of Boards of Inspectors of Artillery
26 May 1918

(1) Inspectors of Artillery

Colonels	No. of horses	Annual salary
8	8	7200

Explanatory note

(1) These are the posts of Inspectors of Artillery appointed to 8 active service detachments (of Generals Fitskhelaurov, Mamontov and Bykadorov, Colonels Kireyev and Alferov, and in the Districts of Cherkassk, Rostov and 1st Don District). We may expect new detachments to be formed.

(2) Senior officers of field rank are being appointed to collect and register arms from people in the towns and stanitsas.

(4) Inspectors of Artillery are completely subordinate to the Heads of Detachments.

Copy attested 26 May 1918

Establishment
Artillery workshops of the Almighty Voysko of the Don

Designation of ranks	number	basic annual pay	notes
Master armourers	3	4200	
Armourers Grade 1	6	3000	
Armourers Grade 2	12	1200	
Quartermaster sergeants	3	300	

[Must be misprint for 3000]

26 May 1918

Establishment of stores of artillery ammunition and harness

Harness-makers	4	3000

(2) The care of horses is in general based on the sums allocated to the Supplies Department, whereas harness, blancards and carts are to be serviced by the Artillery Department.

f. 865, op. 1, d. 237, l.50

Report to Voysko Headquarters of Almighty Voysko of the Don.
From: Administration of General on Duty.
September 1918, Novocherkassk

Having regard to the steady growth of the sphere of activity of Communications Headquarters of the Almighty Voysko of the Don with [Denikin's] Volunteer Army, which inevitably entails corresponding, both with various branches of the Don Government, and also with the Volunteer Army and with the Government of the Kuban Territory, there is an extremely slow postal service or delivery of parcels. In future all communications with Volunteer Army will be effected only through Communications Headquarters. At present the carrying out of all this complicated work is in the hands of one junior officer and one Cossack. Voysko Headquarters recognizes that it is essential right now to lay down a provisional establishment for Communications Headquarters.

Proposed staff of Communications Headquarters

Designation of ranks	number of persons	basic monthly pay
Head of Communications General	1	800
Lieutenant-Colonel or Colonel	1	500
Administrator in Charge	1	450
Assistant Junior Officers	2	450
Clerk	1	20
Cossack messengers	2	10

In January 1919 the Don Cossack Army was being pushed back to the south of the Voysko territory, and many Cossacks were deserting the front to return to their home villages or even to go over to the Reds. The Whites were pushed south and could reform their line only along the right bank of the River Donets, where they stood until Denikin started his last offensive in May 1919.

On 19 February 1919 the 'parliament' (Krug) voted Afrikan Bogayevsky to replace General Krasnov as Ataman. In January the British had already compelled Krasnov to place himself under Denikin's overall command.

Summoning a Krug was costly and time-consuming, resorted to only when major issues of policy were to be decided. In the intervals between meetings of the Krug the Voysko was run by its Council of Executive Heads. The later Don Army table of establishments is marked as confirmed and signed by Krasnov on 30 December 1918. This table was then to be submitted for approval to the Council of Executive Heads.

GARO f. 865, op. 1, d. 237, 1.2 carries the preamble which was inserted after they had seen and approved the scales of manning and pay:

To be brought forward for approval by Council of Executive Heads, and in case of approval for signature.
To: Voysko Secretary, Department of Establishments of Almighty Voysko of the Don.
From: 2nd Quartermaster-General of Voysko staff.
Attached to the above document is an extract from the record of a session of Council of Executive Heads of 24 January 1919, point 3:

Extract from record of session of Council of Executive Heads of 24 January 1919 on the question of the establishment of Don Armoured Car Section and tables of specialized technical equipment of the heavy vehicle maintenance department attached to the Don Vehicle Division:
RESOLVED to confirm the establishment and the table with the appropriate signatures.

This proposal for establishment of units should presumably be re-dated to 12 February (New Style), and must be one of the last orders signed by Krasnov. Further details on the Armoured Car Section are given in the Explanatory Note at end of the following.

f. 865, op. 1, d. 237, I.1

I confirm on 30 January 1919:
Addendum to Order to Almighty Voysko of the Don, January 1919

Provisional establishment of Don Armoured Car Section

Designation of ranks	number of persons	basic monthly pay	notes
Section Commander Senior officer (major or colonel) with specialized education	1	600	
Second in Command for combatant service Senior officer	1	500	
Chief clerks	2	400	1 for stores 1 for technical
Cossacks (combatant)			
Sergeant-major	1	pay according to rank	
Quartermaster-sergeants	2		
Storekeeper	1		
Drivers	5		
Motor-cyclist	1		

<u>Cossacks</u> (non-combatant)

Senior medical assistant	1
Clerks higher grade	4
Clerks medium grade	4
Metal-workers	6
Lathe operators	2
Blacksmiths	3
Electrician	1
Mounted couriers and maintenance men	33
Transport drivers	5

Vehicle section: explanatory note

The Don Armoured Car Section began its existence with only one wrecked vehicle of type *Kazak*. By capturing armoured cars from the Reds, and building one new one, the number of armoured cars rose to 8. It must be added that these armoured cars are definitely divided into four types: Austin, Ergard, Harford and Fiat.

The temporary establishment at present in place has been made up on the basis of 4 armoured cars and 5 lorries. Extra to establishment there has been added a third element consisting of 1 aide-de-camp, 1 senior medical assistant and 2 clerks.

Because of the above-mentioned division of armoured cars under various types, taking also into account the holding of 8 armoured cars, it is absolutely essential to break the establishment down into 4 sections of 2 armoured cars apiece, classified by type. This must be done for operational purposes, besides making provision for fuel, greasing and spare parts. The establishment figures for personnel (officers, Cossacks and technicians) must be increased accordingly.

Section 1: 1 unit of Ergard armoured cars.

Section 2: 1 unit of Harford armoured cars; 4 lorries; 1 car; 8 motorcycles.

Machine-gunners	12
Gunners (37 millimetre cannon)	2
Car driver	1
Motorcyclists	8

Personnel holding rank in Section 1

		Pay
Commanders of armoured cars (Yesaul)	4	450
i/c machine-guns (Sergeants etc.)	4	400

Officers' drivers (Sergeants etc.)	4	400
Gunners (Sergeants etc.)	2	400

Cossacks		
Drivers	9	
Drivers mates	9	
Machine-gunners	12	
Motorcyclists	8	
Gunners	8	

Section 2

Vehicles: 3rd squad of Austin armoured cars 2; machine guns 2
4th squad of Fiat armoured cars: 2. Machine guns: 2. Drivers: 2

Total in Division Senior officers (majors, colonels)	3
Junior officers	28
Officials	2
Cavalry Sergeants	1
Senior medical assistant	1
Senior NCOs	10
Junior NCOs	20
Clerks	20
Cossacks	48

Armoured cars	8
Lorries	11
Cars	4
Quartermaster's carts (for two horses)	3

Note:

(1) Commander of Don Armoured Car Section is subordinate in all respects to Head of Military Technical Management.

(2) Financial allocations for the Section are made for hiring technicians, drivers and acquiring instruments for maintenance, spare parts and materials, if these for some reason cannot be obtained from the motor transport units of the Almighty Voysko of the Don.

(3a) Each armoured car is an operational unit, consisting of 1 armoured vehicle, 1 lorry and 2 motorcycles,

(3b) Armoured squad consists of 2 armoured cars, 2 lorries, 4 motorcycles.

(4) Commander of Armoured Car Section has all the rights of a regimental commander.

(5) Commander of armoured car has the rights of a cavalry squadron commander.

(18) All personnel shown on the establishment have the right to obtain an apartment, at 25 per cent of basic pay.

Shell workshop in Taganrog

Seeing the quarrels to obtain accommodation in Novocherkassk, 'the right to obtain an apartment' must have only been a pious hope.

Krasnov's signature in black ink was entered at the head of the establishment table for 'Shell Workshop in Town of Taganrog' (1.97 follows). Salaries seem roughly ten times greater than the pay of specialists in the armoured car units, no doubt reassessed early in 1919 after the period of severe inflation.

f. 865, op. 1, d. 237, I.97 (extracts)

Establishment
of Shell Workshop in Town of Taganrog,
equipment stores in Taganrog

Designation of ranks	Number of persons	Basic monthly pay	notes
Head of workshop Officer of field rank, graduate of Artillery Academy or engineer	1	12 000	
Explosives experts, senior	5	8 400	
Explosives experts, junior	5	7 200	
Working horses	10		

Notes

(1) All ranks enumerated in the above establishment are provided with maintenance allowances and provisions of all other types, as set up by the existing legal requirements, besides which rooms with heating and lighting are provided directly at the workshop, or if such rooms are not available a rent allowance shall be paid at a scale of 25 per cent of the pay shown in these figures.

(2) The posts enumerated below may be filled by hired personnel, but only by those who have the specialist educational qualifications appropriate for these posts. Those who are enrolled on a voluntary basis receive maintenance allowances as shown in the above table.

Pay

No matter what dramatic developments were taking place at the Front, individuals had to continue with the mundane cares of earning their living – particularly difficult under the currency inflation which follows as an endemic consequence of war.

f. 865, op. 1, d. 237, I.63

To: Duty General at Voysko Headquarters, Almighty Voysko of the Don.
From: Senior medical assistant.
7 September [20 September] 1918

Under the scales for personnel laid down by the General Staff of the Almighty Voysko of the Don my pay has been set at 350 roubles per month in my position as Senior Medical Assistant. I request Your Excellency's good offices to secure me 350 roubles.

Housing

The following squabbles over housing relate to the period May–December 1919 when the Don Army had regained possession of Novocherkassk. The population of the Cossack capital was swollen by refugees, by the families of men serving at the front, and by officers who clung to their posts in the rear, letting others do their fighting for them.

Colonel Polyakov was Chief of Staff of the Don Army in 1918. Because of the shortage of accommodation it was decreed that no one should occupy more than one place of residence.

f. 865, op. 1, d. 224, I.15

Copy of copy
No. 1806, 8 December 1918

... to other junior officers one room, and furthermore persons in the military department who already have apartments, even if the number of rooms is less than that shown above, do not have the right to requisition other apartments.

f. 865, op. 1, d. 224, l.18

REQUEST

In 1917 my wife, Alexandra Filipovna Kurdyumov, acquired by purchase from Ivan Osipovich Polyakov the property at 47 Komitetskaya Street. Colonel Polyakov's wife was living in a wing at the back of this house. The apartment she was occupying she should have vacated in the autumn of 1917. With my permission she stayed on to live for a certain time in the apartment. In the spring of 1918 Mrs Polyakov left a few of her things just in one room. I proceeded to do up that apartment, and in it I installed my wife's own sister with her family, at no charge to them.

Mrs Polyakov brought an accusation against me that allegedly I had evicted her from the apartment. Against Mrs Polyakov my wife brought a counter plea to have Mrs Polyakov removed from the apartment.

The Justice of the Peace examined a series of witnesses and ruled that Mrs Polyakov should be removed from the apartment where her things were held for storage. Against these decisions Mrs Polyakov brought pleas to the Congress of Justices of the Peace and these cases have still not been resolved.

In the meantime, on 24 May this year, Colonel Polyakov turned up in my apartment, at a time when I was away from Novocherkassk. He announced to my wife that his former apartment was requisitioned for him and that my wife's sisters, the Derebaskovs, should immediately leave the apartment.

I have the honour to apply to Your Excellency with a most humble request in disposing of the matter under your jurisdiction to defer the requisition order, until the case is settled by the court on 26 May 1919.

f. 865, op. 1, d. 224, l.11

> To: *Chairman of Commission Requisitioning Apartments.*
> From: *Colonel Babkin GHQ.*

I request you to produce correspondence relating to requisitioning apartment in house of Kurdyumov, sent to you on 3 June (No. 1187).

f. 865, op. 1, d. 224, l.23

To: *Chairman of Commission Requisitioning Apartments.*
From: *Colonel Babkin GHQ, attested Captain Vorobesk. 15 July*

Chairman of Council of Executive Heads requests you to inform him how Colonel Polyakov could come to occupy two apartments, if Mr Kurdyumov's testimony is confirmed.

f. 865, op. 1, d. 224, l.20

4 September
Kurdyumov, I. G.

DECLARATION

According to my information Colonel Polyakov, at the time when he requisitioned my wife's apartment, had an apartment in the house of Mrs Pukhlyakov at 13 Arsenalnaya Street. Having occupied my wife's apartment Colonel Polyakov so constrained the Derepyatskov [sic] family that they were compelled to sell part of their furniture, so that they could fit into the two little rooms which Colonel Polyakov graciously allowed to be set aside for them.

f. 865, op. 1, d. 224, l.14

Novocherkassk Town Office. Copy to Mrs Alexandra Filipovna.
Secretariat 11 September 1919 Kurdyumov.

In reply to your application of 9 August the Town Office encloses herewith a copy of the Order of the Almighty Voysko of the Don of 8 December 1918 No. 1806.
The property document should be with the owner of the apartment.

f. 865, op. 1, d. 224, l.13

To: *Head of Secretariat of Chairman of Council of Executive Heads of Almighty Voysko of the Don.*
From: *Ivan Georgiyevich Kurdyumov, resident at 47 Komitetskaya Street, Novocherkassk.*
18 September (stamped 'Received 18 September 1919')

Further to my application of 4 September, concerning my complaint against the actions of Colonel Polyakov requisitioning the apartment, I have the honour to present a copy of Order No. 1806 of 8 December 1918 on the procedure for requisitioning apartments, received by me from the Novocherkassk Town Office, relating to the Order of 11 September, which Order I had in mind when I made my complaint and showed that Polyakov had an apartment at the time when he requisitioned mine.

f. 865, op. 1, d. 224, l.21

From: *Colonel Babkin GHQ.*
Copy

I request you to inform me in whose apartment and exactly where Colonel Polyakov is living, and also whether Mrs Derepatskov [sic] has been moved out of the apartment which he occupies in your house.

f. 865, op. 1, d. 76, l.6

Report of Manager of the Department of Land Management and Agriculture.
3 September 1919, Novocherkassk

The Novocherkassk College of Land Survey is situated in the house of Kurdyumov on Pribylinskaya Street. In the middle of February this year the premises of the college were requisitioned for a field hospital, but on the night of 29–30 May a fire broke out in the hospital, which destroyed the upper storey and caused such damage on the lower floor that it was impossible to remain there any longer without repairs to the building. The house owner Kurdyumov proposes handing over his property to the Government for 900 000 roubles. I request the Council of Executive

Heads to place a credit for this amount at my disposal for acquiring Mr Kurdyumov's property and for effecting repairs.
Manager of the Department of Land Management and Agriculture.

f. 865, op. 1, d. 225, l.19

Telegram   Urgent   Official
To: The Governor General Rostov on Don.
From: General Popov, Chairman of Council of Executive Heads.

The Requisitioning Commission has decreed to take over for use as a field hospital the gymnasium of the First High School which contains expensive equipment. Give orders to cancel requisition 1709.

f. 865, op. 1, d. 225 l.31

Telegram Novocherkassk   Urgent
To: Head of Department of Public Education.
From: Head of High School No. 1, ?Pannishko.
Received 13 August 1919

The Requisitioning Commission has decreed to take over for use as a field hospital the gymnasium for the two high schools which contains expensive equipment. Since this contradicts the telegraphed decree of the Health Inspector, safeguarding the preservation of premises with teaching equipment, I request Your Excellency to defend the interest of educational establishments.

f. 865, op. 1, d. 224, l.24

20 September

… *re* requisitioning in town of Rostov on Don of the pastry and sweet shop of Oganov and Babul for the needs of the club.
RESOLVED: to turn down the application.

f. 865, op. 1, d. 224 I.26

To: *Chairman of Commission Requisitioning Apartments.*
From: *Lieutenant General Popov, GHQ.*
23 September 1919

A. I. Boyarinov, Deputy of the Voysko Parliament has informed us by a letter addressed to the Don Ataman, that you have given instructions to block up the floor, leading from the 'dining room' into the rooms assigned to Boyarinov, whereby Boyarinov is rendered unable to heat his rooms. Boyarinov is also debarred from using the kitchen alongside Vagner, and thus he and his family are condemned during the winter to freeze and die of hunger. Give instructions immediately for all this to be investigated and get the matter settled. Inform me of the outcome.
For Head of Secretariat Serezhit

f. 865, op. 1, d. 224, I.33

To: *Commandant Kazanskaya stanitsa.*
20 September 1919

I request you to release immediately from requisition the premises occupied by the reading room and secretariat of the Information Point in Kazanskaya stanitsa, or to take it away as a matter of urgency.

f. 865, op. 1, d. 215, I.27 (*extract*)

December 1919

DECREED: To hand over to the Chairman of Novocherkassk Garrison Housing and Building Commission for the use of the Department of Communications two rooms occupied by the grocery shop of Binnalshnov at 39 Komitetskaya Street.

f. 865, op. 1, d. 215, l.24 (*abbreviated*)

December 1919

Expenses sustained in connection with taking over Khotsri's house on Aleksandrovsky Street: The credit demanded for maintenance of the house for two months of the current year is made up as follows: heating 62 700 roubles, pay for the yard man 2400 roubles, cleaning up garbage 2000 roubles, repair of water heating boiler 3000 roubles, repair of stoves in bath house and laundry 2000 roubles, electricity 1200 roubles, water 600 roubles and construction of gates 400 roubles.

Hygiene in Novocherkassk

The documents which follow bear witness to difficulties in administering Novocherkassk early in 1919, when the Don Army was being driven south in headlong retreat.

f. 865, op. 1, d. 237, l.74 (extract)

Paymaster's Office.
From: Don Ataman Krasnov.
30 January (12 February) 1919

III.   Each year the accounts lay down the sums necessary for paying the personnel who are employed to carry out technical tasks which require specialized knowledge, and the medical personnel (1 doctor and 1 medical attendant) for serving the Krug (Parliament) while it is at work, as also the Voysko Second in Command and his assistants in dealing with business arising from the Krug.

Concerning measures against cholera, although the lack of paper for printing these articles means that the Bureau is unable to bring them to the notice of the public. It has become clear from exchanging opinions with members of the Conference that the only sure way of making healthy sanitary conditions in the town is by constructing the necessary number of large containers to carry out the sewage by motor transport. The Conference recognized that it would be necessary to have 4 containers operating constantly, and for them we shall need 5 lorries. One of these should be held in reserve to replace other vehicles when the inevitable breakdowns occur. Although the Municipal Authorities are taking steps to enlarge the fleet of vehicles at their disposal for dealing with sanitation, none the less they are hardly likely to have much success in increasing its capacity, because on the one hand there are not enough horses, and besides that not enough materials for making the framework of carts and casks.

It is the town's inhabitants who are responsible for cleaning streets and yards. However, in view of the serious shortage of means of transport in the town, the Conference acknowledged that the inhabitants will not be able to meet this obligation. It is therefore more sensible to concentrate everything connected with the cleaning of streets and yards in the hands of the Municipal Authorities, and they will seek to recover the money from the inhabitants for the expense they incur under that heading. The Mayor, A. S. Dronov, has declared that this measure should be given legal status, and furthermore that the town must hold considerable funds, since it is no easy matter to get the inhabitants to meet their financial obligations.

At the end of the session the Head of Department of Internal Affairs came to announce that the Chairman of the Council of Executive Heads and other members of the Government had expressed their willingness to provide every possible form of help to the municipal social services in their fight against cholera.

Attested [in black ink]: Don Ataman Krasnov.

Conscription

Order to the garrison of Rostov and Nakhichevan on Don

No. 72, 26 March 1919

I command all prisoners of war to register by 1 April. They shall be assigned to work both in government institutions and also with private individuals.

Order to the Almighty Voysko of the Don

No. 642, 12 April 1919

To bring the ranks of the Don Army up to strength I order to be called up for service all those liable to serve from 1916 and 1917 (those who were born in 1895 and 1896) and drafts from 1900 to 1909 (i.e. those born from 1884 to 1889 inclusive).

Order to Cherkassk District of Almighty Voysko of the Don

17 March 1917 Novocherkassk
12 April Yekaterinodar

Non-Cossacks [*inogoródniye*], as also Cossacks who had been called up from the territory administered by me were sent with the Main Squad. Some of them hid along the route before they got to the (?) GE and some went away from the squad of their own accord.

Order of the Commander-in-Chief of armed forces in South Russia, Yekaterinodar

Sufficient uniforms have now been brought up, but vile thieves are stealing them and selling them.

Supplies

f. 865, op. 1, d. 224 I.28

CONFERENCE
on Urban Needs, 12 [25] June 1919 in Aleksandrovsk-Grushevsky

The Mayor, N. G. Kharchevnikov, stated that: expenditure would amount to approximately 1 200 000 roubles, with income only at 800 000 roubles. In the light of this the town was requesting a subsidy from the Voysko amounting to 500 000 roubles.

The Chairman of the Town Food Supply Commission announced that the town was experiencing severe difficulties in food supply. The transport of food products was working very badly. Food prices were rising at an incredible rate. The price of flour had reached 200 roubles a pood. There were no potatoes on the market.

The Chairman of the Coal Industry declared that potatoes which they hold, having received them from the Food Supply Department, they can sell to the town, without any limit in quantity at 30 roubles a pood.

Director, Department of Internal Affairs recommended seeking information from the Novocherkassk Town Administration as to how they organized the purchase of flour and other food products in the Kuban, and that they should themselves set up the same kind of purchasing system.

The Mayor: The Director of the Department of Food Supply, General Yaroshensky, gave the town of Novocherkassk the sort of authorization to buy flour in the Kuban, which it would be almost impossible to use. Authorization was given for buying food for the town on an independent basis, not using the food products account as laid down in the convention for the Department of Food Supply. Purchases of this nature could always be requisitioned on their way to us.

K. P. Kaklyugin promised to hold talks on this subject with General Proshevsky [Kaklyugin noted below as Director, Department of Internal Affairs].

The Chairman of the Finance Commission: *re* the tax raised on property in the town (this is the main part of our income, yielding up to 700 000 roubles), from the market, the stock pens and the abattoir. If the town does not get any help from the Voysko, then we shall have to cut down our expenditure on public education.

Panchenko, as representative of the Savings and Loan Association, requested that prisoners of war should be sent to unload wagons and similar tasks connected with supplying the population with food.

The agricultural workers' representative in the Duma asked us to support his petition about sending POWs for work in the fields, in view of the very severe lack of labour, and also to extend exemption from conscription to agricultural workers living in the towns (from the age of 37, not 47), as has been done for the agricultural labour force in settlements outside the town.

Recommendations of this conference referred to below:

f. 865, op. 1, d. 224 I.27

To: His Excellency, Ataman of the Don.
Report of Director of Secretariat of Department of Internal Affairs Almighty Voysko of the Don, Novocherkassk
24 September 1919

On 12 June this year in the town of Aleksandrovsk-Grushevsky I convened a Conference on Urban Needs. I have the honour to report to Your Excellency that in my opinion (1) the plea made at the Conference to send POWs to work in the fields as also (2) to extend exemption from conscription to agricultural workers living in the towns, as has been done for those working in agriculture in settlements outside the town, both merit your approval.

Director, Department of Internal Affairs   K. Kaklyugin

f. 865, op. 1, d. 237, l.51

To: *Council of Executive Heads, Almighty Voysko of the Don.*
       From: *Clergy of Novocherkassk Cathedral.*
                        Petition
                23 August 1919

On 18 August this year a law was promulgated concerning stipends of priests in the Don diocese.

In our parish there are a great many private chapels. In these churches our parishioners fast, celebrate services and requiem masses. The money collected in each parish is divided into 60 parts, so that on average a clerk receives 150–200 roubles. Thus the total monthly earnings of a clerk do not amount to more than 600 roubles, i.e. 200 roubles less than the wages of a cathedral watchman.

The clergy in the cathedral have a great deal of unpaid work (special services for this or that event in the life of our country, funerals of renowned warriors, liturgies for the souls of the dead, and requiem masses for them, as also for other people who have rendered public service).

The cathedral clergy beg most humbly to ask Council of Executive Heads of the Almighty Voysko of the Don to understand our plight and to set our normal pay scales as follows:

Since the pay of a cathedral watchman equals 800 roubles, so it will be right to allocate:

Clerk	950 roubles per month
Priest with secondary education	1350
Priest with higher education	1450
Archpriest	1650

                                                            signatures

f. 865, op. 1, d. 224, l.4

To: *Chairman Council of Executive Heads.*
From: *Voysko Secretary of the Almighty Voysko of the Don.*
30 August 1919

re credit for grain preparation operations.
RESOLVED: To open at the disposal of Director of Department of Finance an extra-budgetary credit amounting to one million (1 000 000) roubles for making a subsidy of 4% annually for a period of six months to the Don Mutual Aid Society for those serving in Novocherkassk for grain preparation operations.
Original with relevant signatures
Attested   Voysko Secretary

f. 865, op. 1, d. 224 l.31

Extract from record of session of Council of Executive Heads of 11 September *re* petition by Greek citizen I. A. Baylas to revise payment from 30 roubles to 75 roubles per pood for wheat requisitioned from him RESOLVED to refuse the application.

Finance

Novocherkassk and Rostov fell to the Red Army in the first days of January (New Style) 1920. Doubtless *list* 8 envisages evacuation from Rostov. In spite of the threat from the north the second document below, also dated 13 December (*list* 5) seems to indicate that on 13/26 December the Whites still hoped to hold Novocherkassk, although this was only a few days before the Reds were to enter.

GARO f. 865, op. 1, d. 215, l.8

Extract from Proceedings of Council of Executive Heads of Almighty Voysko of the Don, meeting of 13 December 1919.

HEARD: Report of Manager of Justice Department on improving economic conditions for members of Governing Senate and on giving the officials an evacuation subsidy.

DECREED: (I) To enlarge from 1 November this year the effect of point 7 of the urgent decree of the Special Session of 3 December (minute 117), confirmed on 4 December by the Commander-in-Chief in that part which affects the officers of the General Administration to embrace officials of the Governing Senate, so that a special sort of food supply (category VI) should be granted to those in classes 4, 5 and 6 in the highest measure: Higher Investigating Magistrates 3500 roubles per head, their Assistants 2500 roubles and Higher Secretaries 1500 roubles per month. (II) New scale to be back-dated to 1 November. (III) To issue immediately to officials of the Governing Senate a subsidy for their evacuation, amounting to two months maintenance allowance, with supplements to meet the rise in prices and for family men. (IV) To propose to the Director of the Department of Finance to open for the Director of the Justice Department of the Almighty Voysko of the Don an immediate credit for this, amounting to 615 762 roubles 72 kopecks.

f. 865, op. 1, d. 215, l.27

Decree

HEARD: Report of the Head of the Department of Internal Affairs
DECREED: (1) From the December account of the Army Council for providing help to refugees to the sum of 6797 roubles

(1) To	Roubles
Ust-Medveditsky District Soviet	6 925 962
Upper Don District Soviet	43 387 962
Second Don District Soviet	
for December	1 589 862
for November	950 000

(2) Calculated on these accounts a credit of 12 860 580 placed at the disposal of Head of Department of Internal Affairs.

f. 865, op. 1, d. 215, l.3

To: Department of Finance.
From: Director of Military Department.

In view of the exceptional need for large expenses to meet operational costs I request that there may be placed at my disposal 10 million roubles.

signed Lieutenant General
pp. Chief of Staff

f. 865, op. 1, d. 215, l.19

To: Council of Executive Heads.
From: Department of Trade and Industry.
December 1919

In the town of Taganrog at the end of November 1919 a series of sessions was held of a Commission under the chairmanship of the Assistant Mayor of Taganrog to examine the question of raising wages for workers in the Russo-Baltic metallurgical and leather factories. The Commission had regard to the desire of the Metalworkers Union to raise wages, starting with 54 roubles for 8 working hours for an unskilled worker and going up to 100 roubles 80 kopecks for a Category 1 worker. A minimum living wage was sought, calculated by the Union on 1 October at 59 roubles 85 kopecks, on 15 October 76 roubles 25 kopecks, and on 20 November 112 roubles.

The Leather Workers Union, basing its claim on the more difficult working conditions and the fact that they do not receive any sort of food supply from the factory managers should have a wage for 8 hours from 80 to 100 roubles for Category 3.

It is interesting to note from the following *list* 38 that small stanitsa units were still being formed into regiments as late as 12 December 1919.

f. 865, op. 1, d. 215, l.38

To: *Council of Executive Heads, Almighty Voysko of the Don.*
From: *Head of Military Department, Novocherkassk.*
13 December 1919

REPORT *re* issue of 2 million roubles for food and running costs for cavalry companies from the stanitsas.
The Ataman of the Cherkassk District of the Almighty Voysko of the Don in his report of 12 December 1919 no. 46406 is asking about speedily opening a credit amounting to two million (2 000 000) roubles to be given to the commanders of three cavalry regiments, now brought together from stanitsa companies, to meet expenses for their food and running costs.
As I find it essential to release the said sum, I would propose that an extra-budgetary credit should be opened as a matter of urgency, placing two million (2 000 000) roubles at my disposal, for me to distribute 800 000 roubles to the regiment which comprises six squadrons, and 600 000 to each of the regiments with four squadrons. pp. Director of Military Department at GHQ, Lieutenant-General
Acting Head of Supplies of Almighty Voysko of the Don,

Lieutenant-General

f. 865, op. 1, d. 215, l.39

To: *Finance Department.*
From: *Don Army Finance.*
DECREE granting two million roubles as requested in list 38. **GARO f. 865,**
op. 1, d. 215, l.5
13 December 1919

Taking into account that the costs of labour and materials have increased from September to December three or four times over – we need:
(1) For adapting the military hospitals we have evacuated and are setting up anew.
(2) For finding quarters for the reserve units which have been re-formed 16 million roubles for the 1920 building season.
Summary of building work to be carried out in 1920 – in Novocherkassk:
Repair and adaptation of private and public buildings for military units and institutions 5 million roubles (+ Rostov: 11 building schemes).

f. 865, op. 1, d. 215, I.34

From: Lieutenant General.
30 December 1919

Arising from the Bolsheviks invading the boundaries of the Donetsk District the Voysko Council for aid to refugees seeks for an advance of 5 million roubles to be placed urgently at the disposition of the District Ataman of Donetsk District.

Czechs

Allied with Germany in the First World War the Austro-Hungarian Empire contained many Slavs, impatient to be free of Austrian domination. Soldiers captured by the Russians included many from the area which the Treaty of Versailles would later create as Czechoslavakia. The Russians built them up into two divisions, which contained some 40 000 men.

The peace of Brest-Litovsk introduced a confusing period for the Czechs and Slovaks. Only the defeat of Austria and Germany could allow them to form the independent Slav state they wanted to bring into being. They remained firm in their resolve to see this through. In contrast to most of the Russian troops around them, they maintained their discipline, and as a result became one of the most redoubtable units to survive the chaos of the Revolution. In 1918 they saved themselves from falling into German hands in Ukraine. On 26 March they obtained an agreement from local Soviets to leave Russia via the Trans-Siberian railway, to be shipped back to fight against the Germans on the Western Front.

The Czechs and the Soviets always remained suspicious of each others's intentions, and in May 1918 this hostility was to break out into open conflict.

f. 3440, op. 1, d. 7, I.4

To: *Voysko Ataman of the Don Army.*
From: *O. I. Shkor, authorized representative of Union of Czechoslovak*
Associations in Russia.
10 April 1917 Rostov on Don, Bolshaya Sadovaya No. 33

re forming teams of workers from Czech prisoners of war, who, although they have not been handed over to us, I propose that the Czech prisoner of war, Franktishka Kopechek should be transferred to the shell factories of the Russo-Baltic Factory in Taganrog.

I request the Commission for Accommodation to free from occupation Bolshaya Sadovaya No. 33.

f. 3440, op. 1, d. 4, I.2

To: *Don Oblast Revolutionary Military Council.*
From: *Authorized representative of Union of Czechoslovak Associations in*
Russia.
Note of Report
Rostov 9/22 March 1918

Acting on comrade Syrtsov's proposal I am presenting to Rostov the present Note of Report.

Leather and Winter clothing

f. 865, op. 1, d. 235, I.1

To: *Head of the Secretariat of the Chairman of Executive Heads of the*
Almighty Voysko of the Don.
From: *Deputy Supplies Officer for Head of Department, Colonel Bobrikov*
Urgent
February 1919

Today there have been delivered to Inspector Vasily Filipovich Rudukhin for the Society of Aid to the Front ten thousand (10 000) sacks.

f. 865, op. 1, d. 235, l.4

March [number] 37

An inter-Union Commission has been organized for distributing goods coming from abroad. Until a plenipotentiary representative of the Don arrives, for the time being there has entered into the body of the Commission [illegible]. 2500 poods of China tea have been assigned. Large sums of money will be required to pay for goods which arrive. I propose 10 millions, which must be transferred to the appointed representative to cover immediate payment for goods. I am sending by special courier a statement of accounts of the Commission. The appointed representative must be equipped with wide powers and have a list of the raw material which it is proposed to send abroad, and he must have up-to-date knowledge of the state of commerce and industry on the Don.

The firm of Coates were producing thread as a by-product of their linen industry. Herz were at this time one of the best-known firms manufacturing optical devices.

f. 865, op. 1, d. 235, l.31a verso

Act no. 87

On 23 march 1919, in Novocherkassk, a Commission consisting of Chairman Lt.-Col Aivazov and members: Collegiate Secretary Chernetsov, V. I. Yermakov, and Chairman of Don Chamber of Auditors, Accounts Clerk Olofinsky, took into store goods and materials, delivered by Lieutenant Flak from Colonel Bobrikov in Odessa:

(1) Threads
(2) Metal buttons
(3) Khaki coloured buttons
(4) Glass buttons
(5) Coates threads – 10 dozen
(6) Used binoculars (Herz) 2
(7) Binoculars (Lenera) 1
(8) Used telescope (Herz)
(9) Calf skins – 445 fus
(10) Sleeves of jackets and scarves 245 pairs
(11) Fronts to dresses 83 pairs

The calf skins are very bad quality, showing cracks when bent and tearing under the slightest strain.

f. 865, op. 1, d. 235, I.38

From the Commission's Act of 23 March among the articles accepted by Colonel Bobrikov there has turned out to be calf skin of poor quality.

f. 865, op. 1, d. 235, I.31a

To: *The Voysko Quartermaster-General.*
From: *Colonel Vakar and Colonel Zotov, Head of Department.*
10 May 1919
Copy

A batch of boxcalf and goat skin of unsatisfactory quality. Inform me urgently whether this is true.

f. 865, op. 1, d. 235, I.29

To: *Head of Secretariat of Principal Head of Military Supplies.*
From: *Colonel Lesnikov, Assistant Quartermaster-General, Head of Department, Lieutenant-Colonel, Chief Clerk of Stocktaking, Collegiate Assessor Zolotov.*
12 August 1919
Copy

445 fus of calf leather sent from Odessa by the Purchasing Bureau have been used for the inner linings of boots, since its price is no higher than sheepskin. Signature attested: Head of Inspector's Department (signed).

f. 865, op. 1, d. 235, l.29

To: Odessa Purchasing Bureau of Almighty Voysko of the Don.
From: Colonel Bobrikov, Director of Purchasing Bureau. 6 August

In forwarding the current correspondence I wish to inform you that I sent from Odessa a total of 15 000 fus of chrome leather @ 17 roubles 50 copecks per fus, and 445 fus of chrome calf skin at 10 roubles per fus.

Fully aware from my service experience how incompetent and captious are the Commissions which take in materials for government institutions, I addressed myself to the Principal Head of Military Supplies with my report No. 51 of 26 May this year, in which I asked for arrangements to be made to return this leather to me, since I am firmly convinced that its market price is immeasurably higher than the price I have paid; but up to now I have received no reply to that report.

f. 865, op. 1, d. 235, l.28

To: Principal Head of Military Supplies of Almighty Voysko of the Don.
From: Major-General ? Bomenuoek.
12 August 1919

There was no unsatisfactory quality of boxcalf and goat skin. 445 fus of chrome calf skin was despatched by Colonel Bobrikov @ 10 roubles per fus. In the Commission of the Oblast Materials Store this calf skin was found to be of bad quality: rotten, breaking when bent, and tearing under the slightest strain.

Chrome calf skin was received by Lieutenant-Colonel Semenchenkovanyy according to a completely satisfactory sample which was shown to him. Colonel Bobrikov does not allow that it would be possible for him to have accepted completely unsuitable leather.

This calf skin went to the inner linings of boots, since its price was no higher than sheepskin.

The Treasury did not suffer any loss, since the cost of a fus of calf skin was 10 roubles, whereas the cost of a fus of imitation chrome leather was 30–38 roubles in Rostov. Thus from the goods purchased by Colonel Bobrikov the Quartermaster General got boots with a lining @ 10 roubles, while by making up boots with Rostov leather they paid 30–38 roubles a fus with no inner lining.

f. 865, op. 1, d. 235, I.28

Telegram
To: *Novocherkassk, addressed to General Sidorin copies to: Chairman,*
Council of Executive Heads and General Chernozubov.
From: Yaroshevsky.
20 May 1919

Colonel Merzhanov is again trying to requisition motor vehicles of the Department of Food Supply. Having regard to the decree of the Council of Executive Heads, that vehicles can be requisitioned only when they carry the decrees of that Council concerning the mutual consent of the Army Commander with the representative of the Council, be so kind as to convey an appropriate order to Colonel Merzhanov.

f. 865, op. 1, d. 235, I.24

To: *P. Kh. Popov, Chairman Council of Executive Heads, Almighty Voysko of*
the Don.
From: Principal Head of Supplies of Armed Forces of South Russia,
Yekterinodar.
11 July 1919. Received by Secretariat of Council of Executive Heads
17 July 1919

Dear Sir Pyotr Kharitonovich,
In order to unify the evolution of proposals for restitution of losses caused by the enemy during the late war in the Don and Kuban Oblasts and in localities subordinate to the Commander-in-Chief of Armed Forces of South Russia, the Head of Military Administration has instructed me to form an inter-departmental Commission, to contain representatives of the Departments of External Affairs, Finance and Justice of the Don and the Kuban.
   Informing you of this, I beg you not to refuse to make arrangements to send Your Representative to the session of the Commission, which is to take place under my chairmanship at 19.00 hours on 18 July in my Office

With esteem
[illegible signature]

f. 865, op. 1, d. 76 I.3

Decree
3 September 1919

of Council of Executive Heads of Almighty Voysko of the Don, HEARD: Resolution of Director of Military and Naval Sections, DECREED: to grant Director of Military and Naval Sections power to advance sums to the Provisional Committee of the All-Russian Land Union when the latter is ordering warm things and footwear for the Don Army, to amount to not more than 50 per cent of the cost of the things on order from agreed sums allowed.

f. 865, op. 1, d. 76, I.4

Decreed
3 September 1919

To open for use by Administration of Military and Naval Sections 86 accounts for extraordinary expenses by the Principal Artillery Administration amounting to FORTY MILLION roubles for purchases, in accordance with resolutions of 30 August to acquire through the Purchasing Office in Constantinople forty thousand poods of cartridge brass and five thousand poods of American powder for rifles, which are required by the artillery department to produce rifle cartridges.

f. 865, op. 1, d. 76, I.5

September 1919

HEARD: Report of Manager of Department of Land Management and Agriculture concerning premises for a college for surveyors.

DECREED: to open an extra credit to be placed at the disposal of the Manager of the Department of Land Management and Agriculture 815 st. 1 lit of ? *asmet* / of the aforesaid department for 1919 in the Agricultural section amounting to one million four hundred thousand (1 400 000) roubles, of which 900 000 roubles to be assigned for buying Kurdyumov's property on Pribylinskaya Street and 500 000 roubles for carrying out repairs to buildings in the property thus acquired.

Chairman of the Council
Manager of the Departments
Secretary of the Voysko

f. 865, op. 1, d. 215, l.9

To: *Director of Military and Naval Departments.*
From: *Lieutenant-General, acting Head of Military Supplies.*
December 1919

Colonel Bobrikov, representing the Odessa Purchasing Bureau, has reported on a proposal which has come to him from a British subject, Foster, to get from Constantinople, within ten days from signing the contract, 40 000 sheepskin coats and 40 000 pairs of felt boots in exchange for grain, counting 13 poods, 20 lbs against one sheepskin and one pair of boots, ranked as one item, on condition that they receive grain amounting to 200 000 poods not later than 21 days after the sheepskins and boots have been delivered to Novorossiysk, and the remainder within two months from the signing of the contract.

In view of the pressing need for warm things for the Army, I request you to authorize the Odessa Purchasing Bureau to acquire from the British subject, Foster, 40 000 sheepskin coats and 40 000 pairs of felt boots in exchange for grain, counting 13 poods, 20 lbs to be exchanged for one sheepskin and one pair of boots on the terms set out above.

f. 865, op. 1, d. 215, l.10

Decree of Council of Executive Heads Almighty Voysko of the Don

HEARD: Report concerning the acquisition of 40 000 sheepskin coats and 40 000 pairs of felt boots in exchange for grain.

DECREED: to authorize the Odessa Purchasing Bureau to acquire from the British subject, Foster, 40 000 sheepskin coats and 40 000 pairs of felt boots in exchange for grain, on condition that the coats and boots are handed over in Novorossiysk not later than 14 days from the signing of the contract. The grain due to be delivered in exchange for the boots and sheepskins should be handed over in Novorossiysk on two dates, to wit (1) 120 000 poods after 21 days from the signing of the contract, (2) the remainder to come through after the Sea of Azov has become free for navigation.

f. 865, op. 1, d. 215, l.34

From: Lieutenant-General.

An offer has been made by the Company of Moscow United Trade and Industry to deliver to Novorossiysk the following goods for the Army:

(1) 15 000 pieces of shirt material, measuring about 900 000 arshins at 65 roubles an arshin.
(2) 149 pieces of trouser material of No. 1? thickness measuring about 7000 arshins at 250 roubles per arshin.
(3) 1000 pieces of double trouser material.
(4) 756 pieces of standard trouser material.

All the material listed above is in Novorossiysk and can be delivered immediately to the Don. 10 deposits amounting to 10% of the cost of the whole consignment, and the remaining 90% to be paid in Novorossiysk on receipt of the goods. Prices prepaid to Novorossiysk including all expenses and customs dues.

The Company, taking on all responsibility and expenses for receiving and delivering the goods as I have indicated above, allocates itself a 6% recompense.

The Army needs warm clothing, the prices are relatively inexpensive. I therefore find this offer acceptable and request permission to acquire all the cloth on offer, but setting the profit margin at not more than 5%.

f. 865, op. 1 d. 215, l.3

DECREED: To permit Manager of ?VMO to acquire in Novorossiysk through the services of Company of Moscow United Trade and Industry cloth as follows:

(1) 15 000 pieces of ?shirt material ? etc. ?

Payment to be effected as follows: 10% of cost of whole consignment to be paid in advance at time of purchase and the remaining 90% when the goods are received in Novorossiysk. Expenditure to be met from credits allocated under this heading.

Based in the south of Russia, the Don Army and the Volunteer Army found themselves in an area which was relatively well-supplied with food, at least in comparison with the Reds' bases in central Russia. On the other hand the dry steppes of the Don and the Kuban had no extensive woodlands and only some trees, mainly in the river valleys, hence the reference in *list* 16 to the shortage of timber.

f. 865, op. 1, d. 215, I.16

To: Council of Executive Heads Almighty Voysko of the Don.
From: Manager of Military and ? M Sections of Almighty Voysko of the Don.
10 December 1919, Novocherkassk

Since in the Building Section of the Military Engineers Department there is no timber, as is essential for carrying out building work, since it is completely off the market and none can be brought from Tsaritsyn, in consequence of its being urgently transported to the Kuban I request that the Council of Executive Heads make a decree to permit the Head of the Building Section to requisition the fencing of the Polytechnic Institute and the Horse Racing Club, as also fences and suitable buildings and sheds of brick factories etc. in Rostov, Taganrog, Aleksandrovsk-Grushevsky, Novocherkassk and Kamenskaya stanitsa.

For Director of Military ? M Section   Lieutenant-General
For Head of Supplies   Major-General Rodionov

DECREED: Permission given to Head of Building Section of the Military Engineers Department to take fences etc. for building.

3
1919: Red Strategy

Situation reports

As long as Germany was at war with the Western Allies, the Kaiser's government feared that a new Eastern Front might be formed against them. The Volunteer Army was opposed to them in theory, though in practice Denikin tried to avoid open conflict with German units, as he wished to concentrate his efforts on overthrowing the Soviets.

The outcome of the civil war would depend largely on which side could hold the loyalty of their own supporters and capture the allegiance of the mass of the population, who had little understanding of politics and had seldom been called on to exercise any political choice. Swings in the military situation on the Don may be seen as reflecting changing sympathies among its inhabitants. For eight months from May 1918, the Don Army re-established its power.

In May 1918 Denikin insisted on returning to the Kuban, took Tikhoretskaya, and on 18 August, Yekaterinodar, which the Reds had named as the capital of their North Caucasus Soviet Republic. In December 1918 the Whites tried to persuade the Cossacks to carry the campaign outside the territory of the Voysko, but those serving at the front were becoming disillusioned, and several regiments returned to their homes, opening a large gap through which the Communists could advance. The Red Army conquered most of the Don territory in the first months of 1919, and the Whites fell back to the south bank of the River Donets.

The Red Army report which follows is a curious mixture of fact and fantasy, typical of a time when it was difficult for even the commanders to find reliable sources of news. In December 1918 Britain had forced the Cossacks to accept a unified command, the Almighty

Voysko of the Don agreeing to place itself under Denikin's overall direction. But Cossack morale was already weakening, and in January the Red Army poured through the large gap in the front which had been stripped of defenders. Most rank and file Cossacks did not see any sense in going beyond the boundaries of their homeland, and were reluctant to join in a general advance on Moscow. Krasnov's efforts to persuade them to fight on led to a drastic split in the allegiance of those fighting at the front. Many went over to the Reds, as mentioned in the second paragraph of the report. The majority of the Cossacks simply returned to their own villages, carrying their rifles with them, according to their long-standing traditions. As the Reds proceeded south the more prosperous Cossack villages remained loyal to the Don Army, and the commander rightly warns of 'a hard fight' to take each stanitsa. Britain was now starting to send equipment and arms to the Whites, but the 'two Scottish regiments' on the Georgian highway can only have been one of the many baseless rumours which circulated during the civil war.

Taken all in all the commander's confident tone reflects the Red Army's success in the early months of 1919, when they were pushing the Whites down to the south of the Don territory.

f. 17, op. 109, d. 50, I.1

To: *Revolutionary Military Council 8th Army.*
From: *Head of 12th Rifle Division.*
Report
21 February 1919

Pressed back by the Red armies, and thanks to the successful movements of the Ukrainian Army, which has occupied Starobelsk, Bakhmut, Lugansk, and penetrated deeply round General Krasnov's left flank, the Cossacks have recently begun to retreat on their left flank, and at the moment this retreat can be observed on the whole of their northern front.

The Kazanskaya Regiment has come over completely to the side of the Soviet troops, the Meshkovskaya and Migulinskaya Regiments have come over in part. The Red Army's superiority in numbers on our right flank, as also the threat from the direction of Bakhmut and Lugansk, all these factors have forced the Cossacks to pull back more speedily on their let flank than on their right. The rapid movement of Soviet forces along the Liski-Yevstratovsk railway, demoralization among Cossacks of Meshkovakaya,

Kazanskaya and Migulinskaya stanitsas influenced the commanders, so that they considered Cossack resistance to be broken. They decided just to exploit their victory by a rapid march, setting themselves as a final objective even the capture of Novocherkassk and Rostov.

Acting on the information available to me on 4 February I reported that I cannot share this point of view. The Cossacks are putting up a stiff resistance and we shall have to take each stanitsa after a hard fight. There are villages where all the men have departed, and our transport is effected only by Cossack women, because there are no males left. I have made a careful study of interrogations carried out with Red Army men who have escaped captivity and with Cossacks who have come over to our side. I have tried to get to the root of the moral force which makes other Cossacks fight so stubbornly.

Under the direction of the Allies the Whites have carried out a complete unification of all their forces operating in South Russia. Denikin has been appointed supreme commander of all these forces, and he is acting as the Allies decree.

Odessa, Kherson, the Crimean peninsula and Mariupol are being made into the bases for a future advance. 120 tanks have already been unloaded in Odessa, and 60 tanks in Novorossiysk.

In the Caucasus the English have helped the Volunteer Army to finish off the remains of the 11th and 12th Soviet Armies. The units who come from these bases are equipped with all the latest Western technology. Their troops will be headed by armoured cars and tanks.

[dates in Old Style] 6 January Zheleznovodsk taken, 7 January Kislovodsk, 9 January Georgiyevskaya.

In the area of Naurskaya upwards of 10 000 Red Army men have been taken prisoner. The English have sent two Scottish regiments along the Georgian Military Highway.

8th Army is now faced with new divisions of the Volunteer Army from the Caucasus. On our divisional front we have today discovered the 17th Volunteer Regiment.

After Germany collapsed the Bolsheviks set Ukraine up as a Soviet republic, but they alienated the rural population by confiscating grain to feed the cities in central Russia. Antonov-Ovseyenko was in overall command of Red Army units in Ukraine. Trying to exercise control over local partisans meant he found himself tied down dealing with insurrections, like those of Grigorev who changed sides in May 1919. Antonov was consequently unable to spare any troops to aid the Reds attacking the Whites along the Donets.

Since entering the Don territory in January the red regiments had suffered many casualties during four months of relentless fighting. Their ranks had been further depleted by typhus, and they were running short of supplies of food, clothing and equipment. These exhausted remnants could hardly be strong enough to withstand Denikin, as he struck north up towards the Soviet heartland. Two weeks after this despatch the Volunteer Army launched its most successful offensive of the war, crossing the Donets on 24 May.

The Southern Front was where the outcome of the civil war would be decided. Vatsetis' dissatisfaction with Antonov was well-founded. He suggests Ukraine might be a source from which to recruit large reserves of Red Army men. But such recruits should be posted elsewhere, so that they do not become infected by any of the different strains of separatism.

f. 17, op. 109, d. 41, 11.12–14

To: Chairman of Defence Council, comrade Lenin, copy to comrade Trotsky
From: Vatsetis, Commander-in Chief of all Armed Forces of the Republic;
Aralov, Military Commissar, Member of Revolutionary Military Council of the
Republic.
7 May 1919 Serpukhov (received 8 May)
Urgent. Secret.

In the last few days war in the south of the RSFSR has taken a turn for the worse. In the eastern parts of the south, i. e. in the Don Oblast, we cannot strike a decisive blow, in spite of sending down there the last forces we have at our disposal at this time. On the Southern Front the enemy already has a numerical superiority over us. The military units which we are sending to the Southern Front are not in sufficient numbers to make up for our losses in killed, wounded and illness in the 8th, 9th and 13th Armies, whose ranks have been greatly thinned in ceaseless hard battles. The armies of the Southern Front are getting no more than 40% of the necessary replacements. In the area of the Donets Basin our units have been forced back step by step.

To the west of the Manych the 10th Army have come up against an enemy superior in numbers. The successes achieved by our 10th Army have evidently reached their maximum, and from now on they will have to go over to the defensive.

The enemy's river fleet, and his superiority in land forces, with the river fleet thrown into action ... The threat of Kolchak on the Volga has required all our reserves to be transferred there, thanks to which we have managed to check the further advance of his armies.

Ukraine, advancing along the path of independence, appears weaker than had seemed at first glance.

My instructions about the need to form a strategic reserve met with statements from Antonov, Commander of the Ukrainian Front, that to create this he would have to clear out the whole Ukraine. Petlyura is threatening Kiev from the north west. The uprising to the north-east of Kiev is evidently growing. We have had to send the 3rd Division which was stationed in Chernigov Province. According to Antonov's reports the rebels have 8 guns. This rebellion in the rear of the Ukrainian front now makes for the same unfavourable circumstances as have been created in the rear of the Southern Front in the Don Oblast.

The national governments formed in Lithuania and Belarus have turned out to be not of the slightest use to us. The two divisions, that were handed over to them to have their numbers made up, have completely fallen apart. All that is left of the Lithuanian division are three headquarters, while the soldiers have turned to plundering. Both Ukraine and also all the southern and south-western oblasts of the former Russian Empire are a source we could draw on to fill the thinning ranks of our armies.

I would propose the following steps be taken:

1. In the name of the Central Government of the RSFSR declare mobilization in Ukraine for the western, south-western and southern oblasts of the former Russian Empire, and send all those who are conscripted into reserve battalions stationed outside Ukraine, so that, after training in the reserve battalions, squads of reinforcements made up from them may be taken into army units on the Eastern, Southern and Western Fronts.
2. Since the Command of the Ukrainian Front can hardly manage to move towards Budapest, and since equally we must allow for Romania to act against us, as a result of the ultimatum which she has been offered, with Petlyura advancing from the direction of Galitsiya, I consider it imperative to appoint a member of the General Staff as assistant to Antonov, Commander of the Ukrainian Front. We can in no wise consider satisfactory the present state of affairs on the Ukrainian Front, since control of the troops of the Ukrainian Front has to such an extent passed out of the hands of the Commander, that he cannot even allocate four brigades to render timely assistance, as so desperately

needed to help the Southern Front. At this juncture in time, when the strain of battle on the Don and on the Eastern Front demands all our reserves, when we have no reserves in the interior of our country, this weakness of command on the Ukrainian Front may have a very dire effect in our civil war.

3. On the Western Front we must attain complete unity of military and political command. The measures we are taking to achieve this in the western parts of our Republic are being given effect extremely slowly, which fails to meet the way events are quickly developing against us, both from the armies of Kolchak and Denikin, and also from Europe in the West.

f. 17, op. 109, d. 44, l.34

From: Trotsky, Chairman of Revolutionary Military Council of the Republic.
1 June 1919 No. 79/s

Voroshilov and Mezhlauk have carried out in full the real task which they were expected to perform to create a strong Ukrainian Army. I propose tomorrow or the day after to summon to Izyum as a central location the commanders of 8, 13 and 2 Armies, i. e. Voroshilov, as also Mezhlauk and Podvoysky and the Quartermasters, in order to unify everything that can properly be centralized, but certainly not creating any sort of Donets Military Republic.

f. 17, op. 109, d. 44, l.43

To: Sklyansky for Lenin.
From: Trotsky, Chairman Revolutionary Military Council.
5 June 1919 Kharkov

The situation on the Southern Front is extremely difficult. The only way we can make a real change will be by concentrating a powerful striking force on the shortest and most exposed direction towards Mariupol and Taganrog. It has therefore been decided to build up as quickly as possible a strong 14th Army in the area of the former 2nd Ukrainian Army. It is my intention to turn over the counter-insurgency forces to form part of that Army after the area of the rebellion has been subdued. One rifle division and one cavalry division are being formed in haste. Kharkov is providing 500 Communists. Our best hope of success lies in forming the 14th Army speedily and in secrecy. I request Central Committee to take special pains over this exceptionally important task. The first thing is to see whether the demand I sent to Sklyansky has been fully met. The second thing is to send as many extra forces of political workers and military commanders and reliable units, even if they are small in numbers, to crush *en route* the trouble Makhno is causing.

f. 17, op. 65,. d. 35, l.86

To: Chairman Soviet Defence, Kiev; copies to Chairman Sovnarkom, Lenin; Chairman of Revolutionary Military Council of the Republic, Trotsky, to find at current address, acknowledge receipt.
From: Ukraine People's Commissar for Military Matters, Podvoysky, 2 July Berdichev Station (decoded 4 July in Secretariat of Deputy Chairman of Revolutionary Military Council of the Republic).
Telegram (cypher)   *Secret*

On 28 June there were sent to 14th Army the personnel of the brigade commanded by Dmitriyev, consisting of Brigade Headquarters, the commandant's office, two regiments of 600 infantry, one squadron of 100 men with 50 horses, 12 light field pieces with 130 horses, communication companies, bakeries, a machine-gun section, transport for bringing up food supplies, a medical unit, and 49th Regiment of 6th Division with 1800 infantry. On 30 June orders were given for sending 10 000 sailors to reinforce Dmitriyev's brigade and to take workers to swell the strength of the Brigade – that is all that can still be taken.

The 14th Army was ordered to transfer 54th Regiment with 1200 infantry. In order to forestall the Whites moving out of the Crimea at the Perekop position an order was made that the 2nd Regiment of sailors should be detached and its strength augmented with workers, and to form a light battery and a series of heavy batteries. In the meantime, until the Regiment and artillery as specified could take up their positions, it was directed that a holding battalion should be sent from Nikolayev, consisting of some men of the Spartakovsky Regiment with a section of heavy artillery. In the direction of Proskurov there have been despatched 40th Regiment and towards Yekaterinoslav 2 armoured cars and the armoured car squad of 14th Army, consisting of 4 armoured cars.

f. 17, op. 109, d. 41

Telegram (cypher)   *Secret*
To: *Commander Eastern Army Group; copies to Lenin, Trotsky, Sklyansky*
From: *Vatsetis, Commander-in-Chief; Gusev, Member of Revolutionary
Military Council of the Republic 123 PTK 264 568 2/7 23 50 3 July (received
3 July 3. 05)*

2 July 1919 OPERATIONAL
The forces of our Southern Army Group have left Tsaritsyn. The 10th Army,
which had been defending that city, is now taking up positions to the
north of Tsaritsyn between the Volga and the Kama. By taking Tsaritsyn the
enemy has cut our communications down the Volga to Astrakhan and to
the 34th Division, which is operating on the northern shore of the Caspian,
and has cut our communications with the Volga and Caspian Flotillas. The
loss of Tsaritsyn and the withdrawal of the 10th Army north of that point,
coupled with us losing Nikolayevsk, poses a threat to the right flank of our
Eastern Front, since the enemy may move forces to the east bank of the
Volga, starting to advance towards Urbakh and Saratov, and making a
common front by linking up Denikin's forces with the Ural and Orenburg
Cossacks. Our troops of Southern Army Group, who have retreated from
Tsaritsyn, have been seriously shaken up, and they are facing an enemy
numerically superior, possessing tanks and good technical equipment. For
this reason it is still difficult to predict what line our 10th Army will eventually manage to hold. Because of this it seems quite possible that Denikin
will move part of his forces east of the Volga to cut the Astrakhan–Urbakh
railway, and begin to advance towards Saratov, perhaps even further
north, to Aran', i.e. bringing pressure to bear on the rear of our Eastern
Front. If the enemy carries out this sort of manœuvre then you will have to
put in your best fighting units as a real reinforcement to our Eastern Front's
right flank. From what we have said it follows? [nonsensical sequence indicated by question mark in text] right flank of Eastern Front and left flank of
Eastern Front because of the mountainous terrain the war has been long
spun out, and that in the Ural Mountains you might achieve the same
success by using smaller numbers of men for pursuing the enemy. Do you
not think it is a good time for you to reconsider how your forces are
grouped in the centre and east flank of the Eastern Front with a view to
building up sufficient reserves as necessary, for them to be transferred to
the area of Saratov and other points that are under threat? We must both
strengthen the right flank and the rear of the Eastern Front and also stop
the enemy moving up the Volga and interfering with the mid-Volga area

where we are building up new formations. We are awaiting your conclusions about what actions you propose, depending on establishing a demarcation line between our Eastern and Southern Fronts along the lower course of the Volga.   Nr. 3232/on

Commissars versus commanders

The Reds had almost no experienced military commanders. In the face of considerable opposition General Bonch-Bruyevich and Trotsky enlisted many former officers of the old Imperial Army to serve the Reds as so-called 'military specialists'. Mawdesley (1987, pp. 59–63), provides a succinct account of the creation of the Red Army. He states that in 1918, 22 000 ex-officers were enlisted to serve in the Red Army, and by the end of the Civil War this had risen to the astonishing total of 48 000. This must stand to Trotsky's credit as one of the main factors which led to victory. In many cases the Communists held the officers' wives and families hostage as a guarantee of their husband's loyalty to the Bolshevik cause. The officers' submission to the aim of the Party was also ensured by appointing known Communist activists as 'military commissars', who exercised close supervision over military operations.

Many documents are filled with appeals from commisars to assign more 'political workers' (*politrabotniki*), to strengthen their hold over their units in the field. Large numbers of dedicated Communists could not be made available, and the constant recurrence of this theme is a useful reminder that in the first years after the revolution the Communists were only a tiny minority in the great mass of the population.

1. 182/4

1 February 1919   9th Army
Concerning artillery units of 9th Army

Army's complete lack of commissars. Political Section of Southern Army Group has none. We must have eighteen battalion commissars, not essential to have artillery specialists. Position serious. Urgent measures essential.

When commissars were originally attached to active service units, operational orders had to be countersigned by them. The 'unity of command', which Vatsetis wanted to establish, would have meant subordinating the political commissars to the unit commander and giving the final control over operations unequivocally into the hands of the latter. The controversy over how to organize their duties remained a point of dispute through to 1924, when the ultimate say in all decisions was finally assigned to the military commanders.

f. 17, op. 109, d. 44, I.7

To: *Revolutionary Military Council*
From: *Trotsky, Chairman of Revolutionary Military Council, Serpukhov*
Telegram by direct line
Received 19 January 1919

I am completely and wholly in agreement with the opinion of the Commander-in-Chief that it would be quite wrong to replace V. Gittis as Army Commander. We cannot get rid of people who are working conscientiously, and this applies to Iskratsky. We know he has declared himself to be ill, and apparently there is little hope of his coming back soon to the Southern Army Group. So the question about a temporary replacement takes on a more serious meaning. I am afraid that Tukhachevsky may not be the best man for the job. Would it not be better to appoint Tukhachevsky to the 8th Army and Gittis to command the Army Group? I request an up to date report about the situation at the Front.

f. 17, op. 65, d. 136, I.16

On the Eastern front the political workers are too taken up with questions of military operations and devote too little time to political education.. They may again fail to note the demoralization of the army.

f. 17, op. 109, d. 44 cont I.10

To: ? M People's Commissar of State Supervision copy to Lenin.
From: Trotsky.
Telegram   Copy
23 April

Congress of principal field controllers of Southern Front has declared it unnecessary to appoint commissars for us. Field controllers are officials. Our Party commissars are attached to them to give them authority.

Nr 359

f. 17, op. 65, d. 136, l.16

To: [Secretary of] Central Committee.
From: Trotsky.
14 June 1919

I am passing to you for Central Committee a telegram sent by me to comrade Smirnov at Ufa: 'I do not know of any telegram which is supposed to allocate to you a whole series of separate individuals to go into the 7th Army. No such order was given by me.'

f. 17, op. 109, d. 44, l.47

Moscow to Sklyansky.
From: Chairman of Revolutionary Military Council, Trotsky.
(4th of 4 telegrams)
? June 1919

The Kharkov and Oryol Districts come under the Revolutionary Military Council of Southern Army Group on the same basis as the Volga and Ural Districts are subordinate to the Eastern Front; give them orders over the signatures of myself, Vatsetis and Aralov.   No. 1880

f. 17, op. 109, d. 44, I.146

To: *Central Committee of Russian Communist of Party*
From: *Smilga, member of Revolutionary Military Council of Southern Army Group, Volsk*
16 August 1919

Report
I
General situation

The situation on the Southern Front remains extremely serious. Our right flank is continuing to fall back, while our centre and left flank are at present marking time, being unable to go over to the offensive because no reserves have come up. Headquarters, communications and supplies are everywhere extremely badly organized. Army staffs do not have reliable information on the fighting capacity or numerical strength of their units, nor about the state of their equipment. Very often the headquarters of the Armies lose touch for a long time with the headquarters of their divisions.

The organization of political indoctrination is only now beginning to be set up (at least in the 9th and 10th Armies).

II
The reasons for our failures

The main basic reason for our failures lies with the INABILITY of the Southern Army Group's Revolutionary Military Council to lead and direct our forces.

The Southern Army Group's Revolutionary Military Councils are noteworthy for their large numbers of personnel, and the very short space of time each member spends in any one Army. This unwieldy organization has been set up on a false principle, which is fatal to any military activity, namely that each member of the Council should become expert on one or other aspect of our work. One person 'supervises' the Political Section, the Special Section and the Tribunal, a second person 'does' supplies, medical services and military communications, a third the units in reserve, a fourth the headquarters, a fifth accompanies the commander – and so on *ad infinitum*. This hapless form of organization results in decentralizing control of the troops. Instead of one single will we have a multitude of voices – with the most varied aims, understanding and ideas in view. On certain solemn days this body of elders gets together and decides the 'main' questions by means of formalized decrees. One could not imagine a more absurd mockery of the basic principles of warfare. In the Southern Army Group they have brought into being the most stupid demands of our 'lefties' for a collective command. I have always considered (and think to this day) that the best type of command is concentrated in the hands of one leader, that 'Councils' are only a passing phase, brought about by dozens of ideas of different people. I have tried to make small councils, with not more than two Communists and one military specialist, hoping to move on to having just one Communist. All the other Communists have had to go into military tasks, acting in some specialized capacity – as supply officers, commanders, chief clerks etc.

Here we are dominated by other conceptions. I maintain that military specialists in the South are placed in a completely false position. They are followed by a whole train of people speaking specialized military jargon, while in practice the Army Group is managed by comrades who have no idea of military affairs. The other trouble on the Southern Front is the constant switching about of staff. A person will work for two or three months in such and such an Army, just get to know its organization and personnel – and then he is moved on. This applies both to the members of Revolutionary Military Councils and also to the military specialists. According to comrade Sokolnikov, over the course of about half a year the 13th Army has seen change-overs of from five to six Heads of Supplies. Because of this we hear perpetual urgent cries about the lack of bread and trousers. Anyone can see only too clearly that this system of frequently replacing personnel – a system of organized panic – inflicts nothing but terrible harm on our work.

I can guarantee to quote many facts to support any of the statements I have made.

III
THE REVOLUTIONARY MILITARY COUNCIL

The Revolutionary Military Council simply could not work in the way it is at present constituted. There is such a gap of mutual incomprehension that it is impossible to imagine how they could come to any agreement on the best way to work. In order to avoid the Southern Army Group HQ becoming a battleground for a tussle which would be quite inexcusable at such a difficult time, I have determined to refrain from work at the front and to stay 'in the group'. I must add that Yegorev is absolutely not up to his duties.

IV

The Southern Army Group is sick. It can only be cured by <u>surgical</u> intervention.

As a conclusion: Those at present in charge must be recalled and a normal Revolutionary Military Council must be set up, which is capable of working.

16 August   Smilga

PS I must add that in the 10th Army, where the numerous individual members of the Revolutionary Military Council 'take an interest' in various aspects of their work, added to the way the structure of the Army is itself falling apart – we have reached such a pitch that one member of the Council has given orders for the others to be kept under observation. That is not the way to make war.

f. 17, op. 109, d. 44, I.149

To: Central Committee.
From: Trotsky.
30 September 1919

With regard to the report by comrade Smilga I consider it necessary to make the following points:

(1) The overall appreciation of the situation shows a certain lack of perspective. In the organization of the Southern Army Group there are no particular features, in view of its special factors which would distinguish it from the Eastern Front. In the latter during the time of our retreat one could see the same features of collapse and demoralization as on the Southern Front. In exactly the same way members of the Revolutionary Military Council were replaced, and this had a very positive effect.

(2) I met the author of the report in Volsk. My proposals were accepted without any objections. I heard no counter-proposals being put forward. The report's author did not point out to me any faults in our work on the Southern Front. I consider this type of behaviour is not right, judged either from the point of view of the military chain of command or from our work as comrades in the Party.

f. 17, op. 65, d. 136, l.3

From: *Chief Clerk of Secretariat of Commissar of Headquarters.*

Special Section of Republic has decided to abolish Special Section of Southern Army Group, finding it quite sufficient to subordinate Special Sections of Armies directly to Moscow, without going through the Group. That sort of arrangement shows complete incomprehension and ignorance of the Republic's Special Section with work in the Armies.

f. 17, op. 65, d. 136, l.3

From: *comrade Trotsky.*
(received) 12 September 1919

According to the report of Anokin, Chairman of the Tribunal, the court has declared on the criminal part played by Orlovsky, Chairman of the Provincial Communist Party. He led a Detachment of Special Assignments men from Tambov to go into action without the knowledge of the Council of the Fortified District.

f. 17, op. 109, d. 44, l.188

To: *Central Committee Russian Communist Party.*
From: *Member of Revolutionary Military Council of 14th Army, A. Bubnov.*
16 September 1919

After working for a month as a member of the Revolutionary Military Council of the 14th Army I made the quite unexpected discovery that the general line of my work was considered to have an element of undisciplined individualism [*partizanshchina*].

It has turned out that this opinion is based on a written declaration by comrades Natsarenus and Kizelteyn, who testify that with my connection and my arts and devices I hindered the reform and reconstitution of the 14th Army. I firmly maintain that:

(1) During my time in the Revolutionary Military Council there were never any disagreements about the organization of the 14th Army.

(2) In particular, with regard to converting the former 'Crimean' Army into a normal division (after my first visit there), all decisions about the current reconstruction were accepted unanimously.

(3) It was in fact I who set out the scheme for a practical, thorough reconstruction of the Crimean Division.

That was done by me after my first visit in a written report, from which 14th Army Revolutionary Military Council learnt of the exact nature of the Crimean Division.

(4) When I took on the post of Chairman of the Commission to reform the Ukraine Division I carried out completely the decree of the Revolutionary Military Council.

I would refer you to comrade Epstein, who was working in the Commission as political commissar.

With comradely greetings

A. Bubnov

In *list* 20 below, it is curious to see the unwitting survival of the old term 'officers' rather than the normal Red Army designation 'commanders'. There is a similar lapse in the *Report on the Bryansk Rebellion* (f. 17, op. 65, d. 136, 1. 16 below), though in that case there may have been an intentional warning in retaining the word 'officers'.

f. 17, op. 65, d. 136, l.20

To: *Revolutionary Military Council.*
From: *Sklyansky.*
8 August 1919

One member of Revolutionary Military Council must proceed immediately to the Don estuary with a group of political workers and take measures to stop the moods of panic in headquarters of the divisions. We shall hold talks tomorrow morning, give you the Red officers, except those intended for the Seventh Army.

f. 17, op. 65, d. 136, l.21

To: *Political Sections of all Armies, copy to Trotsky.*
From: *Member of Revolutionary Military Council, Yurenev. 1919.*
Telegram

Former chain of command from Armies to Centre via Army Groups is cancelled by the Political Section, as we have acknowledged it necessary to abolish Political Sections of Army Groups. All questions raised by political life in the Army should be reported on directly to all offices of People's Commissar for Military Affairs.

NR 107

Military intelligence reports

During the Civil War when fronts were changing rapidly and many units were not firm in their allegiance, it was extremely difficult for headquarters staff to get a reliable picture of the situation at any given time. Their task was further complicated by the fact that few units were operating at their correct strength, as for example in the report of 16 June, the so-called 'battalion' which mustered only 120 men, and even more unrealistically the two 'regiments' of 150 – 200 men apiece.

f. 17, op. 109, d. 44, l.2

To: *Nizhni Novgorod Provincial Military Commissar.*
From: *Chairman of Revolutionary Military Council, Trotsky.*
Telegram
10 January No. 199

What have you done with soldiers of 11th Division who have returned?

f. 554, op. 1. d. 3, l.88

From: *Report on Party work in Novocherkassk, Rostov on Don and*
Taganrog.
May 1919

During this period *agents provocateurs* from our cells helped the counter-intelligence service to carry out arrests in the Taganrog District

Organization. Several *agents provocateurs* were at work. In the collapse up to 60 men were arrested out of the whole Organization.

It is extremely difficult to send documents and money across the Front.

f. 554, op. 1. d. 3, l.90

From: *Papers of the Donburo.*

'Treacherous bag woman'
Denikin has concluded a 15-year deal with England, calling in all surplus supplies of grain in the Don and Kuban areas.

f. 17, op. 109, d. 44, l.54

To: *Russian Communist Party (Bolshevik).*
From: *Syrtsov.*
16 June 1919 (received by Central Committee 3306 20 June)

I request the following message be sent to Bychkov by some agreed method:
'The critical situation at the front means that we must urgently consider some action in the enemy's rear. Inform us urgently of what chances there are for coordinating these actions. Step up to the maximum activity for disorganizing the enemy's rear. Donburo Syrtsov'.
527 14 June

f. 554, op. 1, d. 10, l.17

Agents' reports
9th Army.   *14 June*

Commanders of gangs Roshchenko and Bakyu have been arrested by our agents and handed over to the Special Section. In the area of Ambga and Mekhadyr there are obviously few men in the settlements, since they have evidently taken to the hills and some have joined gangs. There is an intense campaign of anti-Soviet propaganda, putting it about that the Red Army wants to advance.

10th Army

From the area of Vladikavkaz, according to reliable reports of 3 June, in the settlement of Alagirskaya (30 versts west of Vladikavkaz) former officers are carrying on intense propaganda among men serving in the 2nd Ossetian Regiment, claiming that all those serving in the 2nd Ossetian Regiment will be arrested and handed over. As a result the men from Alagirskaya in the 2nd Ossetian Regiment are hiding in the nearest woods and are hostile to the Soviet regime. The officers from Alagirskaya believe that the whole population of Alagirskaya sides with them, and any attempt to enrol them will be resisted. Alagirskaya is guarded by patrols of officers. According to the same information we should keep an eye on the Chairman of the Alagirskaya Revolutionary Committee, the former Lieutenant Nagarev. No gangs were discovered in the upper reaches of the River Uruk. 5 versts lower down the iron mountains a gang of 150 men attacked, and 76 rifles were seized. Those who took them declared that they were Red Army men. Attested: Senior Scientific Worker of Rostov Oblast Party archive

V. Perelygin

Agents' reports by 6 a.m. 16 June

9th Army: The remains of Denisov's detachment, which went from here, are active on the Kerch peninsula from Kerch to Mama Headland. Although they are not numerous they still do represent a certain force. A special service battalion, stationed at Adzhimushka has been called on to deal with them. A detachment that is hiding in the ravines maintains contact with Denisov's squad, and he has stated that at the slightest action against the forces holding the coast of the peninsula he will strike at their rear with his detachment. The soldiers in Kerch and along the coast are not in a mood to fight. When our aeroplanes appear they reduce them to panic. The remnants of Denisov's squad declare that given the slightest pressure by the Red Army they will be able to occupy and hold the coast from Kerch to Mama headland. The militia and the fishermen are inclined to side with the revolution and will come over to join the Reds. According to the same source, Eupatoria and Saki contain the 8th and 9th Regiments of men from the Kuban and the Don, with the strength of about 150–200 men in each regiment. The regiments were assigned to guard the shore of the Kerch Peninsula, but the soldiers have refused this duty, saying that they will only proceed as a mounted formation. Five versts to the north of Simferopol' trenches and barbed wire fences are being put in place. In the area of the Kozmo-Demyanovsky monastery a detachment of up to 150 Communists is operating under the command of the oblast Party committee. A detachment, under the command of Vasily Denisov and political commissar Grereda, formerly active in the area of Kerch, is now operating 25 versts north-east of the said monastery on the hill No-otyl (not on the map). It includes 1000 men and several guns. This detachment is maintaining contact with a unit from the oblast Communist organization. To the east of it as far as ? old ? units of Captain Orlov are deployed, amounting to 10 000 men, according to what the peasants say, including cavalry and up to 12 guns of various calibres. His detachment is constantly sending patrols along the road to Karisu-Bazar and Feodosiya, and makes raids on ? On 4 June Orlov's detachment along with Denisov's carried out a raid on Islamt Terek station, where they took various articles of property from the men of the Volunteer Army.

f. 17, op. 65, d. 136, I.17

To: *Pravda.*
From: *Military Censorship Section.*
18 July 1919

Military Censorship Section has repeatedly requested the editorial department of *Pravda* to submit military-type material for preliminary examination by the military censor in the editor's department. Almost every day the newspaper contains material which constitutes a military secret.

d. 155, 11. 80–81

(extracts)
To: *the Administration of the Special Section of the All-Union Cheka / copies to the Special Section of the Southern Front, to comrade Minin, member of Revolutionary Military Council of 10th Army.*
Report and statement
5 September

On 3 July this year, acting on the order of Revolutionary Military Council of 10th Army, No. 326, comrade Genkin is appointed as the new Chairman to replace comrade Novitsky as Chairman of Special Section.

(I)   State of the Special Section on 4 July this year. Even a cursory glance reveals the state of Special Section of 10th Army to be chaotic. We do take into account that 4 July was the moment of the evacuation from Tsaritsyn, which fell to the enemy. Comrade Novitsky is handing over to his successor only a certain part of the secret papers and documents. Why does he not hand over the Special Section as a whole?

The papers which comrade Genkin has received are no longer secret from him. They have come in as multiple copies, there are no top copies.

Information. Have measures often been taken to organize a network of informants? There are none of them in one part. The establishment is for one or two persons.

(II) Work on organizing the Special Section of 10th Army. The Army is retreating, together with it must retreat the steamer in which the Special Section is quartered. Taking advantage of that time an assessment of Party workers was carried out. As a result we are left with a small number of workers, but those who remain are reliable.

Work of the Information Unit
Two objectives:

(1)   Infiltration, i.e. through its informants, through reports, extracts from political communiqués and such like – it should gather materials which pick out criminal personnel in various institutions, units and Army staffs.

(2)   By drawing up reports, summaries of operations etc., it should keep the centre and the Revolutionary Military Council informed about the work of the Special Section. In the active part of the Section there are in all about 35 agents, of whom only 6–7 are capable of undertaking serious counter-intelligence work in depth.

The Head of Staff for All-Russia has assigned to us the responsibility of examining prisoners of war and people who have come across to us.

Managerial Unit
Department No. 4 has been moved into the occupied town of Kamyshin for work in the town and on the Army's left flank.
Department No. 2 is placed on the left bank of the Volga (at present in the Nikolayevsky Workers' Settlement).

Three points of the Special Section have been organized on the River Volga. They are responsible for observing all passing steamers and for military intelligence work.

(III) Coded report on the work of the Special Section of 10th Army, from 4 July to 1 September this year.

Total number of cases processed by Special Section 10th Army,	326
Out of which cases completed:	
charged with spying	6
charged with counter-revolutionary activities	3
charged with dereliction of duty	69
charged with belonging to a White Guard organization	3

f. 554, op. 1. , d. 3, l.98

Information received by the Donburo at Oryol from partisan organizations on the Don.
30 September 1919

Taganrog: Main artillery base. The Baltic Factory: the Whites' only shell and cartridge factory on Gimnazicheskaya Street No. 7.
English tank detachment. With the section there are 8 mobile workshops fitted out for repairing motor vehicles, and much technical equipment carried in the back of a lorry.
Overall quantity of tanks in Volunteer and Don Armies?
2 Voisin aircraft without engines.
The Baltic Factory produces 15 000 cartridges a day.

Rostov on Don
Factory producing 3 inch shells
In Taganrog District there is grain in sufficient quantity. The harvest has been good.

f. 17, op. 109, d. 66, l.1

To: Red Army.
From: Red intelligence.
30 September 1919

English supplies to Denikin and Don Army.
All teaching staff have been called up, in view of which the spring exam-inations have been cancelled. Conscription applies to all men born between 1891 and 1900.

A new officers' school has been opened in Rostov. Denikin has issued an order forbidding the killing of Red army men who have surrendered voluntarily.

f. 17, op. 65, d. 136, l.51

To: Smilga, Head of Political Exercises.
List of Sorting Offices of the Republic.
5 November 1919

In view of the importance of Sorting Offices both for Army Groups, Armies and those attached to Post and Telegraph offices the staff are in charge of distributing and sending out military correspondence by telephone and telegraph. By the nature of their work they are bound to know and have in their possession the most secret information in the form of lists of our Armies, showing where various units are placed. I have taken on the coun-trywide task of reforming these Offices by gradually infiltrating our specialists in among the White specialists.
12 November 1919

Cheka reports

The Bolsheviks had been an underground illegal group up to 1917. They retained many conspiratorial attitudes and theories throughout the whole history of the Soviet Union. Their constant fear of counter-revolution found its sharpest expression in the secret police, which started under Dzerzhinsky in December 1917. Originally known as the Cheká it was a dominant force in the Soviet Union, being renamed at various stages as NKVD, MVD, and KGB.

f. 17, op. 109, d. 44, l.77

To: *Moscow, Mokhovaya, Central Committee of the Party, to Stasovaya,*
c.c. Smilga, Petrograd RVS.
From: *Raskolnikov, Fleet Commander, Astrakhan naval 1108 130 21–6.*
Received: 27 June 1919

I completely support the accusation against Adamovich. Appointed by Flotilla order to be in charge of the political section. Adamovich asked to be released from that duty, but his resignation was not accepted. Taking advantage of my going to Tsaritsyn for a short time, he quite flatly announced to the Staff Commissar his decisive intention to leave Astrakhan, and when I returned I found that Adamovich was not here.

Since I consider that Adamovich, who had been appointed to his post by flotilla order, had no right to quit his duties without the commander's permission and went to Moscow without the proper authorization, I find Adamovich's conduct absolutely impermissible and not as befits members of the Party, and I request the Central Committee to carry out an enquiry into his conduct. As witnesses we could call on Deshevoy, Raioner, Kalin and Kirilov, who are at present in Astrakhan.

f. 17, op. 109, d. 44, 11. 71 – 72

... concentrate political work with work of the punishment squads with a sensible combination of repression and propaganda.

f. 17, op. 109, d. 44, l.161

To: *Dzerzhinsky, All-Russian Cheka, Copy to Lenin, Kremlin.*
From: *10th Army Special Section.*
Cipher telegram   Top secret
10 August 1919 (received 23 August)

Special Section 10 has discovered one of Denikin's main networks of agents in Saratov and beyond the Volga. The local Provincial Cheka has a very large forgery set-up. In order to protect our rear areas the army has sent me a telegram empowering me to keep some supervision over the Provincial Cheka.

Decoded in the secretariat of the Deputy Chairman of the Revolutionary Military Council of the Republic.

After the Bolsheviks assumed power in 1917 they had to learn the skills of administering a vast territory and adjusting to an ever-changing pattern of political relationships. Colossal blunders were made at times, but overall we may be surprised at how well they coped in the early years of establishing the Soviet regime. It was common practice for officials to classify potential adherents as 'sympathizers' alongside the more select lists of those who had been formally enrolled as full Party members.

f. 17, op. 109, d. 44, I.163

> To: *Dzerzhinsky, All-Russian Cheka, Copy to Lenin, Kremlin*
> *From: Southern Army Group*
> *Telegram   Top secret (coded)*
> *10 August 1919*

Information on numbers of Party cells and sympathizers in Armies on Southern Front:

1. 164 Total	670 Communists	971 sympathizers
1. 165	560	910
1. 166	806	1159
1. 167	52	112
1. 168	649	478
1. 169 verso	652	783

Personnel

f. 17, op. 65, d. 35, I.23

> To: *Board of People's Commissar for Land of Central Committee.*
> *Declaration*
> *November 1919*

On 22 November I submitted an invoice to the accounts department of the Property Nationalization Board pursuant to the warrant of 21 November, signed by comrade Sereda. This assignment of funds at 5 January this year still has not been acted on by the accounts department.

I protest against this delay of 43 days, and I accuse the chief accountant of sabotage, together with the young lady who is responsible for the list of assignments. I request that they should be removed from their posts.

Instructor of the Property Nationalization Board   M. Shurilin

f. 17, op. 65, d. 136, l.26

Minutes of Revolutionary Military Council of Republic
22 August 1919

Minute 25
Resolved:
(3)   Comrade Kurayev, member of Revolutionary Military Council of 11th Army is appointed as a member of Revolutionary Military Council of 9th Army.

To: Ye. D. Stasovaya.
From: Chief Clerk of Secretariat of Commissar of Field Staff of Revolutionary Military Council of Republic.
September 1919

In view of the forthcoming change whereby Special Group Southern Army Group is to be made into an independent Army Group I consider that it is an inappropriate moment to abolish that group's Special Section. It must be preserved and converted into Special Section Southern Front.

The greatest change in the Red Army was its rapid growth. The army's strength in October 1918 was about 430 000 men; the figure given by one official source of 3 000 000 men in October 1919 seems exaggerated, but numbers were probably approaching that at the end of 1919.   (Mawdesley, 1987, p. 181)

With this extraordinary expansion it is small wonder that individuals were sometimes appointed to the wrong posts.

Supplies: January to June 1919

From 1914 the war against Germany had put pressure on many of Russia's resources. With the collapse of the Tsarist army German forces advanced across Ukraine and south Russia, pushing east to occupy Rostov-on-Don in May 1918. This placed all the black earth region in their hands, and for the last six months of the war they were exporting large quantities of grain from these rich areas to feed the German homeland.

After Germany surrendered to Britain and France, the Don Cossacks pushed out the remnants of the Don Soviet Republic to make themselves masters in their own territory. The White generals tried to use them in further offensives against the Communists in Moscow, but they did not consider this larger war to be any concern of theirs. In January 1919 there were mass desertions from the front as the Cossacks streamed back to their own villages.

Food supplies had already run short in 1918. That summer the Soviet government resolved to implement a policy of procuring grain directly from farmers in the food-producing areas. In 1918 this applied to provinces surrounding Moscow, and from 1919 to all areas under Soviet control. Theoretically the grain was to be paid for at prices fixed by the government. Theoretically it was to be taken mainly from the richer peasants – the kulaks – who might be regarded as a class enemy. Theoretically only surplus grain was to be taken. Theoretically the yield from each area was to be assessed on the basis of what they had provided in previous years. In practice, all these conditions were a dead letter.

Food-requisitioning squads scoured farmsteads for every morsel to be found. Often they did not even spare enough seed for the farmer to sow next year's crop, so that many families were left to starve to death. The Communists came to be hated in the countryside: there were frequent clashes with the scratch teams of soldiers, sailors and workers, and some 5000 lost their lives trying to collect food for the hungry cities. Serious disturbances built up, which broke out into large-scale rebellions against Soviet power in 1920–21.

In the opening months of 1919 when the Reds were again pushing forward, they recovered much potentially fertile land. But strong resentment against Soviet power arose from Communists requisitioning foodstuffs and farm animals, as shown in the piece which follows.

f. 17, op. 109, d. 44, I.6

To: *Revolutionary Military Council of Southern and South-Eastern Army Groups and Special Food Supply Committee for Southern Army Group.*
Project
Undated, but filed before telegram of 19 January 1919

(1) It is proposed to Revolutionary Military Council of Southern and South-Eastern Army Groups to assign military units not directly committed to military operational requirements to be re-employed for food supply work.
(2) Military units carry out the operational food supply tasks of the Special Food Supply Committee for taking from the population grain, meat, animal fats and other food products.
(3) The areas in which the Red Army's food supply work is to be put into effect are defined by the Revolutionary Military Council of the Army Groups as agreed with Special Food Supply Committee.
(4) The responsibility for checking rests on the Revolutionary Military Council of the Army Groups and Special Food Supply Committee of Southern Army Group.
(5) This directive is to take effect without delay.

For most of 1919 it was impossible for the Soviets to exploit the coal mines of the Donets Basin, and their locomotives had to run on supplies of wood. Constant fighting had played havoc with Russia's railway system and this caused further dislocation of supplies.

f. 17, op. 109, d. 44, I.11

From: *Gotovitsky, Head of Administration for Chairman of Revolutionary Military Council.*
27 January, Moscow

Acting on comrade Trotsky's instruction I am forwarding a copy of a telegram which has been received:

'The transfer of reinforcements assigned to the South and the East is coming up against the failure to provide rail transport when needed. For several weeks the Head of Revolutionary Forces of the Town has had the responsibility of working out such a plan, which has been hindered by rolling stock being delivered several weeks late. It is the responsibility of the Head of Revolutionary Armed Forces to work out such a plan.

By the summer of 1919 not only were there difficulties in transport, but the Red Army was experiencing severe shortages of many essential items. The most acute need was to supply the front line troops facing Denikin across the River Donets. After months of incessant fighting these units were pitifully under strength; the men were ill-clad, almost starving, and short of equipment and ammunition. 1919 was the most critical year for the Soviet Republic, threatened firstly by Kolchak in the Urals and then by enemies from north, west and south. It is open to question whether Moscow could have sent substantial reinforcements to the Donets front. The document which follows is an eloquent warning of the retreat which was forced on the Reds when Denikin launched his offensive in June.

f. 17, op. 109, d. 44, l.16

To: *Central Committee of Communist Party, Moscow.*
From: *Political Commissar of Second Artillery Section of 1st Brigade of Niza*
Division.
Copy
7 May 1919

I must bring to your attention that our Front will be in a disastrous situation if the most exceptional and energetic steps are not taken for supplies – both food supplies and supplies of forage. Speaking for myself I fully recognize my own shortcomings in both these respects, but I would all the same suggest we must find more sensible ways of doing things. The general picture shows that there is no fodder of the normal dry sort and that, however regrettable it may be, it is not always possible to make use of fresh pasture. Our horses are falling down, which has a serious effect on the fighting capacity of the army. The men get nothing to eat for two days at a time, and it is beyond our powers to talk them round. Here is one example for you: our 5th Battery got one day's fodder over six months and days. However, the battery was not stationary but moving from place to place, as we had to manœuvre, so that when we crossed the Donets our artillery was not able to move ten versts in a day. Other batteries seem to be in the same state. In short I am not in the slightest exaggerating when I

say 'disastrous' in the full sense of that word. Men are so worn out with cold and hunger that we can really expect terrible consequences if supplies are not provided for both men and horses. There is a great shortage of horses.
Political Commissar of the Section (signature attested)

Most of the conscripts in the Red Army came from peasant villages. They were only too aware of how their people were suffering, and it is no wonder they lost what little enthusiasm they had for the Soviet cause. At times even whole units would go over to the Whites, such as the Serdobsk Regiment in April 1919.

f. 17, op. 109, d. 44, I.17

To: *Temporary Executive Head First Cavalry Army.*
copy to: *Chairman of Supply for Reserve, comrade Goldbor, Commander of Supply Troops. Head of Staff of the Republic (Moscow only).*
Telegram

On 12 May in Kharkov units of 4 Cavalry Division in the areas of Orzhitsa, Denisovsk and Veliko-Seletsk interrupted the work of the Food Supply Organs, who were carrying out food requisitioning, while the Red Cavalrymen of the division carried on agitation for requisitioning not to be carried out, and everything subject to requisition was given out to peasant cavalrymen.

The Commander of Forces in Ukraine categorically orders the responsible leaders and Commissars of units of 4th Division to cease this sort of misconduct and to take the most energetic measures to prevent it recurring in the future. Please inform us of what measures you have taken. Temporary Executive Head of Chief of Staff Shuvayev
Duty Military Commissar / signature
Resolution of comrade Sklyansky: 'Personal.. Top secret. Copies to comrade Lenin and comrade Molotov, 16 May Sklyansky.'

As Chairman of the Republic's Revolutionary Military Council, Trotsky held the supreme authority over all fronts of the Civil War. Tsaritsyn was a key centre of communications in the region of the Volga, and the Whites made strenuous effort to capture it. In October 1918 the forces defending the city were regrouped into three Armies, 8th, 9th and 10th. Almost independently of other fronts in the war, Stalin and his supporters in Tsaritsyn were making a bid to set up a separate centre of power, Trotsky realized that in practical terms he could do little to influence decisions taken in that city. Hence his reluctance assent to Minin's appointment, and he returned forcefully to the question of supplies which had become so crucial for the whole outcome of the war.

f. 17, op. 109, d. 44, l.43

To: *Lenin.*
From: Trotsky.
Message by direct line   Secret
June 1919 (received 5 June 21.00)

In reply to Lenin's message I consider that Minin can be transferred to Tsaritsyn only if the Revolutionary Military Council of 10th Army agree, and this is recognized as their direct responsibility. As a general rule I consider it extremely dangerous to pile up the numbers of individuals with plenipotentiary powers – and particularly in cases where functional relationships are ill-defined. It is far more important to deal properly with the question of supply, and especially the supply of cartridges.

This most vital heavy responsibility lies on the shoulders of a person who is dealing with it just as one of his other duties. All the matters of military supply have been entrusted to Veynberg, who is quite incapable of facing up to the task. All warnings have gone unheeded, with no means of providing cartridges. The Extraordinary Supply Commission and the Military Procurements Department are exposed as being completely useless by their failure to supply ammunition or to get wheeled transport organized. From the moment when Southern Front was threatening to collapse I made repeated proposals to hand the Lugansk factory over to Southern Army Group. They put me off with a bureaucratic pretext that Southern Army Group had no technical resources, as if the Council for the National Economy could not let Southern Army Group have the essential technical resources if the necessity arose. On the other hand Southern Army Group could have evacuated the factory in good time and used it in various units depending on circumstances at the front. I saw with my own eyes how three and half full days were senselessly wasted, during which the factory might have been evacuated, as Kolegayev was insisting, and as the Centre kept refusing. Now the evacuation has been carried out God knows how. The best workers from all departments are made over to the War

Department, while the most important military task, i.e. supply, remains in the hands of chance survivors in other departments and is dealt with any old how. I must really draw Central Committee's attention to the way the whole business of military supplies has been set up in the most impossible and criminal way.

There is also a grave threat to our supplies of forage. We need cavalry at all costs. The People's Commissariat of Supply issues orders on paper for fodder, dry or fresh cut. It simply is not true that the whole of our country cannot get a sufficient quantity of oats to feed the horses in our army. We have just got to realize that this makes the difference between victory and defeat.

f. 17, op. 109, d. 44, l.51

To: *Defence Council, received in Moscow by Sklyansky, decoding of note received by direct transmission from Trotsky's train, Voronezh.*
From: *Trotsky, Chairman of Revolutionary Military Council of the Republic.*
10 June 1919 (Decoded in the Secretariat of Deputy Chairman of the Republic 11 June 1919)
Secret

1.   The state of the medical services is an appalling affliction. We cannot make war if sick and wounded soldiers are treated like dogs.
2.   What I have said about medical services can be applied overall to the general position of supplies. It is on these very questions of supply that we may well come to grief. I can see two ways out of our difficulties: either (1) Krasin is really placed at the head of our supply services, and concentrates in his hands all the preparation of material. He should set off without delay to go round Russia and Ukraine, visiting the most important centres of production, organizing the production of cartridges, shells, guns, equipment, – or else (2) the preparation of military material is put completely under the control of the military department, and Kolegayev is placed at their head with complete authority over the means and resources of the Higher Council of the National Economy. If this second course is decided upon then the Emergency Committee for Supplies is completely abolished. If there is no agreement among us on this point I insist that we should convene a plenum of the Central Committee to examine the question in all its dimensions, for all other matters hinge on this question.

True signature

d. 155, l.2a

Revolutionary Military Council Eastern Front,
Revolutionary Military Council 5th Army
received 26 June 1919

Fifty per cent of the Red Army men have no footwear, greatcoats or under-clothes. As the cold nights set in, illnesses from catching cold are increasing every day.

1. 4
Head of Supplies of the Eastern Front will try to take in our workshops which are our only salvation in the present situation.

Supplies: July 1919 to April 1921

f. 17, op. 109, d. 44, l.1

To: *Head of Supplies for Southern Front (at Kozlov); Copies to Central Supply Administration, Moscow; Head of Administration, Chairman of Revolutionary Military Council, Gotovitsky.*
From: *Trotsky, Chairman Revolutionary Military Council.*
Telegram

Southern Front needs underclothes. Soldiers are covered in lice. On the personal responsibility of the Head of Supply Administration and Chief Supplies Officer for Southern Front I charge you to deliver the necessary quantity of linen within the next two weeks.

f. 17, op. 109, d. 44, l.91

To: *Moscow, Sklyansky, Central Committee, All Russian Chief of Staff,*
        Central Supply Administration, Rykov.
    From: *Trotsky, Chairman Revolutionary Military Council.*
9 July 1919
Message by direct line from Voronezh, received 9 July 1800 hrs

Reinforcements are coming to Southern Army Group in absurdly small numbers. The main reason is the lack of supplies on the spot. If everything moves so slowly it is impossible to re-establish Southern Army Group. Just in order to build up the divisions which are held in reserve for Southern Army Group we must have 85 000 men. I propose: (1) to mobilize two-thirds of all types of the necessary personnel, and send them off straight away to destinations appointed for them to be formed up and brought up to strength, to be at the disposal of Southern Army Group. Principal Head of Supplies should be made responsible for this. (2) All-Russian Chief of Staff should be directed to send the reinforcements without arms or uniform. (3) To give immediate authorization for Southern Army Group to mobilize eighteen and nineteen-year-olds in Oryol and Kharkov Districts. (4) Bring in a general decree for the conscription of eighteen-year-olds. (5) In the shortest possible time enforce orders to bring Southern Army Group's command and administrative staff up to strength, giving Districts and Provinces definite time limits under the supervision of the military commissars. (6) Principal Head of Supplies to check immediately that this has been carried out to meet requisition forms of Southern Army Group (see Southern Army Group Revolutionary Military Council's telegram No. 7554). (7) See that Southern Army Group is adequately supplied with credits and currency notes, since all work is paralysed by lack of same. (8) Once more I propose that Central Supply Administration should equip 14th Army and the Kharkov group with Japanese rifles, making exceptional efforts to achieve this. (9) I expect those responsible to report within 48 hours on what steps they have taken to meet the instructions in this telegram.

f. 17, op. 109, d. 44, l.91

To: *Moscow, Sklyansky, Principal Military Engineering Administration, Central Supply Administration.*
From: *Trotsky, Chairman Revolutionary Military Council.*
9 July 1919 (received 19. 18 hrs)

To a demand for telegraphic cable and paint Principal Military Engineering Administration replies that there is none. Such an answer is not acceptable. Principal Military Engineering Administration can more easily find a way of producing telegraph paint. Have steps been taken to get telegraph cable from Ukraine? I propose that the Head of Principal Military Engineering Administration should apply exceptionally energetic measures to supplying Southern Army Group with telegraph equipment.

After Budyonny's victory over Shkuro his Corps was made up to become the First Cavalry Army. As a member of its Revolutionary Military Council Voroshilov was Budyonny's right-hand man, and backed him up at times when his men were behaving in a quite outrageous way. In view of his record we must view with considerable scepticism his assurance that the Cavalry Army's conduct was 'exemplary'.

f. 17, op. 65, d. 571, l.122

To: *Comrade Molotov, Central Committee Russian Communist Party.*
From: *Voroshilov, Member of Central Committee.*

The troops have received no forage for twenty days. The men of the Cavalry Army are in excellent spirits, and up to now their conduct has been exemplary. If food supplies continue to be difficult then undesirable excesses may arise from hunger. The Don Oblast is a completely hungry area, particularly the Salsk District, where the people have absolutely no bread, and the families of Red Army men are in the most frightful state. Since there is no grain forage for the cavalry divisions some of the best horses have started dying.   Voroshilov

By 1 August the troops in the District will be brought under the jurisdiction of the People's Commissar for Supplies. Supplies not guaranteed. Essential to feed, ? otherwise disband the units.

As the Whites advanced in 1919, Shorin was placed in charge of a Red Army strike force, which was intended to deliver a decisive blow and push Denikin into retreat.

f. 17, op. 109, d. 44, l.179

To: *Sklyansky.*
From: *Trotsky's train.*
16 September 1919

In the area of Shorin's group the supply organizations are extremely bad. Quite often the divisions are starving, in spite of the fact that there is plenty of grain around. We cannot even find small agents, since almost all those who are literate have gone away with the Whites.

f. 17, op. 109, d. 44, l.67

To: *Chairman of Revolutionary Military Council, Trotsky, to find at current address.*

I am transporting 75 carriages of recently appointed Red commanders. I request you arrange to despatch to HQ 14 Army special type revolvers, sabres, binoculars, compasses.
                                    Bubnov

The urgent plea that follows is reinforced by the Commissar's haste to get everything down, leading to repetitive and jumbled syntax.

f. 17, op. 109, d. 44, l.216

To: *Lev Semyonovich.*
From: *Military Commissar of 8th artillery division.*
6 February 1920

Highly esteemed Lev Semyonovich,
Our units are starving in the full sense of that word. No more than 30 per cent of them have clothing, as a result of which absolutely no training is being carried out, and complications may ensue. Horses are falling because there is no forage; can any improvement be expected? Our units have gone over to rations allowed for troops in the front line. Since 29 January they

have received nothing but bread. As a result of our agitation their fighting spirit has still not gone. Regarding the level of [revolutionary] consciousness in the Army one can predict that we are nearly at the point when talk will not work, and people will have no faith in what we are saying. When we were inspecting the units there was one reply – can anything be improved? If not, then let us go straight home. At home they will put their own things right, and will make up for lost time in their work for the country, will help to deal with the general destruction. At the moment their sitting around here brings nothing but harm and demoralization. Previously the peasants gave the troops a little food, but now even that is not forthcoming. Local inhabitants gave what they could, gave everything – even more. Do not believe the military specialists. We need to [?] let some of the men go, slim down the Army quickly, as a matter of urgency. If the Army remains in this state till the spring, then firstly everything is going to come apart in our hands, in the second place more than half the Army will run off in all directions and will not stand the hunger and privations.

We must immediately decide what is the proper strength for the Army to have in the future, and give it a presentable appearance by getting rid of spare capacity. That is our strength and victory. We have an awful lot of men on the ground and that is an unnecessary burden. For one example on 6 February the artillery units of the 8th Rifle Division are 1400 men over their proper strength. There are further reinforcements of 2180 coming – what are we to do with them? If we let go the six years of oldest men, then we'll still have the same number to spare. And if everything goes on as it is at present, then by the spring we'll have neither men nor horses: the men will run off and the horses will die.

f. 17, op. 65, d. 571, l.109

To: *Central Executive Committee, Moscow; Copies to Don Committee, Rostov, Caucasus Office of Russian Communist Party.*
From: *Chairman of Revolutionary Committee of TMO.*
Telegram
11 April 1921

Novocherkassk Commander of Armed Forces in Don Oblast have repeatedly sent messages to Don Supply Committee and Don Executive Committee that there are no supplies of food in the District. The population is really starving, military units and workers are being supplied only on a very uncertain basis. At present there is completely no food supply.

Acting on the resolution of responsible official in the District we are forced to cut up edible foodstuffs into tens of thousands of poods for feeding the children and military units. The amount of food allotted will suffice for two weeks, and beyond that there is no solution to this problem. We insist absolutely that arrangements are made to supply military units and the needs of the District within the prescribed time.

Chairman of Revolutionary Committee of TMO Bysarov

Large numbers of deserters

The following documents show what a large-scale problem desertion was right throughout the civil war. In one province government measures (or fear of starvation) brought in no less than 48 000 in just two weeks.

f. 17, op. 109, d. 61, l.1

[Minutes 33   Secret]

Sessions of Central Commission for combating desertions 23 June 1919.
   Families of deserters who come in voluntarily from the day of amnesty for the deserter have the right to have restored the aid to Red Army men, which they lost as being the dependents of a deserter.
(1)   In Ryazan Province eleven to twelve thousand deserters have been recovered, about seven thousand of whom came in of their own accord.
(3)   We may recover deserters for Southern Front in Provinces of Oryol, Kursk and Voronezh.

Trotsky

f. 17, op. 109, d. 61, l.13

From 16 to 29 February 1920 there came in voluntarily 25 715.
Caught in round-ups 22 654.

Greens

Alongside the regular forces, at least nominally under central command, many bands of guerrillas sprang up – 'partisans', both Red and White. The origin of the 'Greens' is described in *list* 92 below.

They took this name because at the beginning they found refuge in the woods. Even though their total strength is probably exaggerated, it is clear that they represented a substantial force. It was a constant objective of Bolshevik policy to try and bring the Greens and other partisans under regular army discipline.

The Soviet government knew the valuable contribution such rebels could make, especially when they were operating behind enemy lines. On the other hand these independent forces were slow to obey orders from Moscow or from regular Red Army units. In the most extreme cases, leaders, such as Grigor'ev or the anarchist Makhno, operated with large bodies of men who were not controlled by either Reds or Whites. Trotsky and others used the pejorative word *partizanshchina* to describe the activity of leaders such as Colonel Mironov, who were not always eager to place themselves under Party discipline.

The Party tried to enforce its will through Revolutionary Military Councils, and through military commissars attached to commanders in the Red Army. The most celebrated of these was the writer Furmanov. He later described the difficult task he had faced in controlling Chapayev, the partisan leader, whose exploits on the Eastern Front gave him a legendary status as almost a Soviet Robin Hood.

f. 17, op. 65,. D. 35, I.83

To: Moscow, All-Russian Central Executive Committee, Sovnarkom, Central Committee, copy to Tambov, Podbedsky.
From: Head of Defence, Dolen.
Telegram with highest priority
1 July 1919

Yesterday, 30 June, gangs of Greens came to join the atamans. Supported by artillery fire they started to advance towards the station of Tavolchanka. Having taken it they resumed their advance against Romanovka station. Our units made a fighting retreat covered by the armoured train 'Comrade Lenin '. Romanovka station was taken that night. The advancing forces had up to 2000 infantry and 300 cavalry. Our detachments had too few men to defend themselves against the gangs. The people of the area are hostile to Soviet power. Sometimes, as our forces moved to cut off enemy who had broken through, they have been fired on from behind corners. We need stronger military units with a sufficient back up of artillery for us to be able to cut them off at source and eliminate any desire to rebel. Cossacks and officers with shoulder straps have been observed going into villages and calling meetings which all the people join in. The Centre should pay serious attention to the Southern Front and we must realize that our army will be left without the forces it needs in its rear if rail links are cut between Tambov and Balashov or Balashov-Rtishchevo.

f. 554, op. 1,. D. 3, l.92

To: Donburo.
From: Novorossiysk.
Copy of report sent to Donburo 14 September 1919 (extract)
3/ [following 2/ pp. 17–18]

What is the Green Army and where did it come from? After the retreat of the Caucasus Army, caused by those traitors Soporan and K, a group of Red Army men, who had been thrown on the mercy of fate, found themselves a refuge in the mountain, and from 1918 they have been carrying out raids on houses in the country and on trains which passed by. As they had at their disposal both light artillery and several machine-guns, their raids began to spread panic in those parts – and they added to their stock of weapons, of which they now possess a large quantity. Peasants persecuted by the Volunteer Army began to come over to them, and then thus were able to field an impressive figure of up to 60 000 Greens, who under good leaders and able commanders were able to wreak havoc in the enemy's rear. Their political beliefs are too diverse, but they do have leanings towards Soviet power.

The Green Army is divided into three groups: the first group is operating in the area of Tuapse and Sochi, and poses a threat to Tuapse. The second group is at Novorossiysk itself, and consists of three regiments under the command of the well known leader of the Novorossiysk Mensheviks, Vasil'ev. There is a third small group towards the right hand coast of Novorossiysk, but it contains many of our loyal Communists. Up to now the headquarters of the Green Army has been linked with a group of anarchists. They were trapped by a false report that the town was ready to rise, as a result of which the town was ringed with White Guards; an English cruiser shone its searchlights and opened fire with its heavy guns. The Greens broke through the ring of Whites around them and escaped to the mountains without many casualties. Considering the importance of Novorossiysk it has been decided to send political literature and a special appeal to the Green Army to set up a committee in Novorossiysk and to unify these masses of men into one whole. We have decided to send Party workers there in order to make up a strong organization there and to carry on our work on a wide scale. We have not been able as yet to make contact with Novorossiysk. Cold weather is setting in, and the Green Army lack clothing and footwear. Send personnel and material help as an urgent matter.

P. S. In Novorossiysk the English steamer Borodino is unloading 8 light tanks and up to 400 guns of various calibre, up to 6-inch field guns. They have also unloaded a large quantity of shells for these guns, and 4000 mules that were brought out from the southern Caucasus. They are forcing 1200 prisoners of war from the Balkan peninsula to go to the front, but the POWs beg to be allowed to go home, and to receive English clothes to wear. Parts for steam locomotives have come from America and masses of machine-guns.

f. 554, op. 1. d. 3, l.76

To: *Central Committee, Russian Communist Party (Bolshevik).*
From: *Don Oblast Revolutionary Committee.*
22 October 1919

After several unsuccessful attempts on our part to enter into contact with the organization in Novorossiysk and the Green Army, at the beginning of August we finally managed to contact a group of Communists in Novorossiysk, consisting of a small number of long-standing Party members… Only by blowing up the tunnel near Novorossiysk will it be possible for us to cut off the transport of all military material from the port of Novorossiysk. This material passes on to all the fronts of the Volunteer Army, in action against us.

At the present moment there has built up in Novorossiysk an enormous number of our prisoners of war, who are being held in appalling conditions.

The Green Army has a total strength of approximately 70 000 men, counting those who are on the eastern and western flanks of the mountains. They are dispersed in groups, starting just south of the Taman peninsula, along the main range of the Caucasus mountains almost as far as Elbrus. Each group operates independently, having a strength of no more than 4000, and usually 2000 to 3000 men.

(We have sent contacts to the Green Army).

On 14 October we again received an impassioned appeal from our loyal comrades to give immediate aid in support of the Green Army.

At 9 a.m. on 1 October explosions of shells occurred simultaneously on the shore and at sea, on board an English cruiser loaded with shells and which were to be unloaded. The English authorities barely managed to tow the exploding cruiser out of the bay into the open sea where it sank.

(1)   The whole eastern coast of the Black Sea is by now in the hands of the Green Army.

(2)   We should now call a conference in order to arrive at a unified command.

On 17 October an emergency meeting of the Don Oblast Committee resolved to send without delay all our best forces of Party and military activists to a total of 5 men.

f. 554, op. 1. d. 3, I.97

> To: Comrade Beloborodov.
> From: Donburo, Oryol.
> 30 October 1919

The Donburo is now being evacuated and we have to write in a goods wagon.

We should transfer a complete staff for the partisans or two or three partisans who can lead the Greens Army against Denikin's rear. 60 000 may be an exaggerated estimate of the number of Greens, but there may well be 30–45 000.

The following document, penned from quite a humble source, advises on policy to be pursued towards Makhno's men, as the Red Army advance into Ukraine in late autumn 1919. The writer has uncertain syntax and punctuation, which we have tried to amend in our translation. Many ordinary people reacted against the name 'Communists', but felt less hostile to 'Soviets' or 'Bolsheviks'. They had not realized that by 1919 these terms were virtually synonymous, since other revolutionary groupings, such as Mensheviks or Socialist Revolutionaries, were now powerless in the face of the Bolshevik take-over.

f. 17, op. 109. d. 44, I.205

> To: Trotsky.
> From: A. Kondratenko, 14th Army.
> 25 November 1919

Dear Senior comrades, in the not too distant future our Party can expect to face an unpleasant business, which may bear on the process of the social revolution. I mean that kind of anarchy we find under Makhno *makhnovshchina*.

As our troops move further into Ukraine, especially the Donets Basin, we shall be faced with the break up of our units:

(1) All Ukrainian Red Army men who get as far as their homes are unlikely to go any further. They will begin to absent themselves from their units, dispersing to where they live – and what is more, taking their arms with them.

(2) Worked on by the propaganda, which not so long ago came from the Socialist Revolutionaries and anarchists – and from real hardliners who pass under the general label of 'Makhno's men' – our men may begin to go over from us to Makhno's band, not only as individuals, but even whole units at a time.

(3) As a result of this, units will begin to break up, and may go down to their minimum strength – which will have a bad effect on morale – and we may start to see a recurrence of the disastrous retreats which happened in the spring of this year. To forestall this sort of thing we must work out ways to stop it at the beginning and immediately eliminate this kind of demoralization. In my opinion we must: (a) at all costs keep our international units, (b) when our regular units first come into contact with partisan detachments we must behave with careful diplomacy towards them, so as to avoid clashes, until we have got rid of Denikin's people. As already happened in the spring of this year, it would be desirable to use these same partisans for further pressure against the enemy on the Don. This in itself may lead to breaking down the partisan units, while it will help to preserve our regular units in a fit state to go into action. It is they who will be the suitable ones for our further advance, in contrast to the partisans who tend to be enthusiastic for the revolution only when the enemy is right on their doorstep. (c) We must put in a big effort to persuade bands of the more reliable partisans to recreate themselves as regular units of Soviet troops. In general we have to mobilize all available resources for wide-scale agitation, both in detachments of partisans and in our own units. We have to proclaim the virtues of the Communist Party, of the Soviet system, its centralization of authority, and how the regular forces of the Red Army are better than bands of partisans. In general we must conduct our business in such a way that we do not fall into our previous errors, do not allow our units to disintegrate and begin to go over to Makhno – rather than that, we should be breaking down his units and bringing them over to our side. Many of the partisans acknowledge Bolsheviks, but not Communists, so that we must explain

widely by means of leaflets and by word of mouth, both to them and to Ukrainian peasants in the areas we occupy, that there is no Party of Bolsheviks who are not Communists, that comrade Lenin, who headed the Bolsheviks, is now the leader of the Bolshevik Communists. It would be very useful to slip some good Communists secretly into Makhno's forces as an undercover operation, not holding Party cards, reliable men – not those half-converted to Makhno, as we can already see sometimes in our Party, especially among the Ukrainians. A good man like this should join a band as a rank and file partisan, without declaring himself a Communist, spend a little time in the squad until he wins sympathy among the partisans he is with, as being an excellent guerilla fighter, or as a man – and then carry on propaganda for our Party in an indirect way, i.e. pointing to all the faults that exist in the bands, but are not in the Red Army (particularly looting). These can be shown up for the Party committee to see, and we can claim that this sort of thing does not happen in Soviet regiments. In general we must use every suitable chance and occasion for the good of our Party. Circumstances now are particularly favourable for our propaganda to be effective, and this idea could have a tremendous effect on breaking up Makhno's bands and preparing them to come over to our side.

These agents must be slipped in with the most complete secrecy, and we must be extremely careful about choosing who is to be sent. Selecting them should be the responsibility of active Party workers and long-standing members of the Communist Party, in order to ensure that they do not contain any people who are half-sympathetic to Makhno and who might give away this secret. I beg you to pay the most serious attention to everything I have said here, not just limiting yourselves to a formal bureaucratic acknowledgement, and to give effect to all suitable measures in the very near future.

Communist of the army organization of the 14th Army.

Andrey Kondratenko

25. XI. 19
It is essential to send Communists into Makhno's bands without delay, so that those sent may have the chance to earn widespread trust as old hands 'who came to the partisans before the coming of Soviet forces', and under these circumstances this will give them every chance to make arguments in favour of the Soviet way of doing things and especially for our Party. If on

the contrary they are sent as an open and above board policy we may have the partisans lynching our Party specialists – besides other very harmful consequences.

We should call up several years of those liable for military service, all the young Party men who are pro-Revolution in the areas we have occupied and by this simple means fill up the ranks which have been depleted for one reason or another, whether by desertions or wounds etc., and it is also necessary to proceed to organize reserves from these same people in the areas we are occupying.

A. Kondratenko　　　　　　　　　　　　　　　Signature attested M. Shaver

Bryansk rebellion

In November 1917 quite a wide range of the population had elected a Constituent Assembly, in which the Socialist Revolutionaries formed the largest party. The Bolsheviks dissolved the Assembly after it had met for one day on 5 January 1918. The most serious attempt to revive it was made by the Committee of Members of the Constituent Assembly, which held a large area in Siberia and the Urals till it was overthrown by Kolchak's authoritarian rule in November 1918. In the minds of many people the Constituent Assembly held a certain promise of democracy, and there were other outbreaks in its name. After the February revolution the railwaymen had shown themselves to be sympathetic to the Mensheviks and other parties.

f. 17, op. 65, d. 136, I.18

Report on the Bryansk Rebellion
March 1919

The rebellion took a Left Socialist Revolutionary type of political line. The uprising was headed by several officers from the command staff and the last class of Red officers to graduate. The majority of our command staff were passive in their attitude to the uprising, while some of the former officers came out actively to put down the rebellion.

It began on 1 March in the town of Orzha, where it was quickly suppressed. It then spread in small uprisings throughout the whole province. It proclaimed everywhere its main slogan 'Long live the Constituent Assembly'. There was fertile soil for dissatisfaction to grow because of the food crisis. In February there were rumours that most of the Red Army men were in open rebellion under arms. In the Thirty First Regiment, on top of the scanty and filthy food and poor uniform clothing, the men were discontented with their commanders.

An organization under the name of 'The Iron Union' is kept up by funds from the bourgeoisie. Railwaymen represent a real pillar of counter-revolution.

4
1919: Who will Win?

Policy towards Cossacks

February to May 1919

Communists held contradictory views on how to administer the Voysko territory. In 1918 the failure to set up any normal system of government was largely responsible for turning almost the whole population against them. In later years, as the Soviet Union was established, it became the practice for the Politburo or the Central Committee to lay down the main lines of policy, and these policies were promulgated through channels of the Communist Party. The various branches of the administration were managed by People's Commissars (eventually in 1946 changed to the title of Ministers or Deputy Ministers). These latter really exercised the role of officials, carrying out the functions of permanent civil servants, implementing policies which had been decided by the highest organs of the Party.

In 1919 this distinction was not always followed. It was later recognized as a serious weakness in Soviet handling of the Don area that Syrtsov was both Chairman of the Party organization and head of the so-called Civil Authority.

The Communists felt they had learnt a bitter lesson from the events of the previous spring. As a sop to Cossack pride Lenin had in 1918 approved the creation of an independent Don Soviet Republic. Largely under German pressure this collapsed in May 1918, and the Red Army was driven out of the whole Don territory. In 1919 Moscow repeatedly declared there must be no more trifling with Cossack separatism. The proposal to split up the Don Oblast was part of the hard-line idea of destroying Cossack society (*raskazachivaniye*). It was hoped to abolish the Cossacks' separatist leanings by dividing their lands among several Provinces.

In May, when the Don rebellion proved difficult to put down, Lenin expressed his astonishment that many Cossacks had retained their weapons in the rear areas of the Red Army. From the beginning of their advance, Southern Army Group were all too conscious that they should call in the arms, but the problem had no easy solution. Firstly, many Cossacks who had abandoned the Whites' front in January thought that they had some sort of agreement for the Red Army not to enter the Voysko lands. Besides this, long-hallowed tradition meant that Cossack units returning from active service took their small-arms back to their home villages. One of the fictional characters in Sholokhov's *Quiet flows the Don* gives graphic expression to their feelings: 'Without my rifle I'd be naked like a woman with her skirts up'. Most of the active service Cossacks took steps to hide their personal weapons, and when the rebellion broke out in March there were enough arms in Cossack hands to present a serious threat to Soviet power. The insurgents rapidly captured more rifles, and even machine guns, from Red Army stores. As some 30 000 men joined the rebellion, they did not have enough to arm every individual soldier, but set about making their own supplies of sabres, and also cartridges. The rebels were hampered by a crucial shortage of ammunition until the Whites broke through to join them in June.

From March to June 1919 the Upper Don Rebellion held an area about 150 kilometres across, centred on Vyoshenskaya stanitsa. As was common in the civil war the front was not manned in a continuous line, and it swung to and fro with the changing fortunes of the rebels and the Red Army forces trying to contain them.

Syrtsov had spent his early years in Rostov, and the sight of Cossacks suppressing the disturbances of 1905 left a lasting impression on his young mind. In 1919 he was appointed Chairman of the Donburo, and was largely responsible for harsh measures against the Cossacks which led to the Don Rebellion.

f. 17, op. 65, d. 34, l. 48

To: *Sverdlov and Khodorovsky.*
From: *Kozlov.*
4 February 1919

Hullo, Yakov Mikhaylovich. Firstly, Syrtsov has been here for two days and there has been a whole series of conferences. Even before his arrival, as we advanced into the heart of the Don country, temporary administrative units began to be set up under the Revolutionary Military Council of Southern Army Group. The posts were filled by reliable comrades from the Party. The Khopyor District Revolutionary Committee has been put together and is working well. The Ust-Medveditskaya Revolutionary Committee has been organized. Tomorrow Revolutionary Committees will be created for the Donets and the Upper Don. Acting on Trotsky's communiqué of yesterday, until fresh intructions are received, both military and civil powers on the Don are completely subordinated to the Revolutionary Military Council of Southern Army Group. We have received the Central Committee's directive and have already passed it on to the Armies. In order to combat counter-revolution, to ensure speedy implementation of the necessary measures, as also for security and maximum efficiency, we have felt it essential for every military unit which occupies a stanitsa to organize a temporary tribunal, chaired by the commissar, backed by two responsible members of the Party cell.

The Revolutionary Military Council of Southern Army Group has issued an order for arms to be handed in by the population in areas that we occupy. So that arms may be collected in a proper manner, and in order to prevent looting and disorderly conduct, Commissions for the collection of arms have been set up, these also to be under the chairmanship of the commissar, with two comrades from the party. Armed detachments are attached to these Commissions. Member of the Commission and all personnel in the detachment bear personal resonsibility for seeing that these measures are carried out in an orderly way. Any persons found with arms after the declared time limit will be shot on the spot. Detailed instructions for carrying out the Central Committee's directive are being worked out. They will be ready tomorrow and communicated to those in charge in the Armies for implementation. The Political Section is transferring almost all its Party workers to the Political Sections of the divisions and also to the new organs of power. We are not clear about how the centre views the establishment of a structure of government to administer the oblast. Is it seen as essential to create a Don Executive Committee of responsible Party comrades or would it be preferable to set up a Soviet regime on the Don? In the latter case are we to entrust matters to the neighbouring Provincial Executive Committees? If that is done it is not clear to us how to ensure a single management for all our work, especially when we take into account that the tasks laid on us by the Central Committee necessitate a strictly centralized system. Trotsky has promised to give an official answer to these points today. Every hour is vital, since if we do not reach a solution there is a risk that independent initiatives may start up on the spot, and that would be harmful to our cause.

f. 17, op. 65, d. 34, l.64

To: *People's Commissar for Internal Affairs.*
From: *Donburo at Kozlov, Head of Administrative Section, Syrtsov.*
2 March 1919

There is a very difficult problem about creating a people's police force in the areas of the Don Oblast which we have liberated. The lack of reliable and experienced comrades makes it impossible to set up a proper organization. Rogues and counter-revolutionaries push in. We request you urgently to send some Communists who have had experience of organizing a people's police force. We ask you to send them via the administrative section of Southern Army Group.

The Donburo of the Communist Party, in accord with the provisions of the Party's Central Committee, and with the participation of local organizations, is working out a plan for dismembering the Don Oblast. We request you to send someone down who can ratify our work.

Head of Administrative Section, Syrtsov

f. 17, op. 65, d. 34, l.69

To: *Central Committee.*
From: *Donburo at Chertkovo.*
5 March 1919

In the Districts of the Don Oblast there is a complete lack of technical personnel – agricultural or forestry specialists, telegraph operators, accounts clerks, accountants, finance officers. They have either run off or been taken away by the Cossacks. We demand that you send this type of officer immediately. There is an epidemic of typhus; there are no medicines or medical staff. It is essential that you take urgent measures to send some. We must have specialists in food supply and land use. There are no units of currency apart from the local Don money. It is essential to find a speedy solution to this question.

Secretary of the Donburo, Doroshev

f. 17, op. 65, d. 34, l.66

To: Cheka

From: People's Commissariat for Internal Affairs.

8 March 1919

On 2 March the People's Commissariat for Internal Affairs received a telegram from the Donburo inviting us to send a representative of the People's Commissariat for Internal Affairs to participate in work on breaking the Don Oblast into new administrative and economic units.

Seeing that the decision to break up the Don Oblast has already been agreed in principle and that all that remains to be done is to define the boundaries and to establish centres for the newly formed units, the People's Commissariat for Internal Affairs requests the Central Committee of the Russian Communist Party to entrust this work to the Department for Local Affairs of the People's Commissariat for Internal Affairs, which hitherto has worked out all questions of changing boundaries and carving out new administrative and economic units. The Department for Local Affairs has the necessary staff for this kind of work and the materials to go with it. It follows that it will be more convenient and advantageous to hand the technical measures for dividing the Don Oblast to that Department rather than to create a special apparatus for this under any other institution. [Written in ink and underlined on top of crossed out typescript] If for some reason it is not convenient to give this business to the People's Commissariat for Internal Affairs then it is essential that we tackle this task as a joint endeavour. To get the work done quickly it will be sufficient to make a temporary transfer of one or two representatives of the Donburo to the Department for Local Affairs.

With comradely greetings

For the People's Commissar for Internal Affairs

Secretary of the Department

Part of the campaign to suppress the old Cossack identity was to divide the Don Voysko between oblasts, placing most of its territory under Rostov, but some in the Tsaritsyn oblast.

Revolutionary Tribunals started carrying out indiscriminate executions which provoked the local population into widespread rebellion.

f. 17, op. 65, d. 34, I.71

To: *Secretariat of Central Committee, Mokhovaya 7; copy to Soviet of People's Deputies, Petersburg.*
From: *Member of Donburo and Head of Civil Admisnistration, Syrtsov.*
20 March 1919

The Donburo and Civil Administration Section of the Revolutionary Military Council of Southern Army Group request that you send as soon as possible, to be at the disposal of Shaliyevsky's Section, comrade Gorrakon, member of the Soviet of People's Deputies, and the comrades on the list which comrade Shaliyevsky has. The rebellions which have broken out on the Don due to badly organized administration mean that we have really urgent need for political workers.

f. 17, op. 65, d. 34, I. 72 (extract)

To: *Secretariat of Central Committee.*
From: *Members of Donburo; Chairman of Tsaritsyn Executive Committee.*
28 March 1919

On the question of changing the boundaries of the former Don Oblast ... to include in the territory of Tsaritsyn province, which is being formed:

1) Ust-Medveditskaya and Second Don Districts along the boundaries laid down on 1 January 1917.
2) Part of the Salsk and First Don District along the following boundaries.... Note: the boundaries indicated in point 2 are to be regarded as temporary until we have put down the counter-revolutionary rising on the Don – when Tsaritsyn and Rostov Provincial Soviets will be in a position to establish definitive boundaries.
3) For the time being the whole Khopyor District is to be divided between the neighbouring Provinces.
4) The remaining parts of the former Don Oblast will go to form Rostov Province.

f. 17, op. 65, d. 34, 11. 163–6

To: Administrative organs in Don area.
From: Central Committee.
Resolution on how to treat Cossacks. Transfer of population
24 April

In so far as general circumstances permit we should carry out a large-scale resettlement of peasant classes from central Russia.

It is essential to make a large transfer of Cossacks beyond the borders of the Oblast; to do this we must develop a system of partial mobilizations, under which Cossacks concerned are sent off into work battalions as military engineers, construction workers and to forced labour of every type.

With the addendum that peasants living on the Don must be armed, as must also be those who are moved in.

f. 17, op. 65, d. 34, l.77 [handwritten]

To: Secretariat of Central Committee.
From: Syrtsov.
23 April

Further to the explanations which I gave to comrade Novgorodskaya I attach herewith a copy of my telegram to areas of the Don Oblast.

The telegram with this message was sent by me to Millerovo to be transmitted to the other ?local committees. I think the contents of the telegram are sufficient evidence to refute comrade Sokolnikov's reproach that I had in some way been disloyal to the Central Committee's resolution, as announced in its original directive.

With its query regarding Beloborodov the following *list* 79 of 25 April must precede *list* 78, which is dated 24 April, and admits no knowledge of his whereabouts.

f. 17, op. 65, d. 34, l.79

To: Donburo *[in pencil below] In the area of the uprising, to be forwarded to Kozlov.*
From: *Central Committee, Moscow, Mokhovaya 7.*

I am using this opportunity to send the report from the Yekaterinodar Committee. I request Bychkova to pass on by the agreed channel that the report from Anna Fen has been received. The intelligence information is extremely valuable. Continue to keep us informed. The task has been assigned. We are sending money. Where is Beloborodov?

f. 17, op. 109, d. 44, l.78 (in pencil)

To: *Secretariat of Central Committee.*
From: *Syrtsov.*
24 April 1919

To inform you about the position with regard to the Centre of Civil Authority. To agree to the formation of two Centres, one of which is for that part of the Oblast whose Revolutionary Military Council the Orgburo has proposed should transfer to Tsaritsyn Province.

As against this plan comrade Sokolnikov has proposed the creation of a Don Revolutionary Military Council (under the name of 'Civil Authority'). I have expressed my opposition to this plan, as against anything of the sort which may give the population of the Oblast a chance of preserving the status quo. Parts will be artificially attached to Tsaritsyn as to an artificial centre. We have no information on the whereabouts of comrade Beloborodov. Comrades are beginning to arrive to be placed at his disposal.

f. 17, op. 109, d. 54, 1.1

To: *Nikolay Nikolayevich.*
From: *Rail station Log 10–18.*
3 May 1919

In general one must say that the work of neither the Donburo, nor the [indecipherable] commissars is particularly noteworthy. The commissars sent from the Donburo to the stanitsas and villages are awaiting instructions from the Civil Authority. I do not know where the commissars have hidden themselves away. I strongly suspect that they are hanging back in Kozlov.

f. 17, op. 65, d. 34, l.80

To: *Donburo at Kozlov.*
From: *Central Committee.*
9 May 1919

Membership of Don Revolutionary Committee confirmed by Central Committee: Beloborodov, Syrtsov, Plyatt, Feynchold, Yakubov.

Kantemirovka is a district centre on the railway south from Voronezh. Lenin repeatedly expressed his impatience with the failure to suppress the Don Rebellion. On 24 April he even proposed buying the rebels off with an amnesty, although he prefaced this by asking with his usual ruthlessness whether they could not be crushed by really 'merciless' methods.

f. 17, op. 109, d. 44, l.21

To: *Sklyansky, Lenin.*
From: *Trotsky, Chairman of Revolutionary Military Council of Republic.*
13 May 1919 Kantemirovka

The length of time to suppress the rebellion has been protracted because of poor morale. More Communists should be sent. Tomorrow I am proposing to go on to Ukraine. I doubt in advance that the Revolutionary Military Council of Ukraine, consisting of Bubkov, Shchadenko and Antonov, are capable of bringing about the necessary change of course.

List 82 has a pencilled note at the end for a copy to be sent to Smilga, who was one of Trotsky's main opponents, particularly over staffing the Red Army with former tsarist officers. One can only conjecture that Syrtsov may as an afterthought have considered Smilga would support more actively the rooting out of treachery in the army.

Syrtsov makes a frank reference to demoralization in the Red Army and attributes this to the men being brought too closely into contact with villagers (and also presumably to the less harsh conditions they enjoyed when not in the field).

Voronezh and Kalach were outside the main area of the rebellion, and it was a matter of grave concern to the Reds that the rebels were receiving ammunition from those places.

In April and May there were a number of occasions on which rebel units tried to negotiate a truce with counter-insurgency forces in the line against them (see Murphy (1993) 'Don Rebellion', pp. 332–3), and this naturally damped down the fighting spirit on both sides.

f. 17, op. 65, d. 34, l.82

To: *Revolutionary Military Council of Southern Army Group; copies to Chairman Defence Council, Lenin; Chairman Revolutionary Military Council, Trotsky, Mokhovaya 2, Moscow; Central Committee of Communists, Millerovo; Smilga.*
From: *Chernyshevskaya – Syrtsov, now at Bokovskaya, Member of Donburo, based in Setrakovskaya.*
Priority telegram
22 May 1919 (received 24 May)

Demoralization of our units can be halted by imposing stern discipline, which has greatly fallen off. We must strengthen our political work, and the main thing is to move Red Army men away from contact with the villages. As we advance, the life of Cossacks in their cottages has a demoralizing effect on our men. We must go over to keeping them under canvas. An additional advantage is that it will be easier to deal with espionage, which is terribly widespread. Tribunals must be brought closer to the front and they must be more active.

Men who come over to us indicate that the rebels are being supplied with cartridges from Kalach and Voronezh. Cartridges are expended in our units at an unbelievable rate. There is no fire discipline. Our Bokovskaya group has fired off nearly a million cartridges over the last three or four weeks, including several thousand during two days when there was no active engagement with the enemy. It may be that cartridges are being sold to enemy agents, and that other items are being supplied to the enemy. The passive attitude of groups of 9th Army and the failure to co-ordinate our operations develop the idea that we are going neither to advance nor retreat, so that we become more inclined to go over to defensive tactics. The enemy is trying to engage in direct talks with Red Army men. Cases have been noted when prisoners have been released to propose that delegates should be chosen from companies and squadrons to carry on peace negotiations. Guard duties at outposts are done in the most negligent way. I travelled 60 versts along the line of the front and was not once questioned by our outposts or patrols.

June 1919

f. 554, op. 1. d. 3, l.86

To: *People's Commissariat for Supplies.*
From: *V. Trifonov, Temporary Executive Head of Civil Administration Section,*
attached to Revolutionary Military Council of Southern Army Group.
9 June 1919 No. 1985

Local areas of the Don Oblast (with a population of approximately one million) are suffering severe shortages of cloth, milk products, tobacco, sugar, tea, besides many small culinary requirements and articles of household use. They particularly need driving shafts, nails, bar iron, parts for agricultural machines etc. It would have a tremendous effect if we could satisfy people's needs for cloth, for lubricants (even in the form of crude oil), and tobacco.

The time is approaching for work in the fields. Neither Cossacks, nor peasants on the Don have anything at all for greasing the wheels of their wagons or the moving parts of agricultural machines. Since people on the Don have never grown flax or hemp, they have absolutely no way of replacing their tattered clothing, even with any homespun cloth, as many districts do in Russia and Ukraine. The lack of tobacco has a very bad psychological effect on the male population of the Don Oblast, who happen to believe that this shortage is having a particularly bad effect on the spread of epidemic diseases in villages and stanitsas. The most effective form of propaganda to strengthen the Soviet regime on the Don would be by meeting the Cossacks' basic needs. It will be a bad mistake if we do not take advantage of their present frame of mind, and it will be hard to put things right at a later stage.

Cossack morale is at a definite turning point, and all information on the ground makes us quite convinced that their sympathy for the new regime could only be secured by 'just a little piece of cloth for each of them and a small pouchful of tobacco'. That is the only thing that would get them to bring in the contents of their grain stores to our collection points.

We should work on the basis of supplying a million people for the next three months. We need to send at least five tanker wagons of fuel supplies for the many agricultural machines which have come to a halt, for tanneries and so on. For lubricating agricultural machines it is essential that we release without delay at least a thousands poods of mineral oil. To grease wagon wheels etc. we must give out the necessary quantity of either pitch or axle-grease.

Given the chaotic state of transport, and the dire shortages in the Soviet Republic, the above request must have seemed absurdly unrealistic to meet, even in part. In any case it was much too late, for the Whites from the Donets were now breaking through to join with the rebel Cossacks, and the whole Don Oblast was passing into Denikin's hands.

As a Cossack himself, Valentin Trifonov was prone to take a less harsh view of his fellow countrymen than did many of his contemporaries. He was perhaps unduly optimistic in assessing the mood of the Cossacks in June, when the war was swinging so decisively in favour of the Whites. Farmers would no doubt have been glad of anything they received, but it seems highly unlikely they would give up their grain and welcome the Communists simply for a scrap of cloth and a little tobacco.

f. 554, op. 1. d. 3, l.85

To: *Central Committee, Russian Communist Party.*
From: *Reyngolts and V. Trifonov, Members of Don Revolutionary Committee.*
10 June 1919

Through the Department of Civil Administration, attached to Revolutionary Council of Southern Army Group, we have forwarded to the People's Commissariat for Supplies a demand to send a sufficient quantity of cloth for people in the Don Oblast. Our failures on the Southern Front have been due not only to errors of strategy, but our unsuccessful policy towards the Cossacks was also at fault.

Endless confiscations, requisitioning, and extortions – and sometimes shootings like a monstrous form of sport could in no wise make Cossacks feel well-disposed towards the Soviets. We of course do not count on the Cossacks for reliable support for Soviet power, but we suppose that with them we need to use not only stick but also carrot. This incentive must be based on the cloth which we have asked for in an insignificant quantity.

Since the outbreak of the Don Rebellion in March Lenin and the Red Army high command had been concerned that the Whites from the Donets might break through to join up with the rebels. Sokolnikov's telegram announces that the worst has happened and that the rebels are no longer encircled. It was now increasingly likely that Cossacks in the north of the Don territory might feel the momentum of the White advance and wish to join it. In general, Cossacks living along the Khopyor River to the north of the Don had smaller land holdings and no fertile black earth soils. Having less to lose, they did not feel inclined to support the richer Cossacks against the Communists. The Reds found many more active supporters along the Khopyor than in the villages further south. It was through this area that the Red Army had to retreat as Denikin pushed them north in the summer of 1919. Kolegayev also was worried that some of the units facing the rebels might go over to them.

The White forces who broke through to the rebels were commanded by General Sekretyov, who was promoted to lead the 9th Cavalry Division in the Mamontov raid.

f. 17, op. 109, d. 44, I.49

6̲7̲ 7364   Secret
To: *Sklyansky (Moscow), [handwritten in red ink 'Sent to People's Commissar for Military Affairs, Chairman of Sovnarkom, Lenin'].*
From: Sokolnikov.
10 June Decoded in the Secretariat of Deputy Chairman of Revolutionary Military Council of Republic.

On the front against the insurgents on 6 and 7 June Kazanskaya has been occupied, also the Shumilinskaya and Vyoshenskaya areas. However, on that same day of 7 June three Cossack regiments, coming from the south, threw our Millerovo group back to the railway line, broke though to Kazanskaya and caused a panic. As a result of our retreat from Kazanskaya we have lost contact with the units operating in the Vyoshenskaya area. We are trying to establish whether the breakthrough has been by a separate Cossack detachment or whether there are other units following it. Because of the general situation on the Southern Front it may be necessary to hold the Front further north along the left bank of the Don.   Nr 371

Sokolnikov had a much more realistic view of Cossack psychology than did Syrstov, or for that matter any of the Bolshevik hardliners who came down to staff the Donburo and impose Soviet power in the most rigidly Marxist terms. It is noteworthy that Sokolnikov could recognize Mironov's qualities as a born Cossack leader, when so many incoming officials were blinded by prejudice against him.

f. 17, op. 109, d. 44, l.50

To: *Chairman of Revolutionary Military Council Trotsky, at current address;*
copy to Chairman of Sovnarkom, Lenin.
From: Sokolnikov, 5th Army TK 2926157.
10 June from Kozlov 22. 15 9 (Decoded in the Secretariat of Deputy
Chairman of Revolutionary Military Council of Republic, 11 June, A. P.).
Telegram   Top secret

One of Denikin's detachments, evidently consisting of three cavalry regiments from the Khopyor, has broken through to Kazanskaya. The risk has been considerably increased that the rebellion may spread into the Khopyor and Medveditsa Districts. Since the front to the south has been opened, the Counter-insurgency Force have now been assigned the task of occupying the left bank of the Don from Boguchar to Ust-Medveditskaya, in order to forestall any spreading of the revolt to the northern districts.

A Revolutionary Military Council has today been set up for the Counter-insurgency Force, but the unit's structure has been renamed as a Counter-insurgency Corps. Khvesin has shown that he is helpless in difficult circumstances. I propose most definitely that Mironov, former commander of 23 Division, should be urgently appointed to command the Counter-insurgency Corps. The make-up of the Counter-insurgency Corps is sufficient guarantee that the men will not depart from Soviet policy, while the name of Mironov will assure the neutrality or even the active support of the northern districts, if it is not too late. I request you to reply urgently to me at Kozlov. I am going to Counter-insurgency Division 9. The command of Southern Army Group are all in agreement.   No. 374

f. 17, op. 65, d. 34, l.92

Cossack Section
Report on the situation in the Khopyor area of the Don Oblast prior to its
being evacuated
28 June 1919

First of all, Cossacks who had been mobilized had nothing to fear, because by the mere fact of their having presented themselves they had already shown they supported the Soviet regime, and because they had no reason to rebel. On the other hand, they had no cause to fear an invasion of the rebel Cossacks, seeing that a battalion of anti-profiteer detachments was stationed in Uryupinsk, and it was loyal to Soviet power. The communiqué circulated to military quarters caused panic among the Communists and their 'sympathizers', since the local Party office did not bother to go into detail about the reasons for mobilization. Besides that, this communiqué spread panic among the population as a whole, and gave rise to a whole series of rumours of the most fantastic sort. Furthermore this mobilization was quite futile, for it transpired that three quarters of the 'sympathizers' had never hald a gun in their hands, so that class of men could be completely written off as a fighting force.

It was with the greatest difficulty that the Communists who had come from the centre managed to insist on the Party being organized correctly, namely by setting up an elected Party committee, regular party meetings, rendering account of our activities, and firm application of Party discipline. Unhappily these measures came too late, and after a week we had to evacuate the area.

At the same time we may take note that in June the centre started to send us really green young people from the Komsomol, some of them no more than sixteen years old. These youngsters demanded responsible posts for themselves. They were reluctant to go to do simple work in village administration, and there were cases when they refused to work and even asked to be taken back. Naturally there there was little hope of getting any real use from these young people.

The local Party office really had not sufficient independence.

f. 17, op. 65, d. 34, l.97

To: *Trotsky.*
From: *Iv. Ye. Popelkin.*
1 July 1919
Report on Soviet work in Don Oblast, particularly in the Khopyor area
<u>*Evacuation in Khopyor Area*</u>

It would be more true to say this was not evacuation but panic. ... *list* 100
Only under these conditions can the party and the Soviets build on firm
foundations.

The harm caused by confusion of functions was strikingly illustrated
in the following report from Valentin Trifonov, who as an educated
Cossack understood only too well the problems confronting the
Soviets on the Don. He was writing after their obvious failure to
deal with them. There was in theory a Civil Authority, but it never
became independent of rule by the Donburo and the military.

   Trifonov understood Cossack susceptibilities better than most. Anti-
Semitism was a long tradition with the Cossacks, and they were deeply
offended at the idea of being submitted to 'foreigners' such as Frenkel,
not to mention the Red Army's Commander-in-Chief, the Latvian
Vatsetis. The Donburo's 5 members, confirmed in *list* 80 of 9 May,
included three with non-Slav names: Plyatt, Feynchol'd, and Yakubov,
who was of Tartar origin.

f. 17, op. 65, d. 34, l.85

To: *Organizational Bureau of Central Committee.*
From: *V. Trifonov.*
Report
10 June 1919

Before the Don Revolutionary Committee was formed, life in Don Oblast,
in areas liberated from the enemy, was settled by the Civil Administration
of Southern Army Group. This institution was headed by comrade Syrtsov,
who was in charge of the Civil Administration, and at the same time
directed the party's Donburo. There might have been definite benefit in
placing in one person's hands both the ideological direction of the Party
and the practical aspects of setting up Soviet power, but benefit would

only have come if circumstances had been different and if politics had been following their normal course. In the present case this uniting of functions did enormous damage to the RSFSR. Instead of one institution keeping a check on the work of the other, instead of our behaviour being corrected by experience and common sense, we got into the position of one single task being subject to one man's will, but a will which had interpreted wrongly both the situation we had to work in and the tasks which that will had to confront.

Comrade Sokolnikov said in response to the question on the causes of the Vyoshenskaya rebellion: 'The rebellion in the area of Vyoshenskaya started because of the military and political actions of the Army'.

For the Don Oblast it is absolutely essential that our organization should be headed by comrades with Russian names.

As the Whites pushed all before them in June 1919, it must have seemed to many Communists that the war was hanging in the balance. Composed no doubt under stress in the crisis the following telegram names Lenin twice as an addressee.

f. 17, op. 109, d. 44, l.53

Priority to: Moscow to Chairman of Sovnarkom, Lenin.
To: Chairman of Revolutionary Military Council, Trotsky; copy to Chairman of Sovnarkom, Lenin.
From: Beloborodov 17 PTK 921 114 130 35.
<u>*Decoded telegram*</u>   *Secret*
12 June (Decoded 13 June in secretariat of Deputy Chairman of Revolutionary Military Council of the Republic) N39

Counter-insurgency Division 9 still has not received the reinforcements which have been sent; its numbers are being made up with Cossacks volunteering from the local stanitsas, which is completely inadmissible. The command staff have even less freedom of manoeuvre. Alekseyev has not given what was expected of him. I have fallen ill with recurrent typhus; now that they have transferred me to Mikhaylovka I have the greatest difficulty in insisting on Khvesin's orders being carried out. Vsevolod's taking over command of 9th Army (!), accompanied by a long trail of capricious decisions has deprived the 9th Army staff of any decisive will, which had already been wavering under the conditions of the retreat.
Authorized to speak for Defence Council Beloborodov

Future Policy for the Don

f. 17, op. 109, d. 44, l.62

> To: *V. Trifonov.*
> From: *Trotsky.*
> *21 June 1919*

We are at present busy organizing a Cossack division. Young Communists are becoming a source of demoralization. It is therefore proposed to send back to Voronezh Province a considerable proportion of the mobilized Communists.

f. 17, op. 65, d. 34, l.70

> To: *Sverdlov, Central Executive Committee, Moscow; Central Committee; Petrovsky, People's Commissariat for Internal Affairs.*
> From: *Member of Revolutionary Military Council of Southern Army Group, Khodorovsky; Chairman of Donburo, Syrtsov.*

Petrovsky's new telegram g. 40/1521 introduces even greater confusion into the situation which is evolving. The Revolutionary Committees do not come under the command of the Political Sections of the Army, but are subordinate to the Revolutionary Military Council of the Southern Front. Acting on Sverdlov's directions the ten million roubles should be transferred immediately to the Revolutionary Military Council of the Southern Front, and not lie unused with the Executive Committees of Tsaritsyn, Astrakhan and Saratov in the expectation of what is to come. We consider that the People's Commissar for Internal Affairs must, as Sverdlov has shown, inform the Executive Committees that all administration on the Don comes under the Revolutionary Military Council of Southern Army Group, and that all the credits for this administration should be made over to the Revolutionary Military Council. Until the Central Committee gives fresh orders to the contrary the Executive Committees are not to interfere in matters concerning the organization of administration on the Don. It is essential to make this clear. Otherwise the disorder and chaos in Tsaritsyn will become even greater.

f. 17, op. 65, d. 34, l.169

Resolution to questions raised by comrade Syrtsov's report

[1. 170 ends] ... it is his responsibility. It is considered essential to direct the attention and activity of our members to strengthening political and organizational work in order to build up a solid foundation (of Party organization) for the work of Soviets.

f. 17, op. 65, d. 34, l.101
[handwritten in ink]

To:
From: A. Popov.
6 July 1919

Short proposals for tactics and measures to be taken when we reconquer the Don Oblast.

I   Create the authority of the State, and back it up with sufficient forces. Relinquish any land reforms.
II   Go over to a definitive Communist system only after victory has been achieved on the main fronts of the Civil War.

Note: the first will be acceptable to Cossacks at the present time as a result of our military victories. The following conditions are required for establishing Soviet power in the Don Oblast and preventing further rebellions.

(1) Sending in masses of Communists.
(2) Setting up an organization of authority concentrated in the hands of a small number of individuals, which authority to be independent of the staff of Southern Army Group...
(3)
(4) Naturally all Cossack prisoners must be evacuated from the area.
(5) All officers, sergeants etc. must be sent away.
(6) As few shootings as possible, and those to be carried out only when there is quite clear cause for them.
(7) Organize the non-Cossacks [*inogorodniye*] to defend Soviet power.

(8) Disarm Cossacks and requisition war horses and saddles. (Carry out wide-scale searches, give large rewards for handing in arms or showing where they are hidden).

(9) Leave intact all Cossack landholdings.

(10) Institute a State monopoly of all stocks of grain. It will be possible to hold the Don Oblast up to the end of the civil war only if we put in sufficient military forces, make a strong organization of authority, and call a temporary halt to our programme for the land.

Member of Communist Party   A. Popov

Grigorev (1878–1919) fought for the Ukrainian Parliament, then Skoropadsky, then Petlyura. In February 1919 he had come over to the Reds and commanded a division in the forces retaking Nikolayev, Kherson and Odessa. On 7 May he raised 20 000 men to rebel against Moscow in the area of Yelizavetgrad, and succeeded in ocupying a substantial territory in southern Ukraine. When defeated by Voroshilov and Parkomenko he tried to join Makhno, but on 27 July was killed on Makhno's orders.

Although Mironov was forthright in condemning Moscow's anti-Cossack policies, he fought long and hard to defend the Soviet regime. It was precisely because doctrinaire Communists were so ham-fisted in handling Cossack susceptibilities that Mironov was invaluable in winning over recruits to the Soviet cause on the Don.

Khodorovsky (1885–1940), an old Bolshevik from 1903, was appointed a member of the Southern Army Group's Revolutionary Military Council in January 1919. His views were directly opposed to those of Trotsky on how the Reds should treat the Cossacks. Trotsky maintained consistently that some of them should be regarded as 'working-class Cossacks', who must be won over to realize their interests coincided with those of the peasants in other parts of Russia. Economic forces should make it particularly easy to find allies in the poorer country in the north of the Don Oblast. Khodorovsky asserted that all Cossacks were irremediably hostile to the Soviet regime, and that the Reds could hope to work only with the non-Cossack population. It has to be recorded that 'the people of the Khopyor and Ust-Medveditsky Districts', whom he specifically mentions, suffered particularly barbarous wholesale killings, as the Red Army retreated through their Districts in the summer of 1919. Khodorovsky found common ground with other critics in deploring the inconclusive efforts to set up a system of civil administration on the Don.

Trotsky pronounced repeatedly that it should be possible to attract many of the less well-off Cossacks to the Soviet regime. History seems to have proved him right. When the Red Army came into the Don territory in January 1919, any men who were absolutely opposed to the Soviets went south with General Krasnov. Those who remained in the villages were unlikely actually to welcome the invasion of their homeland, but they had shown by staying that they at least preferred to try and live with the Reds. The terror introduced by hardline Communists made them feel that every Cossack was at risk, and that the summary tribunals were bent on the indiscriminate killing of any males in the Don Oblast. This led to the massive rebellion, which brought some 30 000 fighting men against the Communists, and cut across the Red Army's lines of communication to its front on the River Donets.

Khodorovsky ascribed to the non-Cossacks a universal hatred of the Cossack rebels. In this he was at odds with other observers of events in the spring of 1919. In spite of his faith in non-Cossacks, the executions carried out by the Reds had been on such a scale that not only Cossacks, but also many *inogorodniye* were turned against the Communists, and the rebels had a number of non-Cossacks fighting on their side.

1919 was the most critical year of the Civil War when the Reds faced a distinct possibility of defeat, not only on the Southern Front. When Khodorovsky blithely wished that the Soviets should have established large garrisons in Cossack villages he ignores the fact that it might not be easy to find men to fulfil this role. It is a common practice for commanders to call for reinforcements. He gave most convincing figures to show how seriously the units on the Southern Front were under strength, but he seemed to share the illusion of many local commanders, imagining reserves of trained manpower to be virtually inexhaustible.

Khodorovsky also exaggerated the hostility of Cossacks towards the Soviets. Rank-and-file Cossacks were not really in sympathy with Krasnov, and some local rebel units even suggested marching south with the Red Army to attack the Whites on the Donets. It is striking that the insurgents even retained the title 'Soviets' for their village administration, and the rebellion proclaimed its official slogan 'For the Soviets against the Communists'. This last provides a clear indication of the Cossacks' motivation: they feared above all that their land would be taken away to be shared out among non-Cossack peasants. Khodorovsky is right in remarking that virtually all Cossacks had a higher standard of living than the peasants in central Russia. The

Communist Party was split from the highest levels down over this question – whether to woo the poorer Cossacks or to destroy the last vestiges of their society. That unresolved controversy proved a fatal weakness in Communist policy in the Don area, and was one of the main factors leading to the setbacks of 1919.

f. 17, op. 65, d. 34, l. 120 repeats Frenkel's report and adds at the foot in ink:

> If we automatically apply to the Don the idea of 'trying to win over the middling peasants' it may lead to more fatal consequences for Soviet power than the 'first' directives of the Central Committee. Frenkel is quite right about Mironov.
>
> A. Beloborodov

Future policy for the Don

In *list* 122, Don Committee refers to a body of the Communist Party, whereas Don Executive Committee was the Soviet institution responsible for giving practical effect to decisions made by the Party, i.e. the local administration acting on behalf of the Soviet government.

f. 17, op. 109, d. 44, l.177

From: *Trotsky, Chairman of Revolutionary Military Council, by direct line from Trotsky's train.*
Note
(received) 13 September 1919

The following disposition to take effect to organize a Civil Administration in the areas of Don Oblast which have been cleared of the enemy:

Firstly: the administration is to be headed by a temporary Executive Committee under the chairmanship of comrade Medvedev. In places cleared of the White Guards local Executive Committees are to be set up, consisting of one representative of Military Power, one representative of Civil Power to be appointed by us, and one representative of the local population to be agreed on with working-class people in the area. This is in order to bring a local authority into force as quickly as possible on the basis of the Soviet constitution.

f. 17, op. 65, d. 34, l.127

To: *Stasovaya, Central Committee, Kremlin, Moscow.*
From: *Syrtsov, Don Committee, Borisoglebsk.*
Military priority telegram

I am leaving on the next train.

f. 17, op. 65, d. 34, l.123

To: *Syrtsov, Don Executive Committee, Saratov.*
From: *Stasovaya, Secretary Central Committee.*
Urgent
13 September 1919

To your telegram No. 19 the Central Committee proposes that you should proceed to work in the the Don Executive Committee. It is quite unnecessary for you to come to Moscow at present.

f. 17, op. 65, d. 34, l.123

To: *All-Russian Executive Committee.*
From: *Syrtsov.*
?13 September 1919

If the question of the Don Executive Committee is to be reviewed by the Donburo I insist on Serebryakov's scheme. In particular I insist on having 5 individuals. If one or two of them have to leave to check on the situation, a proper quorum will always be left in place. The oblast organization is bound to fail if the Donburo of the Don Executive Committee consists of only three persons, without any authoritative representation of the central apparatus of the Party or the Soviets. Part of the Don Oblast is occupied here and there. It is essential for the Don Executive Committee to leave as a matter of urgency. I suggest that as soon as possible its membership should be checked and that some members should be sent from Moscow to work here.

f. 17, op. 65, d. 34, l.122

To: *Central Committee, 7 Mokhovaya, Moscow: Trotsky; Revolutionary Military Council of Southern Army Group, Serebryakov; HQ of Special Group, Smilga.*
From: *Members of Don Committee: Syrtsov, Nikovnik and Reshetkov.*
16 September 1919

The Don Committee of Communists at its first session considered the question of organization. It considers Don Committee and the Don Executive Committee cannot work with only three persons, with colleagues who are not fitted even to run our business from day to day. Don Committee thinks it essential to bring the Don Executive Committee up to five members and to include as two of its members Smilga and Znamensky, the latter to be appointed as Chairman of Don Executive Committee. Znamensky and Syrtsov coming into both Don Committee and Don Executive Committee will establish the necessary link between the work of both organizations. Including Smilga as a member of the Central Committee in the Don Committee will ensure the necessary link with Central Committee, and exclude the possibility of any misunderstanding. It will make the essential clarification of the Don Committee's relations with Central Committee. We consider that our work can be made possible by bringing the membership up to five and including a member of Central Committee in Don Committee. We request you to send your answer urgently to Serebryakov at Oryol for Don Committee and to Saratov for Don Executive Committee.

f. 17, op. 65, d. 34, l.121

To: *Serebryakov at Oryol, for Don Committee.*
From: *Secretary of Central Committee, Stasova.*
[written in ink on unmarked small sheet of paper]
23 September 1919

By decree of Central Committee Smilga is to be included in the personnel of Don Committee.

f. 17, op. 65, d. 34, l.126

To: *All-Russian Executive Committee, Mokhovaya 7.*
From: Syrtsov.
Military telegram
28 September 1919

I have explained how essential my point of view is with the official line prescribed by the Don Revolutionary Committee. I consider it impossible for
me to shoulder the responsibility for that line and I think the Central
Committee must be given the opportunity to bring a powerful personality
into the Don Executive Committee, who can answer up to the demands
which that line entails. I have given the Chairman of the Don Executive
Committee my application to leave the Donburo. I have additional
personal grounds for wishing to do that.

Telegram No. 19 Syrtsov

f. 17, op. 65, d. 34, l.131

Instruction
To: District Committees of Communist Party of Don Oblast

2

District Committee consists of three persons: Chairman, Secretary and
Treasurer

6

One of the tasks of a District Committee is to organize stanitsa and village
Communist cells and sympathizers in their District, this to be done with
the aid of special instructors and organizers, and with stanitsa and area
military commissars, who must definitely be Communists.

9

A District Committee at the same time has to carry out the functions of a
Committee of local organization (e.g. of Uryupinskaya, Mikhaylovka etc.).
The local organization details off a special committee. District Committee
carries out the receipt of members' subscriptions from the members of the
local organization.

13

District Committees must always bear in mind that they are not an administrative authority, and therefore they are not able on their own to carry out any measure of a governmental (Soviet) nature, but these measures must be passed through their own members in the Executive Committees and their sections.

f. 17, op. 109, d. 44, l.9

To: Moscow, Chairman of Defence Council, Lenin.
From: Chairman of Revolutionary Military Council, Trotsky.
Telegram

In Voronezh there is a conflict between Revolutionary Military Council of 8th Army and the University, which has occurred because part of the University's buildings have been occupied. In view of the typhus epidemic, so rife in Voronezh and its environs, it seems absolutely essential to open up a field hospital with 1500 beds.

f. 17, op. 84, d. 32, l.33

To: Lenin.
From: Preobrazhensky.
December 1919

Correspondence with the Cossack Section attached to the All-Russian Central Executive Committee.
Letter to V. I. Lenin and other documents on the Cossack question.
Minutes of the First Army with participation of Kalinin. Refers to Dutov.

f. 17, op. 65, d. 571, l.110

Don Committee and City Committee consider in principle to have one Committee.

Secretary of Don Committee Larin

f. 17, op. 65, d. 136, l.38

From: Trotsky.
Extract
from Minute No. 50 of session of Revolutionary Military Council of the
Republic of 22 September 1919
23 September 1919
Decreed

To summon Yevgeny Trifonov to Commander-in-Chief with the intention (if his service record is satisfactory) of transferring him to the Reserve Army to form a Cossack Division. If this takes effect the Political Section is to appoint an energetic and experienced Commissar to serve that cavalry unit.

Original signed by Chairman of Revolutionary Military Council of the Republic, L. Trotsky, 23 September 1919

f. 17, op. 65, d. 35, l.165

To: All-Russian Central Executive Committee.
From: Secretary of Cossack Section of All-Russian Central Executive Committee (addendum to minutes of 22 November 1919).
26 November 1919

THESES OF COSSACK SECTION OF ALL-RUSSIAN CENTRAL EXECUTIVE COMMITTEE
On formulating policy towards the Cossacks

(1) We, members of Cossack Section of the All-Russian Central Executive Committee, wholeheartedly support the policy which is directed at neutralizing, isolating or expelling from the bounds of Soviet Russia the counter-revolutionary upper strata of Cossack society and any other bourgeois elements which have concealed themselves in Cossack lands.

(2) We insist on the absolute outright need to attract poor Cossacks, and also those who are moderately well-off, to play an active part in establishing Soviet power in Cossack territory, and to help with the central administration of our country.

When we consider the mistakes made in Cossack districts in the past we have come to the definite conclusion that Soviet power can only be established there by a firm administrative policy, carried out by revolutionary Cossacks, acting in conjunction with the non-

Cossack population of the Cossack areas. At the same time we must move cautiously in economic policy, so as not to conflict with the day to day interests of those who are moderately well off but have only a primitive grasp of politics. By all legal means at our disposal we shall try to persuade all comrades that in the Cossack areas, just as in other parts of Russia which our forces have occupied, we should give people the chance to have a good look at our Soviet regime and to realize that Soviet power is not their enemy but rather the real defender of working people as a whole.

(3) We welcome the policy of the Soviet regime that is tending to hand over to Cossacks and peasants the lands which have been freed from the grip of landowners or the counter-revolutionary upper strata of Cossack society.

(4) We shall be pressing the All-Russian Central Executive Committee to grant an amnesty and restoration of citizens' rights to all working-class elements of Cossack society who followed the bourgeoisie against Soviet power without realizing what they were doing.

For the Secretary K?

f. 17, op. 84, d. 32, l.43

To: Lenin.
From: Ye. P. Preobrazhensky.
Autumn 1919

… In the second place I would like to say a few words about our military operations against the Don Cossacks. At the time we first seized the Don Oblast a rebellion broke out there, as you know, and we could not manage to suppress it. Even women and children rose against us. Nowadays, when our units come into villages, some of those people who take up arms against our troops are the sort of people who did not take any part in Denikin's last operations.

It would be perfectly correct for us to go into the Don Oblast as an advance against Denikin's main base, and would lead to a quick and decisive victory.

We have the same numbers of men as Denikin, perhaps even slightly more. In view of this situation the intended plan of advancing into the Don Oblast can only favour Denikin, since it will provide him with new reserves of men.

We must begin to break up the Don Cossacks in a completely new way, which may at first glance even appear somewhat risky.

I should advise the same should be done also in that part of the Ural Cossack territory which we have occupied.

With comradely greetings

Preobrazhensky

Several of those dealing with the Cossacks thought it would be possible to neutralize their nationalist aspirations by sending them to fight on other fronts, away from their Don homeland, and this was actually tried in the case of Mironov.

f. 17, op. 84, d. 33, l.10

From: Trifonov.
Telegram
re Vrangel's advance

It is possible to form Cossack units. They will be suitable for operations on the Western Front.

Colonel Mironov and the Donburo

Throughout 1919, Communists were divided as to how Colonel Mironov should be regarded. In 1918 Mironov had acquired a great reputation as a Red cavalry leader operating in the area south of Tsaritsyn. As a positive figure he was very successful in rallying many Cossacks to the Reds, and this at a time when White superiority in cavalry was proving extremely costly to the Red Army. Against this, Mironov was frequently outspoken in condemning the more extreme application of Communist policy. He fell foul of the Donburo from the beginning of 1919, and this little group of dedicated Communists had its work cut out to establish its authority.

Mironov was promoted to command the Don Cavalry Corps, but some Communists doubted his loyalty, and held him back from the front. He felt that intrigues in the Party had led to this unfair treatment, when his burning desire was to fight for the Soviets at this most critical moment in their fortunes. On 24 August 1919, without any authorization, Mironov led his men to fight the Whites, but was arrested and condemned to death. On the eve of the day appointed for his execution he was pardoned by Moscow and promoted to command 2nd Calvary Army. Znamensky's (1987) novel *Krasnyye dni* exalts Mironov's zeal in pursuing the ideas of the Revolution, as he conceived them.

The main report was not received till 23 September. Kislitsyn (1992 p. 39) quotes from this text. Mironov's comment that the Cossacks had 'not seen any well-educated political workers' pointedly ignores the contribution to the Red cause made by the Trifonov brothers, who were fully fledged Don Cossacks. Yevgeni Trifonov could see the poetic paradox of this ex-tsarist officer fighting with all his might for the cause of the Revolution:

> Whole regiments of Mironov's Cossacks go over to the enemy, to the military gentlemen they once served. And whole regiments run back with all their baggage and technical weapons from the old Don of the Atamans, back to Mironov's Soviet division. Come what may, Mironov, commanding his division for the Reds, shows himself amazingly untroubled by all the ups and downs: he greets quite calmly the reinforcements who stream across to him from the side of the Whites, and he is contemptuous when he hears that his own regiments have deserted to the enemy. He hardly takes account either of deserters or of those who have come to join him – comrade Mironov barely notices the real world, swallowed up as he is by a sort of fierce idealism.   (*Otblesk kostra*, pp. 112 – 3)

Makarov's report of 8 September (f. 17, op. 65, d. 35, 11. 109–33) pays heartfelt tribute to the firm discipline of Mironov's Don Corps, which was in striking contrast to the unbridled license of other Red Army units, especially Budyonny's First Cavalry Army. In May a favourable comment on Mironov was made by a commissar named Suglitsky, who cannot have been predisposed to favour the headstrong Cossack colonel: 'Comrade Mironov's division, and in general the united group under Mironov's command, have distinguished them-selves. In a brief space of time we swept victoriously from Borisoglebsk to Kamenskaya.' (Butt *et al.*, 1996, p. 73). For Mironov's criticisms of Soviet power see Murphy (1993) 'The Don Rebellion', esp. p. 331:

> Food is taken away, they slap on every possible form of taxes, even demanding contributions from men serving in his division and... he is forced to exclaim: 'Well, just look at the commune, God save us from a commune like that.'

In January 1918 the Cossack Section had been introduced into the All-Russian Central Executive Committee to reassure Cossacks that they had some say in the inner councils of the Party. When Mironov's case was being decided they complained, with some justification, that they had simply been side-lined in a matter which should have been primarily their concern. Makarov reveals a serious conflict of interests between Southern Army Group and the Cossack Section of Central Executive Committee, who had resented Mironov being promoted without any reference to them, and subsequently to his being transferred from the Don, where his popular leadership had persuaded many people to back the Soviets. One report of 8 July 1919 regrets that Cossacks were left in ignorance after the revolution. The proposal to add a division to the strength of the Special Don Corps shows Cossack Section's faith in Mironov's power to attract waverers to the cause of the Revolution, whereas more hardline Bolsheviks remained suspicious that he might break away as an independent leader, like Grigorev and Makhno – or Golubov, who had tried to set up as a 'Red ataman' in 1918.

Plainly there was a serious breach of discipline when Mironov moved a large body of men without permission from superior commanders. Trotsky wanted to make the Red Army a firmly disciplined force under proper control of Moscow, and to get away from the time when it had consisted largely of locally organized units, loyal to their own commanders. He was keen to make an example of Mironov's attempt to act independently in August 1919:

> The trial [of Mironov] should have a considerable educative effect for the Cossacks... Among those arrested is a member of the Central Executive Committee, Buladkin, a very close assistant of Mironov.
>
> (f. 17, op. 109, d. 44, l. 178)

Mironov's pleas for the Communists to treat the Cossacks with more humanity found considerable support among Party members who had been entrusted with authority at the highest levels: see Makarov's letter of 8 October, below, in which he names for Lenin some of those who knew Mironov's feelings and made no move to protest against them (f. 17, op. 65, d. 35, l. 146).

Hardline Bolsheviks had Mironov moved to the Western Front, away from the Don, and the protest which follows shows how strong was the feeling in his favour in his home area.

Kupyansk is a railway junction some 50 kilometres east of Kharkov.

f. 17, op. 65, d. 34, l.76

To: Syrtsov, Donburo; copy to Central Committee, Moscow.
From: Communists of Kupyansk.
13 April 1919 (received 14 April)

In number 6 of *Donskaya Pravda* an article has been published, in which it is said: 'Now we have succeeded in liquidating Mironov at Millerovo'. It is intolerable to print pronouncments of this sort, so ill-informed and so harmful. We propose that the next number should carry a special notice in a prominent place about Mironov's appointment as second in command to the Army commander on the Western Front. There should be no polemical attacks, and his services in battle should be recorded. Our men at the front are left to imagine that Mironov has been liquidated, i.e. executed.

Frenkel's suggestions for reforming the Don Oblast reveal the difficulty many Party officials felt in trying to come to terms with Cossacks such as Mironov.

f. 17, op. 65, d. 34, l.116

To: Central Committee.
From: Comrade Frenkel.
Memorandum
July 1919

In future work by our Party on the Don due account must be taken of our past experience, so as not to repeat previous mistakes. Resistance by the kulak upper echelons must be crushed without mercy, just as we must crush the counter-revolution led by the generals. If in the past our forces on the Don appeared weak for a number of reasons, our present task must be to organize in their place a stronger army, which is more tightly knit, better organized, with a higher level of consciousness, better disciplined, and with a larger force of men.

When we crush the kulak upper echelons of the Cossacks, we must at the same time weaken them by other means, by cutting off from [the older Cossacks] all the 'moderate' men who had served on the Western Front, so that we can form [from them] a basis for the Revolution. In the past absolutely no effort has been made in that way (to 'neutralize' the moderate elements, especially the younger Cossacks), as we have done in Soviet

Russia. It is essential for us to work like that in future – and the harder it is to do that all the more persistently we must go on.

With regard to that I welcome the change which the Central Committee has quite rightly made in this spirit. I cannot help feeling alarmed at the experiments of Mironov (who is not a member of our Party), since he may yet land us with a worse set to than the one we had with Grigorev. And his work on neutralizing [the moderates], should be undertaken only by our Party through its most experienced and disciplined members. Mironov should be used only in well-defined limits and circumstances, which would guarantee against any unexpected developments.

Emphasizing this I must draw Central Committee's attention to the danger which Mironov poses for Soviet power on the Don (as witnessed by his previous clashes with the Party and the Revolutionary Committee). It would be imprudent to trust him without any reservations.

I consider the first directives of the Central Committee about policy on the Don to have been wrong, since they placed too great a burden both on our army, with its still imperfect discipline, and on the newly made, very frail Soviet institutions on the Don, while they said absolutely nothing about a cautious, well-evolved way to treat those who were neither rich nor poor. Therefore I think that in future it is most essential to work towards weaning those of modest means away [from the Whites] and draw them over to our side. In my opinion the contest between those who belong to the Cossack class and the peasants (non-Cossack 'outsiders') should be carried on as part of the class struggle. It should not be turned into a shapeless animal battle, since our own interests would suggest a less crude approach.

Over this question I find myself in a minority of two, at odds with the majority of four in the Donburo, since they consider the original directives to have been right. They claim that the sole reason why those policies failed lay with the army, and they are bent on seeking out guilty parties instead of looking for the real causes of that failure. They simply will not hear any suggestion about weaning away those of 'middling' means, and consider that to be a fatal policy. As a minority member (of two) in the Donburo I consider that the Donburo should be replaced by some other persons, for the very good reason that its present members disagree fundamentally with the Central Committee of our Party on the Don. I have furthermore been insisting on changing the personnel of the Donburo, because for a series of subjective reasons – which originally made the Donburo strong, but which now, from losing touch with the broad mass of workers, have become deformed into abnormally intimate and sometimes even family relationships – the whole present personnel of the Donburo have lost their capacity to produce results, although each of the members of the Donburo could be of great benefit in some other place.

In spite of all my most sincere desires, for the last two months I have not been able to do the work for which I am fitted. After three occasions on which I made a most emphatic application, the last plenum of the Donburo found it possible to grant my request to be released from work with those persons who made up the Donburo, and the Central Committee will undoubtedly approve this. Since I consider it essential to step up our work now, at this moment when the Southern Front has collapsed, I made my way to the Political Section of the 8th Army, from where I have been put in charge of the 15th Division.

With comradely greetings, comrade Frenkel

Signature attested

Makarov reports to Cossack Section of VTsIK

I originally intended to present only extracts from Makarov's report. I later decided that the complete report gives the most coherent account of all the duplicity, intrigues and bitterness which surrounded Mironov as one of the most fascinating personalities in the Revolution. The cavalry leader's high-flown oratory should not blind us to his genuine idealism. Here was one man who felt that the original aims of the Soviets had been suborned by the Communist Party. We know from other sources that many powerful Bolsheviks thought all Cossacks were irredeemably hostile, and that their society must be totally destroyed. It is plain that some of those in power saw the Cossack Section of VTsIK as just a sop to Cossack pride, and that they failed to keep the Section informed on crucial questions which should have been its concern. Makarov throws light on several half-hidden problems, and I have translated the full text of his report.

In the later pages of section 1 he reports Mironov attacking 'Olomsky's' writings in *Izvestiya*, no. 75. In Mironov's telegram of 18 August he poured ridicule on *Izvestiya*'s military correspondent, Kholmsky, for his absurdly optimistic assessment of the situation at the very moment when the Red Army was about to lose its hold on so much of South Russia. For some reason Kholmsky's name has been distorted to Olomsky.

Makarov's explanation is reproduced verbatim (pp. 141–63). In the body of his report Makarov introduces extensive quotations: 1] 143–6 Mironov's report of 24 June, culminating in (146) Aralov's approval. 2] 147–8 Mironov's call to join his Corps. 3] (149) Mironov's message to Cossack Section. 4] Mironov announces to 9th Army that he is going to the Front to fight Denikin (150). 5] (150) Mironov wants the Russian people to take industry and the land into their hands. 6] Mironov informs 9th Army that he is building a force to fight the Whites (150–1). 7] (152–3) Makarov quotes Zaytsev's complaint *re* Mironov's criticism of Communists for their harsh treatment of the Cossacks. 8] (153) Larin tries to bypass Cossack Section with a message to Lenin. 9] (154) Zaytsev tells Mironov he will support recruitment for the Corps (but asks him to keep his letter private). 10] (155) Mironov begs the political workers in his unit to deal openly with him. 11] (155–6) The political workers ask whether Mironov can be trusted to lead his men for Communist power. 12] (156) After Mironov has started to march to the Front the political workers declare him a traitor. 13] (157)Makarov quotes earlier minutes of Cossack Section, co-opting Mironov to join Cossack Section. 14] (158) Makarov quotes his own letter to Larin, seeking to renconcile Cossack Section's acceptance of Mironov with the political workers suspicions of him. 15] (160) Cossack Section have not been informed by Larin about their reasons for doubting Mironov. Cossack Section propose replacing Larin and the other political workers with someone from the Section who can work better with Mironov. 16] (160) Mironov complains that recruitment for his Corps has been obstructed by the political workers with whom he is burdened. He points to the confidence which rank and file Cossacks show in his leadership. 15] (162–3) Cossack Section condemns Mironov's breach of discipline in marching his men to the Front without instructions to move.

The controversy between Larin and Makarov reveals how rival bodies were contending for the ultimate say in making decisions. Cossack Section of VTsIK plainly felt affronted that they had not been consulted when Sokolnikov appointed Mironov to form Don Corps, and to be its commander (141–2). In the first half of 1919 Larin had served as commissar in the Khopyor District. Mironov and his men surely have held him responsible for the wholesale massacres which the Reds had perpetrated there on men, women and children (151, 161). In July Larin was appointed commissar of the Don Corps. Mironov firmly opposed his commissar and the team of political workers who were helping to spread Party doctrine among his Cossacks (141, 153, 162). Larin took no effective action to check Mironov (153). He failed to inform Cossack Section of the difficulties his RVS was experiencing. Cossack Section praised Mironov's leadership and raised him up to become one of their members (157–8). When Mironov marched out from Saransk they had to expel him from being a member of their Section (163).

f. 17, op. 65, d. 35, l.109

To: *Cossack Section All-Russian Central Executive Committee.*
From: *Comrade Makarov, Commissar for Cossack Affairs.*
Report
On the case of armed action by MIRONOV, commanding the Don Corps
8 September 1919 (received 23 September)

[Headings of Report]

(I)   Mironov's personality.
(II) Concerning the political workers of Don Corps.
(III) How Cossack Section of Central Executive Committee relates to aforesaid question.

[I]

Mironov has long been well-known as a leading figure, fighting to help working-class Cossacks. Even in 1906, Mironov, at that time holding the rank of squadron commander, was sent to the First State Duma with a revolutionary mandate from the stanitsas and units of Ust-Medveditskaya District. He was arrested on his way back to the Don. In the summer of 1906 and the spring of 1907, while the State Duma was holding its first two sessions, the Don saw many disturbances, gatherings and political meetings, which presented the deputies with revolutionary demands and resolutions.

At the time of the October coup Mironov sided with those who supported the revolution. He was the Commissar in Ust-Medveditskaya stanitsa. Then he called on those people, mainly Cossacks, who came forward to fight against the White Guardists, and gradually formed a division which took the name 'Mironov'.

Comrade Mekhonoshin called him a romantic, and said that he should be given more men. But he did not belong to any political party.

There were no Communist cells in Mironov's division, and he regarded commissars suspiciously, just as was the case in Kikvidze's division. But he was a good strategist, and got through all the most difficult situations with few casualties. For that reason the Cossacks wanted to join his unit. The population were all sympathetic to him, both Cossacks and non-Cossacks. The peasants of Saratov Province came out with a greeting of bread and salt for him. Excellent discipline prevailed among the units under his command. There were no cases of robbery, looting or forcible requisitioning. His troops did not offend the religious feelings of the people. In general people did not regard the units under his command as hostile, and consequently were drawn to the Soviet regime. Mironov gained all the more prestige from this in that the population were hostile to other units fighting alongside Mironov, for example Kikvidze's, because of the unruly way they behaved. (I am thinking of the time when Mironov was on the Southern Front towards the end of 1918).

That is why, seeing what Mironov could do and wanting to make use of his talent as a leader whom the masses would follow, the Revolutionary Military Council of Southern Army Group gave Mironov more men and appointed him Commander of a task force comprising two divisions. It should be noted that he lived up marvellously to all the hopes that had been placed in him: in a short space of time – late January and February 1919 – he moved ahead of 9th Army forces to reach the Northern Donets River, without meeting much resistance from the White Guards, commanded at that time by General Krasnov. Most of Krasnov's regiments were quite willing to surrender to Mironov, who was greatly looked up to – both by the Red Army and by working-class Cossacks in the White forces.

But the greater his popularity grew and the closer he came to Novocherkassk, the greater became the discontent of the population in his rear – thanks to the clumsy way Soviet power was being established, with wholesale requisitioning, masses of people being shot, and so on. In many places there were even rebellions breaking out, as for example in the Upper Don District (Vyoshenskaya and Kazanskaya stanitsas), and also in Ust-Medveditskaya District.

Mironov criticized sharply the mistakes and offensive behaviour of certain Party workers and Communists (see for example his speech in Ust-Medveditskaya). This state of affairs, and the suspicion that he might be aiming to secure power for himself, was what led Revolutionary Military Council of Southern Army Group to move him to the Western Front – though they failed to convey this to the Cossack Section of All-Russian Central Executive Committee.

After Mironov had been moved away his units became demoralized – because they were badly led, and for other reasons. It was at this time that Denikin began his successful advance along through the whole Don front, when we lost the whole of the Don area again in the short space of two or three weeks.

Before we evacuated the Don Oblast we managed to carry out mobilization in Khopyor and Ust-Medveditskaya Districts by using Mironov's name. Conscripts and refugees retreated out of the oblast. This disaster on the Don, and finding a way to form new military units, brought Southern Army Group back forcibly to remember Mironov.

Acting in the name of the Revolutionary Military Council of Southern Army Group, Sokolnikov and Mekhonishin appointed him to command the

Don Corps which was being created. They gave him wide powers, as it used to be for a 'Governor-General'.

It was thus that Mironov appeared in a high position on Southern Front without the Cossack Section having a say in what was done. Mironov's utterances meant that the government were well-informed of his political principles. His first report of 24 June 1919 was dispatched to comrade Kalinin, Chairman of All-Russian Central Executive Committee; comrade Lenin, Chairman of Defence Council; and comrade Trotsky, Chairman of Revolutionary Military Council – Mironov declared therein [1]:

Revolutionary Military Council of Southern Army Groups, when they appointed me Commander of the Special Corps, stated that this former counter-insurgency force was strong, with up to 15 thousand infantry, including up to 5000 young soldiers under training, and that this was one of the front-line fighting units. If you have been given this information, then I must consider it my revolutionary duty to report that this information is completely at variance with the real situation. I cannot accept this, for when we think of our information as a useful asset, it is making us close our eyes to the real danger. Lulled into a false sense of security, we fail to act in good time, or if we do something then it is too late. I have stood – and am standing now – not for a secretive structure of social life, nor for a narrow Party programme – but for a public and open system of society, in which the people would play an active part. When I say this I do not mean to include the bourgeoisie or kulak elements. The sympathy of the mass of the peasants and the real intelligentsia can only be won over by arranging society on such a basis.

I must report that my Special Corps has about three thousand infantry, spread over a long front. Units are worn out and exhausted. Except for three squads of cadets the rest of the young soldiers are worse than useless, and there are only a pitiful handful left, as against the great thousands we had been promised. The Communist Regiment took to flight; it contained men who were incapable even of loading a rifle. The Special Corps could act as a screen. The position on its front has been rescued for the time being only by bringing out the Cossacks who had been conscripted in Khopyorsk District. That District has not quite lived up to General Denikin's expectations. As soon as the White Guards take steps to remedy the situation the Special Corps Screen will be broken.

'It has not only been on the Don that mass rebellion has been provoked by the doings of certain Revolutionary Committees, Special Sections, tribunals and some commissars. In reality this rebellion threatens to spread in a massive wave in peasant villages throughout the whole Republic. We may come to understand the feelings of the mass of the peasantry and why there is such a large percentage of deserters, who go off to form gangs of Greens. To make you realize the true state of affairs we must tell you that in popular meetings in the villages of ?Novy Chigla, Verkh-Tishank and other places voices have been heard saying openly "Let us have the Tsar back". The cause of our social revolution is threatened with complete failure by the uprising in Ilovatka on the River Ters, and by the muffled unrest which is so strongly felt in most districts in Saratov Province.

I do not belong to any political party, but I have given too much health and strength fighting for the social revolution to be able to watch calmly while General Denikin rides the horse of "Commune" to stamp down the red banner of labour.

When I look ahead and see the social revolution coming to grief (since nothing encourages me to be optimistic and my pessimism is rarely proved wrong), I feel a compelling necessity to recommend the following measures to be taken urgently:

(1) We should reinforce the Special Corps with a fresh Division.
(2) A division must be moved onto its strength, as a basis for the future might of a new army, with which Divisional Commander Zolikov and I will go in person to seize the initiative again, so as to give scope to our other divisions and armies – alternatively I could be appointed Commander of 9th Army, where my military reputation still stands so high... [point 4 follows]
(4) The political state of the country makes it essential to convene a national government, not just of one party, so as to knock the ground away from under the feet of the traitor socialists. We would continue to fight a stubborn war at the front and build up the might of the Red Army. That step will bring back the mass of the people to our side – and they will gladly take up their rifles to save our land and freedom. Do not call this representative gathering either "Assembly of the Land" or "Constituent Assembly". Call it what you will, but be sure to convene it.

The people are groaning. I have made many statements to the Revolutionary Military Council of Southern Army Group, among them the case of a peasant in a village whose name had been changed to "Lenin District". A family of twenty-one individuals had formed their own commune with four pairs of oxen. Because they refused to go into the [Party] commune the commissar took away their oxen, and when the peasant protested he was killed. On this matter, there was a report from Yermakov, chairman of one of the tribunals, whose words send a chill down the spine. I must repeat: people are ready to rush into the arms of the landowners' conspiracy, as long as their torments will not be so sharply felt and obvious as they are at present.

(5) The Party must be purged as follows: after the October Revolution had taken place all Communists should have been put into military units and sent to the front. You would be able to see then who was a sincere Communist, and who was just saving his own skin, or a spy, encouraging our people to act foolishly – and who was filling up jobs in all the revolutionary committees and special sections, such as the Morozovskaya Revolutionary Committee, who murdered 67 people and were subsequently executed.

But as Mironov got no reply to that report he went to Moscow himself, and on 8 July 1919 made another report to Kalinin, Chairman of All-Russian Central Executive Committee and to Lenin, Chairman of Defence Council, comrade Makarov being present at this meeting. This report stated:

The decision to call up Don Cossacks for the Western Front had been taken by 15 March 1919 by a decree of Revolutionary Military Council of the Republic. The C-in-C's order of 16 March, No. 2266 had already given me instructions to form a division. Naturally I have no idea why that mobilization was deferred, and the terrible mistake was made. Before the decision about mobilization was taken I submitted the following explanatory note:

The political revolution of 27 February 1917 took place when the younger generation of Cossacks were still serving at the front in the imperialist blood bath. At that time, feeling the spirit of revolution which inspired everyone, the younger Cossacks, felt at one with the rank and file soldiers, and got some inkling of politics, even if only to a limited extent. "Red" Cossack officers went along with that movement, although the Don officer corps should be ashamed that there were so few of them at that great time when the masses of the working class were beginning to be freed from the scourge of capitalism.

The older generations, fathers and grandfathers, were living on the Don, dominated by the police, as they had always been, with their mind and soul completely subjected to the priest, the stanitsa ataman, the district ataman – where the Tsar was regarded with holy reverence, and his overthrow was still attributed to "internal enemies".

Nobody came out against this ignorant nonsense. They almost stoned to death some isolated individuals who tried to explain the meaning of the change that had happened.

Time went by. The social revolution was coming nearer. When that revolution came, Cossacks on active service were still at the former front, but they were already thinking insistently, and in some cases demanding: 'Back home, to the Don!' General Kaledin was preparing another part for these younger Cossacks to play – namely for them to fight the Bolsheviks in Yekaterinoslav Province and the Donets Basin. Cossacks from the front did not support their leaders' scheme and remained faithful to the wishes of the working class. 32nd, 37th and other regiments refused to obey military orders near the town of Aleksandrovsk, and 32nd Regiment was greeted with music by the Bolsheviks. General Kaledin committed suicide.

What General Kaledin had failed to do was achieved by General Krasnov (and recently achieved, even more so, by General Denikin). Front line Cossacks came back to their homes, and there, being out of reach of the political centres, with no education in politics, their primitive level of understanding let them succumb in the end to the influence of their fathers and grandfathers, coupled also with the counter-revolutionary priesthood and officers – and went over, without realizing it themselves, to side with the enemies of the people. We are all grievously to blame for what happened. The Don was abandoned, and left to its own devices, to choke then in its own blood. It must be noted that it was at that very time, March–April, that the districts of of the Don country began to feel the effect of false agents running wild among them – large numbers of men who had joined the ranks of the Red Guards at that time: isolated villages went up in flames, churches were hit by artillery fire when services were going on, etc. There was rejoicing by such as General Mamontov and Colonel Zastegayev – the revolution itself had provided these gendarmes of the Tsar with provocation for a Cossack uprising. History will at some stage show up objectively that terrible experience of the front-line Cossacks. Hundreds of them were shot by a sinister gang, thousands are languishing in the prisons and the mines.

Even now the Don remains politically uneducated and backward. The Revolution made such fundamental changes that the Cossack who lives in his own village cannot get his poor old brain to make sense of what has happened, cannot grasp the huge scope of the proletarian Revolution which has overtaken half the world. He cannot understand the requisitioning of cattle and grain stores on the Don, which we have had to resort to for our country's hunger. With this in mind, being deeply convinced that Cossacks are not so counter-Revolutionary as they are considered and depicted as being, and that we can turn them again into fighters for the interests of the proletariat, as I was leaving for the Western Front I suggested the following measures to the Revolutionary Military Council of the Republic:

'To retain the Cossack people's sympathy for Soviet power:

(1) We must take account of the way their life-style has been formed by their history and their religion. The passage of time and skilful political workers will do away with the Cossacks' ignorance and fanaticism, which was instilled into them by centuries of militaristic upbringing under the old police system, which penetrated every fibre of a Cossack's being.

(2) While we are going through the period of our Revolutionary struggle against the bourgeoisie, as long as counter-Revolution on the Don has not been crushed, the whole situation demands categorically that the idea of Communism should be brought into the minds of Cossacks and our native peasant population by means of lectures, discussion, pamphlets, and so on, but under no circumstances to be imposed or instilled by force, as seems now to be indicated by all the exploits of those who happen to call themselves Communists, and their ways of doing things.

(3) At the present juncture they should not confiscate livestock and equipment, but it would be better to announce firm prices, for which they could insist on people supplying them with food, making this demand from the whole population of any given place – when one must also consider how well-off is the area in question.

(4) Allow the local population to make their own life, under the guidance of experienced political workers, who would watch carefully that counter-Revolutionary elements should not get into positions of authority. To achieve this:

(5) The best way would be to convoke district congresses to elect district Soviets, handing over complete powers to the executive organs of these congresses, and not to individuals appointed at random, *as happens at present.*

'The congresses should be attended by highly placed political workers from Moscow. We must not fail to take account of the Cossacks' complete ignorance, since up to now they have not seen any good examples of political leaders, but have been completely dominated by reactionary officers, the priesthood and these sorts of people. And only one person understood me, only one person agreed with me – comrade Aralov. He wrote on my note: 'I concur whole-heartedly with these political ideas and requirements, and think they are valid.

Aralov, Member of Revolutionary Military Council of the Republic.

And if you had all agreed, as comrade Aralov did – by now we should have had no front on the Don.

Shall we be blind from now on? No, the cost for that is too high. Citizen Vladimir Ilich, I have been entrusted with forming a Corps. I beg you to support me in every possible way, so that I can bring into being as fast as possible that force which will let us take the initiative on the Don Front, and I stake my head on it that in six weeks we shall throw Denikin's gangs out of Soviet Russia. No matter who tells whatever lies against me, no matter what slanders they bring against me, I solemnly declare for the proletariat to hear: that I have not betrayed its cause and shall not betray it. I beg only that you will understand me, understand me as a non-Party man but as one who has striven to defend the Revolution from 1906 to this day.

I feel grieved and hurt by all the suspicions and accusations coming from people who do not understand the essentials of the Communist ideal. It is not only I who feels pain and distress from these 'interpreters' of the doctrine – all working-class peasants also feel distressed.

Comrade Lenin came to know that comrade Aralov, as a member of the Revolutionary Military Council approved of the contents of this report ('I concur whole-heartedly with the political ideas and requirements and think they are valid'). For his part Lenin said: 'It is a pity they did not tell me that before.'

As a result comrade Lenin and comrade Kalinin promised their good offices, but with the proviso that the work should be carried out along with the Cossack Section, and comrade Mironov was not to do anything without them knowing. Moreover comrade Lenin gave his opinion of Mironov's character in the following terms: 'We need people like this. We must make use of them sensibly.' Kalinin on the whole was quite sympathetic, though at the same time he expressed his concern that Mironov might react against the Party because he had been criticized by some individually unworthy Communists.

Armed with the approval of the central authorities Mironov left Moscow in good heart to proceed to the town of Saransk, where the Don Corps was being formed. On arriving there, in order to speed up the work of putting the Corps together, he straight away issued the following appeal 'to refugees of the Don Oblast' [2]:

'Citizen Cossacks and peasants.

'Last year Krasnov's counter-Revolutionary ground-swell forced many of you to leave your native steppes and homesteads. You had to experience great hardship and suffering.

'In January the returning storm of Revolution shook the apparent might of Krasnov's evil domain. In the course of two or three weeks he had to yield all that he had disposed of for long months and at the price of tens of thousands of corpses of Cossacks who had been deceived.

'You returned to your homes, in ruins, it is true, but none the less your very own. In one's own place even the smoke is sweet.

'Our sloppiness and lack of order built up the strength of General Denikin, and once more you have had to seek refuge in alien lands. But this second expulsion is going to be the last.

'If General Denikin wins there will be no salvation for anyone. No matter how far you travel, how far you seek to get away – you will always finish up against the wall where the White Guard gangs will polish you off.

'But if we win, then I can confidently say that for us this is the last time we shall be leaving, for we too will not stand on ceremony with General Denikin, just as we shall not be too gentle with his pack of White Guard dogs. We too, shall line that nice bunch of people up to be shot.

'Everyone can see what we have to realize and what we must do. *We can only come to one conclusion.*

'For the last time I send forth a call: everyone, no matter what age they are, as long as their hands are strong and their trusty eye is accurate – everyone must come to arms, everyone must come to serve the red flag of labour which the Revolution is handing on to me today.

'We shall break those who have driven us out only if we all strive and press forward together, only by a united response to my summons. Do not hope that someone is going to do this for you.

'And thus, citizens in exile – all come to me! Citizens who have the heart of a citizen, and not the heart of a layabout, – all come to me!.

'Beware lest the dead should hear and rise up – while you are still asleep.

'Beware, for the chains of slavery are already hanging over your heads.

'Life or death – there is no other choice.

'Long live the social Revolution!

'Long live unsullied truth!'

But Mironov soon realized that further formation of the Corps had been blocked by someone's hand, that they had even raised the question of disbanding it, while he was himself reduced to being an outcast, i. e. they would not allow him to form his Corps and at the same time would not allow him to proceed to the front line. This can be seen clearly from his telegram of 18 August, addressed to the Cossack Section, which unfortunately did not reach the Cossack Section till 3 September. It contained the following message [3]:

'I am reliably informed by people who are loyal to me and at the same time have been parties to the organization of political workers that the Political Section has spoken to those in charge [about] disbanding the Corps which has not yet been formed – otherwise, according to what they say, there will be another mass treachery like Grigorev's. I could not bring myself to such vile acts, and I shall always remain Mironov. My political views can [be seen] from my telegram of 24 June to citizens Lenin. Trotsky and to Southern Army Group. I declare once again that Denikin and the bourgeoisie are my mortal enemies. But on the other hand I cannot count as friends those people who recently brought about a wholesale rebellion on [the Don] by their bestial behaviour. To the toiling masses of the proletariat and peasantry I affirm that I have struggled and will go on struggling for the socialization of the means of production and for socialism.

'I beg that political dealings with me should be above board, and that the formation of my Corps should be speedily completed, for someone's hand has absolutely closed off the supply of men. Red Army men on the Southern Front were eagerly awaiting that my Corps should be brought up to strength, and saw that as the key to saving the situation. As an honest citizen and an old Revolutionary I declare that the collapse of my Corps may lead to the final collapse of the Southern Front. I am still keeping an eye on Olomsky's ravings in *Izvestiya*'.

Since Mironov received no reply from the Cossack Section, not through any fault of theirs, he began to negotiate with comrade Smilga, member of the Revolutionary Military Council, who was at that time in Penza. Since I cannot tell you the entire contents of what was said, I am passing on the most outstanding features of what passed between them.

To comrade Smilga's request for him to report Mironov replied: 'I am panting to go into action, I cannot stand by and watch the Revolution fail.'

Comrade Smilga asked him to come to Penza, and at Mironov's request allowed him to take a bodyguard of 150 men. However, comrade Murashev, military commandant of Ruzayevka station, when Mironov required him to provide the rolling stock for his train at Saransk station (11 carriages for men and 19 for horses), in spite of headquarters of 9th Army having given permission, not only refused to supply the carriages, but even sent a telegram to the Commission for Examining Officers' Loyalty, requesting them to send forces against Mironov. (It is interesting to note that comrade Muralov, who happened to be passing through from the Eastern Front, advised Murashev to provide the carriages.)

On 23 August Mironov sent a telegram to Headquarters of 9th Army [4]: 'I request you to convey to Southern Army Group that I, witnessing the ruin of the Revolution and open sabotage hindering the formation of my Corps, can no longer remain inactive. From letters received from the front I know that I am expected there. I am setting out with what force I have at my disposal to pursue our stern fight against Denikin and the bourgeoisie.

I may conclude this account of his personality by quoting the following appeal which he issued after he had already set out [5]: Oh, you poor afflicted Russian people, seeing your sufferings and torments, the way you and your conscience have been abused – no honest citizen who loves the truth should have to put up with this abuse or endure it any longer.

'Take all power, all the land, factories and mills into your hands. On 23 August I sent the following telegram [6]:

> '9th Army HQ, Penza. I request you to convey to Southern Army Group that, seeing the Revolution destroyed and the formation of my Corps openly sabotaged. I can no longer stand idly by, for I know from the letters I have received from the front that I am expected there. I am going to the front with what forces I have to pursue the bitter fight against Denikin and the bourgeoisie. The red flags of the Don Revolutionary Corps bear the inscription: "All land to the peasants!" "All factories and mills to the workers!" "All power to working people, with genuine Soviets of workers', peasant and Cossack deputies elected by the workers, based on free socialist speaking!" "Down with the autocratic power of the commissars and the bureaucracy of the Communists who are killing the Revolution.
>
> I am not alone. Along with me goes the true heart of our nation who have suffered so much for righteousness' sake – and that is our guarantee that our Revolution will be saved.
>
> All so-called "deserters" are coming to join me and will make up that fearful force before which Denikin will tremble and which Communists will revere.
>
> Citizen Mironov, Commander of the Don Revolutionary Corps.

I call on all those who love righteousness and real freedom to join the ranks of the Corps'.

In this manner, imagining himself to be the saviour of Russia, Mironov marched out with 4000 men, 14 machine guns, 2000 rifles, 2 guns (unfit for service) and 1000 cavalry to fight on two fronts, against Denikin and against the Communists.

[II]

Right from the outset the Revolutionary Council of the Don Corps were on Mironov's side. Proof of this can be seen in comrade Skalov's letter to comrade Lenin asking him to give every possible assistance to the formation of the Corps.

Friction started on the spot at public meetings and garrison assemblies, where Mironov vented his criticism of so-called Communists who had wormed their way into the Party. He had plenty to go on, since not only Red Army men (Cossacks and peasants), but even Party workers were mainly recruited locally from the Don. Moreover some political workers were among those who had disgraced themselves on the Don by wholesale unbridled terror and senseless 'de-Cossackification'. At that time, thanks to the Civil Authority and the Donburo most of these in power on the Don were people with no tact or sensitivity towards Cossacks – quite the reverse: mindful of former grievances they unleashed a whole series of outrages, and showed themselves to be quite unscrupulous and with a gangster mentality. Several of this sort of people turned up in the Don Corps among the senior political workers: as for example comrade Rogachov, who was in charge of the Political Section of the Don Corps. He had a criminal record (having been tried for taking bribes in the course of his duty). He had previously been a 'maximalist', notorious for carrying out illegal requisitioning. Comrade Lenin himself had marked down his name in his telegram No. 607. Besides him there was comrade Boldyrev, head of the First Don Division, a former officer of the old army. He was a careerist, since, as a Menshevik, at the 4th All-Russian Congress of Soviets he went against the Cossack Section, because they were supporting the Bolshevik programme. Now turning himself into a Communist, he still continued to try to preach treacherous propaganda against the Cossack Section, trying to make out that members of the Cossack Section were representatives of counter-revolutionary Cossack regiments. It has to be noted that there was no unanimity even among the political workers of Don Corps. The Communists split up into what we might call 'various sects'. Some of them knew everything, others knew a certain amount, while the third lot knew nothing about how relations with Mironov had changed. There were so-called 'Don Communists', 'Russian Communists', and Larin's group, the 'Khopyor Communists'.

When Revolutionary Council of Don Corps saw that on the one hand they could not act to harm Mironov and could not sway Red Army men in the mass, on the other hand that Mironov himself from criticizing individual Communists and demanding that the Party should be purged of unsuitable elements had gone over to the preaching for 'real truth', 'genuine Soviets' and 'a proper social revolution', it was at that time that the critical change occurred.

On 6 August this year comrade Larin, a member of the Revolutionary Council of the Don Corps, wrote a report for Southern Army Group, addressed to comrade Sokolnikov, outlining his distrust of Mironov. On 12 August another report was made to the Revolutionary Military Council by comrade Skalov concerning measures taken against Mironov, which could be summarized as follows: to put a stop to the formation of Don Corps and to break it up into separate units. The Cossack Section was not apprised of this important change in the political workers' attitude to Mironov and the formation of his Corps. During all this time the Cossack Section was sent only one report, written by political commissar comrade Zaytsev on 6 August this year [7]:

Officially formation of the Cavalry Division began on 11 July, with up to 2500 Cossacks. Reinforcements are not coming in well. There has not been a satisfactory supply of uniform or equipment, i.e. not up to the amount that should be arriving. The inflow of men and horses is not as it should be. Steps have been taken to satisfy the needs both for men and horses. As for political work in the division it may be noted that there are enough Party activists. All the work which they are concerned with, to provide political education for the Cossacks, has not been very successful. They are up against serious opposition from Mironov, who carries on an open campaign against the Communist Party at meetings and gatherings. He is always calling on the Cossacks to be non-Party men, saying "I am a non-Party man and I hope that you, Cossacks also, will be non-Party". He points out that the Communist Party consists almost entirely of robbers, who have neither sown nor reaped, but who manage to get everything into their hands, taking everything on the Don from both the peasants and from you, the Don Cossacks. He is constantly pointing out all the Party's minor lapses to the Cossacks, in order to turn them against the Party. It must be emphasized that it is impossible for Party activists to work in these circumstances, in the face of Mironov's open campaign, since he tells the Cossacks for almost everyone to hear not to pay heed to the Communists – for the Communists are up to no good. There is a political section attached to the division which carries out propaganda and organizational work at divisional level, while the regiments have education clubs and lectures are given every day. Up to now the

Cossacks have a reasonable frame of mind. The Red officer Bondarenko was sent by the Cossack Section to be at Mironov's disposal. In the Morozovskaya Division he pocketed 300 000 roubles. His fellow soldiers in our Division caught him out; he was arrested and sent off to the Tribunal, but on the way there he managed to run away. Steps have been taken to search him out. We must ask Cossack Section not to send such scoundrels in future but to check them out carefully on the spot.

However, comrade Larin, member of the Revolutionary Council of Don Corps, for some unknown reasons asked that no action should be taken even on this, the only report that had been passed on. To demonstrate further how Don Corps political workers behaved towards Cossack Section, we may mention comrade Larin's letter to comrade Zaytsev from which we can see that a lot of things are undertaken secretly, without informing Cossack Section. The letter reads as follows [8]:

'Comrade Zaytsev,
    'Forgive us that it is not through you that we are transmitting to Ilich the report of the Political Section and the report of the Revolutionary Council. When you receive the letter, proceed to the Secretariat of the Council of People's Commissars, call out the Secretary, comrade Mariya Avilova (she has the reports), and try to go through to Ilich with her, but without the Cossack Section; it strongly believes in Mironov.'

One could see a certain ambivalence in the work of the political workers, as may be observed in the letter from Political Commissar Zaytsev to Mironov [9]:

'Good day, comrade Mironov,
    'My most hearty greetings, and I wish you success in forming your Corps. I got here today, was in the Kremlin, and am setting about organizing our own Base. I hope to get everything. Tomorrow I intend to go to comrade Lenin with comrade Makarov. I am going to talk to him about forming our Corps. I shall explain everything that has been holding it up, and I shall try to get rid of all that sort of people which you talked to me about. They are taking comrade Larin right out of the Corps. Rogachov is apparently being arrested, since a charge has been brought against him that he has engaged in some illegal confiscations and requisitioning. In short, along with the Cossack Section, I shall do my best to get rid of all those scoundrels from our Corps who are impeding the formation of the Corps.

'You, comrade Mironov, must act according to the dictates of every true revolutionary's conscience, as he stands to defend Soviet power. You should know that the central government has shown its absolute faith in you, as someone who is fighting for the Revolution with complete integrity and devotion. The whole of our dialogue and the views we share will be put into action. At a session of the Central Executive Committee I shall make a complete report about forming the Corps, and about the work of the Khopyor Communists on the Don and in our Corps. I hope that more than half of them may be recalled.

'Comrade Mironov, if you have anything important you want to raise, send an urgent telegram to me at the Cossack Section and I shall do everything. Next, I beg you not to tell anyone about this letter but to keep it secret. Comrade Mironov, you and I apparently will have to work together in the Corps, and one more comrade will be sent from Cossack Section. Comrade Mironov, I understand you quite clearly and the ideals you are working for. The Cossack Section and I are completely in sympathy with them. You must realize that all impediments will be removed. In the mean time all the best to you where you are stationed now. I sincerely wish you success in your work to form the Corps. Write now about what you need and I shall immediately press Central Supply Administration to meet our requirements. All for now. Looking forward to our next meeting.'

There was an extraordinary state of affairs: Mironov was afraid of the Party's political workers, and they were afraid of Mironov. Besides that the political workers hid the real situation from Mironov. Because of this, he said to them [10]:

'You do not believe me. Tell me quite straight. I shall leave. I shall not get in your way, but do not keep me locked in a state of uncertainty. They sent me away to the Western Front. I can understand that was to banish me. Now they have called me back. It's turned out that I have just been banished to Saransk. That is what the Communists are doing. All that is left is for me to shoot myself.'

Don Corps' Revolutionary Committee not only avoided keeping in touch with Cossack Section, not only was guilty of concealing from us the change in its attitude to Mironov, but on 16 August even wrote the following perfidious message to Cossack Section of All-Russian Central Executive Committee [11]:

'Dear comrades: Using a chance opportunity, Revolutionary Committee of Don Corps (its political wing), in its work which we all know is quite difficult, would like to get from you a series of views which have been recorded after an exchange of opinions and decrees on the following questions:

(1) Do you consider it necessary to carry out, of course in a tactful way, Communist education of the Cossack masses? Do you think it essential to set up Communist cells? What sort of part should be played by political commissars in Cossack regiments?

(2) If it is essential to build up Communist cells, how shall this be done in practice without undermining the authority of the military commanders, when the commanders are calling on the mass of the Cossacks to remain non-Party men?

(3) Do you think that everyone can be completely free when the Red Army is being built up, or do you think it necessary to set certain limits on all political speeches made to Red Army men, which should not hinder setting up Communist cells?

(4) Do you think it useful to our cause , when responsibility for political education is taken over by commanders, who have demonstrated their devotion to Soviet power many times in practice, but who are not Party members?

(5) Do you consider it useful to the cause of the Revolution to have a compact mass of people, namely the Cossacks, not educated in the Communist spirit, absolutely devoid of Party cells?

(6) Finally, are you not at all uneasy about handing into the hands of a temperamental Cossack a close knit mass of Cossacks, trained to regard it as essential to remain non-Party men (i.e. somewhat prejudiced against Communists)?

'Whatever your reply may be, having your authoritative response to these questions will greatly help our tactical approach to our day to day tasks, and give us the chance to get rid of defects and misconceptions which we encounter as we work. We request that you should reply by messenger.'

As this communication was received late by Cossack Section (only on 4 September), it naturally was not replied to.

On 24 August, at the moment when Mironov made his break, Revolutionary Committee issued the following notice to Red Army men of the Corps [12]:

'Comrades! We have taken every possible step to settle amicably the conflict between Mironov and the Soviet Republic. Now the time for talk has passed. So that you may be aware where you being led, and what they are inciting you to, we are passing on the decision of the Revolutionary Council of the Republic: "Mironov is declared a mutineer, and strong forces have been directed to move against him. He will be treated as an outlaw. Tell this to your soldiers, with the warning that anyone who dares to take up arms against Soviet power will be wiped from the face of the earth. To avoid bloodshed I am proposing to Mironov for the last time to return to carry out his military duty – failing which he will be considered a traitor to the Revolution. If he submits of his own free will I promise his life will be spared. Otherwise he is inevitably doomed".'

But this proclamation was made known by no means to all units of Don Corps. It was not transmitted: (1) to the 'Janissaries', as the political workers called the Red Army commanders most devoted to Mironov, (2) to the machine-gun crews, (3) to those in charge of equipment and stores. From what was said by 400 prisoners who came over to us voluntarily from Mironov's detachment, it was obvious that they were deceived by Mironov when they marched towards the front, and that they did not know that he had been declared an outlaw. Furthermore the political workers themselves said that they had at that time been forced to go underground, for which reason they could not warn the Corps on a wide enough basis.

It would besides be worth noting quite a characteristic feature, that about 18 Communists went with Mironov, <u>Party members:</u> Gorbunov, Ivan; Bagdasorov, Pavel; Klevtsov, Ivan; Izvarin, Aleksander; Mattern, Oskar; Solomatin, Ilya. <u>Sympathizers:</u> Morgunov T.; Khoroshenkov, Ilya; Savraskin, Grigory; Danilov, Mikhail; Yakumov; Sokolov, Nikandr; Strakhov, Kuzma; Chekunov, Nikolay; Bratukhin, Pyotr; Malakhov, Dmitry; Popov, Nikifor; Bulatkin.

[III]

Cossack Section's attitude to this question may be summarized as follows: Mironov was granted great powers by Revolutionary Council of Southern Army Group, as related in the first part of my report. At first, Cossack Section did not fully trust Mironov, which can be seen from members of Cossack Section comrades Chekunov and Stepanov (who is a member of All-Russian Central Executive Committee), reporting to comrade Stasova, Secretary to Party's Central Committee, and to comrade Vladimirsky, Deputy Chairman of All-Russian Central Executive Committee (both reports dating from 22 March 1919).

But after Mironov received his great powers and the trust of the central authorities, he was co-opted into Cossack Section, following the report he made to Cossack Section. I shall cite in its entirety the resolution to that effect which was spelt out in our minute 75 [13]: 'Acknowledging comrade Mironov's report, which clarifies the situation – both of essential questions concerning the Cossacks – and also the attitude towards Soviet power of working-class Cossacks, and which fully acknowledges the working-class Cossacks, we wish to express our deepest gratitude to comrade Mironov for his detailed report. Taking account of the needs of the front, as comrade Mironov has set them out, and the hardships suffered by working-class Cossacks who have volunteered to join the Red Army, we should meet comrade Mironov's plea for sending all Cossacks who come to Moscow into his Corps, and in general all Cossacks who are free of responsible duties and work. I shall also cite in full minute 76 about co-opting him: 'With a feeling of deep and sincere gratitude to comrade Mironov for all his military deeds to strengthen Soviet power, and taking due account of comrade Mironov's devotion to Soviet power, clearly demonstrated by his principles – attested not only by words, but also by two years of battles hard fought by him against the enemies of those who are building up Soviet power, in which comrade Mironov won glory as an invincible leader – to co-opt comrade Mironov to become a member of Cossack Section of All-Russian Central Executive Committee, making use of his knowledge as a military strategist, when he served with the front line army and was well thought of by the highest military authorities. In order to establish strong links with comrade Mironov, and also for the best possible political work, to send as a help to comrade Mironov a member of Cossack Section of All-Russian Central Executive Committee, to be selected by that body.

Without any concealment, Cossack Section tried to cooperate with the political workers of the Corps, as can be seen from my letter to comrade Larin, which reads as follows [14]:

'Through comrade Avilova it has come to the notice of Cossack Section of All-Russian Central Executive Committee that you do not concur with our ideas on comrade Mironov as set out in the Political Commisars' Report No. 1 of 6 August, and that you think it better not to attach any significance to those findings. I completely agree with your opinion, but at the same time I should like to hear how you advise that we should proceed in this matter: firstly, whether comrade Mironov should be informed about the contents of the report, with a view to getting expla- nations from him – and this I should think proper as simple natural justice, but also because he is a member of Cossack Section of the

All-Russian Central Executive Committee, from whom Cossack Section does not have the right to conceal messages and complaints against the members,

Secondly, will you not consider that (without the attached paper) you might hand over to comrade Mironov himself the enclosed copy of the above document, together with your explanation, requesting him to forward his explanation to Cossack Section of All-Russian Central Executive Committee. If you find it inconvenient for you yourself to give a copy of this report to comrade Mironov, then seal this copy up in an envelope, together with the attached paper, and give it in this form to comrade Sonin to hand on to comrade Mironov.

'For myself I have no doubts about comrade Mironov's loyalty to the Revolution. In so far as I know him, both from private conversations with him, and on the basis of his report to Cossack Section, along with the reports he made in my presence to comrade Kalinin, Chairman of All-Russian Central Executive Committee and to comrade Lenin, Chairman of Council of People's Commissars, comrade Mironov impressed me as someone working to help Soviet power, quite clear in his purpose, and a dedicated fighter for the Red Army against counter-revolution.

'As instructed by Cossack Section of All-Russian Central Executive Committee I beg you, comrade Larin, to send a written report about our work in Khopyor District, with your thoughts about what mistakes the Soviet administration has made, in order to avoid repeating them in future – perhaps pass this on to your comrades, and someone among them will compose a written report, dealing particularly with food and requisitioning policy.

'Personally, I myself have some ten detailed reports from responsible colleagues about work on the Don – from the regions of Kotelnikovo, Morozovskaya, Ust-Medveditskaya, Millerovo, and also about the ill-famed Donburo and the Civil Authority. All these reports have already been sent to the Presidium of the All-Russian Central Executive Committee – and, taking account of them, Soviet policy towards the Cossacks has been radically changed: from wholesale, unthinking terror and senseless de-Cossackification, exercised simply by commands and force of arms, such as was practised by Plyatt, Giye and Frenkel, it has gone over to the most careful, reasoned and considerate attitude towards working-class Cossacks, i.e. those who are poor or with only modest means. This policy takes account of the Cossacks' traditional ways and their daily life, besides the factors that have influenced their economic and cultural development.

'To go with this, an appeal (manifesto) to working-class Cossacks has already been worked out, signed by comrade Kalinin, as Chairman of All-Russian Central Executive Committee and comrade Lenin, Chairman of the Council of People's Commissars, and by the Cossack Section of All-Russian Central Executive Committee. Central Committee of the Party (Bolshevik) is also now working on the question of the Cossacks.

'Please urge comrade Mironov to send inspectors with money for cloth. If he does not send them, Cossack Section's order for 5600 arshins of blue and 700 arshins of red cloth will be cancelled. The price of an arshin of cloth is 80 roubles.

'My comradely greetings to you, and I request you to write an answer to be conveyed by the person that brings this to you, comrade Sonin, who has been specially sent to you as a matter of urgency.'

Don Corps' political workers, as has recently become clear, not only were unwilling to work by keeping in touch with Cossack Section, but concealed a great deal from us (see section 2 of this report). They did not give full information, and among other sins they misled in this way comrade Kuzyuberdin, the member of Cossack Section who had been sent to Don Corps to gather information. That explains why his report is not objective, and why Cossack Section's resolution No. 86 is wrong [15]:

'Noting comrade Mironov's position as a popular leader of pro-revolution working-class Cossacks, who stands truly and absolutely for the idea of the social revolution, and therefore gives his complete support to Soviet power, to back comrade Mironov up, both in his forming and commanding a special Don Corps, and in all his political activity. In the light of this, urgent and effective measures should be taken to replace senior political workers attached to the above-mentioned Corps, since they are not popular with pro-revolution working-class Cossacks, and thus are misguided in the way they view comrade Mironov's actions, and are inevitably delaying the Corps being formed as it should. A member of Cossack Section of All-Russian Central Executive Committee and a member of Party Central Committee should be appointed as Political Commissar to the Corps, and full powers are granted to comrades Kuzyuberdin and Makarov to give effect to this present resolution.'

On 16 August Mironov sent a letter to Cossack Section, in which he announced as follows [16]:

'I send my sincere greetings to Cossack Section. I am deeply touched by the attention you have paid to me and to the building up my fighting Corps, but unfortunately I must declare that insuperable obstacles have been placed in my path to prevent me carrying this out. Comrade Kuzyuberdin will report to you in detail on what is stopping me. For the first time I am complaining, and not on my own behalf, but for good reason, since these people do not understand what they are doing. I shall only say one thing: "Dear comrades, I am a member of Cossack Section, and you should know that through all his life Mironov will bear his cross and will not betray the great cause of socializing all the means of production, and hence, accordingly, the social revolution. Help me to disperse the black fog and the dark cloud which hangs over me."

'That's not just what I need, myself. That is what the front desires. Here are some words from a letter from the front which I have received:

> ... however, it is definitely known that, in any case, the central govern-ment are paying attention to you, and that of course means that we don't have to worry about you. There are rumours going about, like this one: some people say that 'Mironov is in Povorino', others say 'he is only starting out now', and a third lot say: 'he has thought up a plan to cut off Tsaritsyn and to drive the Whites down to the Black Sea, what can you expect from him?' There are also rumours that 'he has been given full powers to root out all saboteurs' etc. The Red Army men and all other divisions are eagerly looking forward to your taking command of your division, and also that you will soon be moving – for, to tell the truth, everywhere, and in particular in our division, everyone without exception place all their hopes for getting back home soon on you...

'None of this is exaggerated.

'So I think it is time to give up all these fears about me. I am bold enough to believe that the masses are following me, not just as an individual, but as someone who has a well-defined ideal, dear to the hearts of working class peasants and Cossacks. And I declare again that I shall not betray that ideal.

'It must be said that the political section which Southern Army Group has sent to the Corps consists entirely of people who have been working in Khopyor District. At the start they appointed comrade Larin, former Chairman of the Khopyor Revolutionary Committee. He did not do much to check the terrible things which were being done in his District. The Cossack conscripts, who make up the main body of men in the Corps, hate both him and all the political workers, whom they know through the way they behaved in their home villages. Larin has now been appointed a member of the Revolutionary Military Council of the Corps. These political workers carry over against me their exasperation with the Cossacks, thinking that it is because of my influence that they have no success with the men. When they strive to establish their authority and the authority of the Party, these people resort to every kind of measure, blundering from one extreme another; they end up by discrediting both themselves and the cause they are serving.

'The best thing for the social revolution would be for all the political workers to leave the Corps, and for them to be replaced by people with a more mature approach to politics. If Cossack Section agree with my conclusions then comrade Larin must go. I would like one of the members of the Revolutionary Military Council to be from Cossack Section, since the Corps consists almost entirely of Cossacks or men who come from the Don. I saw the happy expressions of Cossacks from the west of the area when they recognized comrade Kuzyuberdin. That is an important sign for the menacing times we live in, and – as I understand what they are thinking – I would like to put forward his name on their behalf.

'I beg you to send uniforms and footware urgently by rail. Do not allow the men to go around for more than ten days without something to wear. The cold weather will come on: one cannot be certain that they will remain calm. Someone may put them up to mischief – I'm simply afraid that they are ready to blaze up.

'Send me Cossack trousers. Come what may, I'd like to die in them.

'Long live the social revolution!'

But on 22 August at 4 p.m. Mironov made clear his real feelings about Cossack Section to a general meeting of Don Corps, when he called this Section of All-Russian Central Executive Committee 'the Dog Section' and 'a worm-shaped appendix off the blind gut'. Having heard my report, and the extra information supplied by comrade Kuzyuberdin, Cossack Section passed the following resolution (worded by comrade Makarov) [17]:

(1) Having heard reports from comrade Makarov and member of Cossack Section of VTsIK comrade Kuzyuberdin, who have returned from Saransk as fully empowered by VTsIK, assessing Mironov's action in bringing out men under arms, Cossack Section of All-Russian Central Executive Committee finds that, at a moment of real danger for the Soviet Union from Denikin and other hirelings of the imperialists, there should be no place, not only for armed actions, but even for any sort of unauthorized action, no matter how it has been provoked, since any

actions of this sort are gravely damaging to our work to defend Soviet Russia from the onslaught of the imperialists. For this reason the high-handed way in which Mironov has led Red Army men out of Saransk, together with a number of his other actions against the Soviet Republic, must be considered counter-revolutionary.

(2) In view of this, Cossack Section of All-Russian Central Executive Committee, not wishing to have anything in common with an enemy of Soviet Russia, expels Mironov from being a member of the Section.

(3) As a consequence of the irregularities which have been made plain in mutual relationships between Mironov and Soviet workers in Don Corps, and, thinking it desirable to elucidate all the circumstances connected with Mironov's action, Cossack Section requests All-Russian Central Executive Committee to appoint one member of Cossack Section to serve on the Extraordinary Investigative Commission, appointed by Revolutionary Council of Southern Army Group to look into this matter.

(4) Release the proclamation concerning Mironov's indiscipline to Cossacks serving in Soviet regiments of the Red Army.

(5) Instruct comrades Makarov and Kuzyuberdin to make their report to All-Russian Central Executive Committee, to Central Committee (Bolshevik), to Revolutionary Military Council of the Republic and to the Extraordinary Investigative Commission.'

Praesidium:
Head of Cossack Section F. Stepanov
Commissar M. Makarov
Secretary Dolgachev

Makarov's letter to Lenin

f. 17, op. 65, d. 35, l.146

To: Lenin.
From: Makarov.
Letter to comrade Lenin concerning Mironov's armed intervention and Cossack Section's 'involvement' in that affair. Vladimir Ilich,
8 October 1919

It emerges that Cossack Section knew about that business, and all documents of Cossack Section have been placed under seal. At that time people were trying to stir up a campaign against Cossack Section. Comrade Aralov aligned himself with Mironov's political views.

If we are going to consider who was 'in the know' about Mironov then we ought logically to recognize that not only Cossack Section knew what was going on but also Southern Army Group, namely Sokolnikov and Mekhonishin, and the Revolutionary Military Council of the Republic, i.e. comrade Aralov, besides political workers of Don Corps, comrades Larin, Rogachov, Boldyrev, Zaytsev and Skalov.
Third copy signed on *list* 150 by Makarov.

Petrograd: Evacuate or fight in streets

St Petersburg was renamed Petrograd in 1914, and Leningrad in 1924, reverting to its original title with the dissolution of the Soviet Union. The city is both a major port and one of Russia's largest industrial centres. In 1917, as the traditional capital, it saw the February Revolution, and the Winter Palace became the seat of the provisional government. In October the large urban proletariat and sailors from the Baltic Fleet brought about the Bolshevik seizure of power.

During the civil war it would have been a severe blow to the Communists to lose its factories, and even more damaging psychologically if they were driven from this so-called 'cradle of the Revolution'. Kakurin (vol. 2, p. 187 *et seq*) provides useful details on the fighting along the Baltic coast. In the spring of 1919 Kolchak appointed General Yudenich to command the so-called North Western Army. For much of 1919 there was some danger of the Whites advancing to take Petrograd. In October Yudenich's forces posed an acute threat to the city. The Reds were moving up reinforcements, but they realized they might be short of soldiers to defend their base, and Trotsky stirred the workers to put up a fight for every street:

> The northern capital extends over 91 square versts. If the White Guards break through into this enormous city they will be plunged into a labyrinth of buildings, where every house will face them with an enigma or a deadly danger...
>
> What strength has the enemy? Let us suppose he may have 5000 men, or even 10 000. In the streets they will not be able to manœuvre either in tight formations or in extended line. They will have to break up into little groups and separate units, which will be

lost in the streets and byways of Petrograd, out of proper contact with each other, and with every corner menacing them.
(Trotsky, 1924; *Kak vooruzhalas' revolyutsiya* vol. 2, book 1, p. 383).

Petrograd's fate was partly bound up with the naval campaign in the Gulf of Finland, where a British squadron was lending support to the Whites. The following communication from Trotsky was to resolve one of the squabbles over the chain of command which arose in the hastily constituted Red forces.

f. 17, op. 65, d. 136, l.15

To: Lenin.
From: Trotsky.
12 April 1919

The People's Commissar for Military Affairs, the Latvian comrade Peterson, considers that the means for naval defence and the sailors sent to the coast of the Gulf of Riga come under his command and under Zedin, who has been appointed by him. It is essential to put a decisive stop to these petty local interests.

Yudenich hoped for support from the British ships in the Baltic. White spies carried out detailed reconnaissance behind Red Army lines, and on 13 May Yudenich launched a successful attack which took Yamburg and Pskov on 25 May. Red morale on the North Western front was affected by Estonian and Latvian nationalist aspirations, and by a White conspiracy in Petrograd itself. The former Semyonovsky Guards Regiment actually went over to the Whites.

It is hardly surprising that Red commanders in Petrograd felt that they might even have to face the loss of the city. In Petersburg most of the bridges across the main stream of the River Neva have central portions which can be lifted (cf. Tower Bridge, London) to enable ships to pass through.

f.17, op. 109, d. 44, 11. 15–16

To: *Chairman of Defence Council of RSFSR.*
From: *Vatsetis, Commander-in -Chief of all Armed Forces of the Republic, at Serpukhov, & Aralov, Military Commissar, Member of Revolutionary Military Council of the Republic.*
Detailed in telegrams 02769/2103, 2698/verso
[Copy, Secret]
May 1919

Chief of Staff informs us about measures taken to mine and blow up the following bridges in Petrograd: Liteyny, Okhtensky, Soyedinitelny, and to put out of action the opening spans of Nikolayevsky, Dvortsovy and Troitsky Bridges.

At the present moment explosive charges have already been placed at the following bridges: Samsoniyevsky, Grenadersky, Strogonovsky and Yelansky.

In Petrograd and its environs it is planned additionally to prepare to destroy with explosives all military and naval reserve stores, also any factories and workshops engaged on defence production or adapted for that type of work, and all railway installations.

From the military point of view it would not seem sensible to blow up some of the bridges inside the city of Petrograd, namely Liteyny, Okhtensky, nor the wooden bridges Samsoniyevsky, Grenadersky, Strogonovsky and Yelansky. To destroy them might restrict the army's room for manœuvre. In order to preserve the fighting efficiency of our retreating armies their retreat should be directed as far as possible outside the limits of the city.

Discipline may break down if an army retreats through a large city after having fought a number of unsuccessful battles. It may easily turn into a gang of marauders, and become relatively easy for the enemy to eliminate. Trying to hold up the enemy by destroying bridges inside a large city is not likely to hold him back for long, but will certainly inflict senseless sufferings on the city's inhabitants, causing panic and the death of many non-combatants.

Bridges for public traffic, like those in Petrograd, will take no time at all to restore. The enemy's communications will not be interrupted even for twenty-four hours, since he will bring in floating pontoons and boats which are quite impossible to destroy.

Destroying the Petrograd railway bridge can be helpful only if the explosion is carried out at the right time, taking care not to make it difficult for our retreating forces to come across to the right bank of the River Neva. In order to get our rolling stock across and the equipment we are trying to evacuate, besides our units in their retreat, we must ensure that the bridge remains intact until the last Red Army man has come over.

We should place charges on this bridge, but we must put off destroying it until we have given up any hope of making a fight for it.

As for blowing up almost all the important factories and workshops, this physically impossible task should not be undertaken, since it would only distract the most active elements in the army from the real fighting. We must put the factories out of action only by taking away essential pieces of equipment, with the idea of being able to get production going again quickly in the factories after we come back to Petrogard.

The destruction of Petrograd by Soviet forces will certainly have an adverse effect on the morale of the whole country.

On the other hand, while we are still capable of taking active steps, it may be helpful to save even a small part of our property, as has already been proved in the Western theatre of operations.

We must acknowledge that the most rational way to proceed will be to make a systematic and intensive evacuation of all property which may be useful for military purposes.

PROPOSAL: On the basis of my arguments above I would consider it essential:

(1) To instruct Commander Western Front to place charges only on the railway bridge over the River Neva and the bridges of the Finland Railway, between Beloostrov and Petrograd. Charges to be detonated only by special order of Commander of Seventh Army.

(2) To cancel the laying of charges on bridges in Petrograd city, in factories and their machines, since this would not conform with military requirements.

(3) Take all necessary steps to make a speedy and systematic evacuation from the Petrograd area of property which may be valuable for military purposes, and to carry away machines and tooling, with the aim of making the production lines unusable if they are occupied by the enemy.

ATTACHED herewith: Two copies of the telegram and copy of report number 156 with information. Map at two versts to the inch.

Signed Commander-in-Chief of all Armed Forces of the Republic

(Vatsetis)

Military Commissar, member of Revolutionary Military Council of the Republic   Aralov

Signatures attested:

Inspector of Engineers of Field Staff of Revolutionary Military Council of the Republic, Military Engineer Shoshim

f. 17, op. 109, d. 41, l.16

To: *Sklyansky (Moscow), Principal Administration for Military Engineering,*
Central Supply Administration of Ukraine.
From: *Vatsetis, Aralov (signed Inspector of Engineers of Field Staff of*
Revolutionary Military Council of the Republic, Military Engineer Sha...)
Message by direct line from Voronezh, received 9 July 1800

a/ Take all necessary measures to remove immediately, as planned, from the Petrograd district all equipment, which might be used for military purposes and to carry away from factories all machine tools and equipment, so as to render them unusable in the event of the area being occupied by the enemy.

Addenda: Two copies of telegrams and a copy of document No. 156 with relevant information. Map two versts to the inch.

Signed:

C-in-C All armed Forces of the Republic VATSETIS Military Commissar, Member of REVOLUTIONARY MILITARY COUNCIL of Republic ARALOV.

Signatures attested:

Inspector of Field Staff Engineers of Revolutionary Military Council of Republic, Military Engineers.

Sho...

f. 17, op. 84, d 33, l.33

To: *Trotsky, to find at current address, copies to Lenin, Chairman of Council*
of People's Commissars, to Aralov at GHQ, Serpukhov.
From: *O. Kulov.*
7 November 1919

In my opinion one of the main causes of the Western Front's collapse is the special position of the 7th Army, which sometimes acknowledges, and sometimes does not acknowledge the authority of the Command of the Army Group. The 7th Army is actually in the hands of responsible Party officials in Petrograd. We must choose one of two variants: either to subordinate the 7th Army, and the Petrograd group who are so attached to it, categorically and definitely to the command staff and Revolutionary Military Council of the Western Front, or to single out the 7th Army as a special Army coming directly under the General Staff. This latter course would only reinforce the selfish separatism of the Petrograd group, which up to now has enjoyed a disproportionately large amount of various kinds of military property. If we have to give up Petrograd this equipment is going to be lost.

Measures to combat Mamontov raid

On 10 August 1919, Lieutenant-General K. K. Mamontov led some 6000 cavalry and 3000 infantry to break through the Red lines at Novokhopyorsk. They took Tambov on 18 August, and Kozlov on 22 August. The Southern Army Group put a force of 12 000 under the command of M. M. Lashevich, and had to mobilize even the workers from Tula to meet the threat to that centre of their armaments industry. Lashevich's men were mainly infantry and not able to keep pace with the swiftly moving Cossacks. The Red Army tried to make up a flying column of machine guns, but this could not be formed because of a lack of suitable vehicles (f. 17, op. 109, d. 44, l. 173 contains Trotsky's admission that the Reds had not been able to deal effectively with Mamontov).

The Whites took Yelets on 31 August, and Gryazi on 6 September. The major centre of Voronezh lay between the Don and its left bank tributary the River Voronezh, which flowed into the Don south of the town. To get his men across the bridges Mamontov had to take Voronezh, which he held for a day on 11 September. The Mamontov Raid ended on 19 September, when his Cossacks passed back to rejoin Denikin's main forces between Stary Oskol and Korotoyak. Trotsky's collection of documents (1979–81) *How the Revolution Armed Itself* has a section on the measures adopted to deal with the raid. He was keen to prevent the troops in the front line from being affected by the Whites in their rear. Military law was introduced in all the threatened areas, and he proposed that local Revolutionary Committees should report on Mamontov's movements and harry his men.

Danger should be lying in wait for the White bandits round every corner. At their approach peasants must drive away their horses, livestock and carts in good time – must carry away grain and any sort of food. Anything you don't manage to take away must be destroyed. The Soviet government will cover any losses suffered.

(Trotsky, 1924, *Kak vooruzhalas' revolyutsiya*, vol. 2, book 1, p. 271)

At a time of desperate scarcities it is difficult to believe that any attempt could have been made to fulfil this last promise. Trotsky warned that Denikin was issuing false orders, purporting to emanate from the Soviets, hence the need for attesting the signatures on every document. Acting in the name of the Soviets, Trotsky even tried to get some of the Whites to come over to him:

> 24 August 1991, Cossacks deceived by Mamontov! There is only one way you can be saved, by giving up your shameful attack on the workers and peasants. Arrest your officers yourselves – and stretch out the hand of reconciliation to the workers, peasants and Red Army men of the entire country. Under that condition, in the name of the worker–peasant government I undertake to make it possible for you to have a peaceful existence in Soviet Russia, or a free return – at your wish – to your homeland, whenever that may be your desire. A steel trap is closed round you. An inglorious death awaits you. But at this late minute the worker–peasant government is prepared to stretch out to you a hand of reconciliation.
>
> (*Ibid.*, p. 276).

The promise of 'peaceful existence' in their land must have seemed a cruel joke to Cossacks who had recently witnessed savage killings administered by the Reds. In the civil war under conditions of mass conscription, desertion rates were very high for both sides, and appeals of this sort were quite often circulated; cf. the Whites' telephone message to the garrison of Voronezh (f. 17, op. 109, d. 44, l. 182). It was empty bluster to pretend that the ring round Mamontov was 'closed', and on 4 September Trotsky had to admit that measures against the raid had largely failed:

> Mamontov's cavalry have up to now done their plundering with almost complete impunity, because our intelligence gathering and communications have been so badly set up. Instead of giving precise details, our local authorities have often fed on the darkest rumours. It is specially important to check our own cavalry and infantry's reconnaissance, since experience shows that they quite often avoid contact with enemy patrols, and their reports rely on other people's tales. Some of the local defence forces showed absolutely no will to fight and abandoned their positions before they encountered the enemy. (*Ibid.* p. 280)

On 6 September, Trotsky, Serebryakov and Lashevich recognized that the destruction of their lines of communication made it difficult to transfer reinforcements to the area round Voronezh. They proposed ordering Budyonny's cavalry simply to ride across country to the threatened sector.

After the Whites had made their initial gains on the Southern Front, the Soviets formed a striking force under the command of Shorin. It was intended that this so-called 'Special Group' should split Denikin from the Don Army and drive south with the ambitious objective of eventually taking the Whites' main base at Taganrog. Budyonny's Cavalry Corps was placed under Shorin's command, but were then diverted in an attempt to deal with the Mamontov Raid. Shorin was unable to make any real progress, and from 20 September the Whites began their main advance which brought their forces up towards Moscow, and which achieved its furthest point when they took Oryol on 14 October.

Trotsky was anxious to establish partisans to harry White units, but he wished above all to avoid the disorder which had characterized earlier attempts at this kind of warfare. Makhno and Grigorev were prominent examples of useful allies turning against their former allegiance. He referred back to the original guerilla movements who appeared spontaneously to fight for the Reds soon after the revolution:

Do we need partisans?

6 September 1919
By a long struggle we mastered that clumsy, formless mass of irregular fighters and produced proper, well-trained, disciplined regiments and divisions. But it is at this very moment when we have a strong regular army ... (we need partisans) *Kak vooruzhalas' revolyutsiya*, vol. 2, book 1, p. 283

The first of the three following telegrams must be dated before 17 August. In the telegram of 17 August 'operations in the south' refers to Red Headquarter's hopes of Shorin's force being able to put in a decisive counter-offensive.

f. 17, op. 109, d. 44, l.151

To: *Podbelsky (misspelt Podvelsky).*
From: *Stasova, as ordered by Central Committee.*
Copy
? 11 August 1919

Please report immediately on state of Tambov Brigade and other units of Tambov garrison. Have all proper measures been taken to face up to the enemy who have broken through? Have you mobilized Communist detachments, detachments of Kommrod, of the Cheka? Has an order been given to Communist cells and Executive Committees of local organizations to find ways of holding back the enemy wherever that may be possible? We must harry him in every way and try to use our local forces to wear away his strength, until our main forces deal him the *coup de grace.* Hold onto every inch. Give nothing up without the most stubborn resistance.

To: *Trotsky.*
From: *Stasova, as ordered by Central Committee.*
Telegram
17 August 1919

Central Committee is greatly concerned that the enemy who have broken through to the north towards Tambov and Kozlov should not spoil operations in the south. Since Central Committee are not sure that local organizations and forces are putting up a proper resistance to the enemy and are thus allowing him to continue his movements, Central Committee requests you personally to direct the most serious attention to that area, and to set up everything possible to wipe out with no delay the enemy who have broken through.

Encoded 19.00 hrs 17 August. Transmitted by direct line 21.25 hrs 17 August.
Sent by Poletayev. Received Popov.

To: Shorin, commanding special group at Volsk; Central Committee,
Moscow; Yegorov, Commander Southern Army Group at Kozlov;
Commander-in-Chief, Moscow.
From: Trotsky, Chairman Revolutionary Military Council.
[386   Telegram by direct line, Penza   Top secret]
19 August 1919

On the Tambov front there are now operating: (1) 56th Division, coming
under orders from 9th Army, (2) troops of the Fortified District, subordinated to Southern Army Group, (3) units of the Railway Defence forces,
with their own command. Very serious dangers may arise if this type of
situation is allowed to continue. It is quite obviously essential to unify the
command in the said sector, otherwise we may be threatened with a repetition of the history of the sore which festered in the rear of our forces in
the stanitsas of Vyoshenskaya and Kazanskaya. Report immediately what
instructions have been given.   Nr 357

f. 17, op. 109, d. 44, l.170

To: Lenin, in Kremlin, copies to Sklyansky and Central Committee.
From: ? Osinsky, Tula.
28 August 1991 (received 29 August)

According to information just received the enemy has appeared in the
Yepifanov and Yeremovsky districts of Tula Province. Everything has been
put on a war footing. Our scout from the 'Daredevil Team' has personally
seen a patrol numbering 15 Cossacks, and peasants have told him about a
detachment of 200. At the same time a telegram has been received from
Revolutionary Military Council of Central Committee cancelling mobilization in the factories. In my telegram 28 I explained that really this would
mean leaving Tula without any reliable defence. I most earnestly request
you to rescind this order at the latest by morning of 28 August. I am
absolutely furious at Kraynev's conduct, which is a crime against the
revolution, since he is disorganizing the defence of a centre of arms
production. This is something I said today in the presence of Kaminsky.
    Armed with your telegram we asked him whether it was necessary to
make such an order forbidding us [to recruit the workers], and whether in
fact it is possible to mobilize people. The answer was that of course it is
possible, and we can always reach an agreement between ourselves on a
local basis. In view of all that I have explained I request you to cancel the

order, or if you do not believe me to send someone to replace me with full powers to act. In the meantime I consider it my duty in view of the crisis we are faced with to work to the best of my ability.
Message handed in by Vorontsov at 2.05 p.m. 28 August under the supervision of Head of the Province Sinogeykin.

Voronezh: Whites demand surrender

The offensive launched by Denikin in June 1919 took the Whites far up towards Moscow. Important centres passed into their hands: 25 June May-Mayevsky took Kharkov, 20 September Kursk; Shkuro's cavalry took Voronezh.

Denikin tried to build up the numbers of his troops by conscripting, not only civilians in the areas he had conquered, but even ex-Red Army men. This policy greatly weakened the reliability of his forces. His main advance included 58 650 infantry and 48 200 cavalry. Against them on the Southern Front the Reds fielded 113 439 infantry and 27 328 cavalry. These numbers are quoted by Kakurin (vol. 2, p. 276), although Denikin concentrated his forces to achieve some local superiority along the main line of his advance. We must bear in mind that all such figures from the civil war have to be treated with scepticism: commanders' reports often fudged the numbers they had at their disposal, and there were enormous losses from desertions and sickness on both sides. White forces were now at their maximum, whereas the Red Army went on building up towards its eventual total of five million men. In November 1920 when Frunze drove Vrangel from the Crimea his forces outnumbered the Whites by six to one. The tide turned in October 1919. White morale collapsed. The Red Army pushed south to take Novocherkassk on 7 January 1920 and entered Rostov on 8 January. April 1920 marked the end of the civil war in the Kuban, when the Whites were forced to evacuate their forces from Novorossiysk.

One of the most famous of Denikin's units was the division of Kuban Cossacks under General Shkuro, who had earlier been regarded as virtually invincible. In October his cavalry were occupying Voronezh. Budyonny directed his Corps to attack this vital centre. To recommoitre the defences he sent in his agent, Dundich, disguised as a White officer. On 19 October Shkuro brought his cavalry out to attack Budyonny's flank by night. There was thick mist, making it impossible for either side to use artillery or machine guns. The two bodies of horsemen clashed in a battle of sabres and eventually the Whites turned to flee back into Voronezh, but their horses could not outpace the Reds and many were cut down in their flight. The Cavalry Corps still had to overcome some resistance from the Whites' infantry and armoured trains, but on the morning of 24 October they finally broke into Voronezh.

The Whites had taken Voronezh on 6 October, so that the first of the two following documents must have been transmitted before that date. We need not take literally Postovsky's claim that 'the ring is closed', though it was true that most roads out of Voronezh were held by the Whites.

Under Mamontov General Postovsky commanded a division and was later to defend Kastornoye. Budyonny reported that he was cut down by his Cavalry Corps when they took that important railway junction on 15 November. Like many military memoirs Budyonny's account of his exploits is none too modest. We have to approach *Proydenny put'* with some scepticism. This report of Postovsky's death is false. The general survived to fight under Vrangel in the Crimea, and in emigration lived in Paris (see *Rodimy kray*, 1959, 20, p. 15). One could hardly expect someone in Postovsky's position to be a member of the Socialist Revolutionary Party, and his claim to share S. R. views was simply intended to make his offer appear more credible to the Soviet commander.

f. 17, op. 65, d. 136, l.43

To: General ? Postakovky, commander of the Fortified District
From: Major-General Postovsky
October 1919

Talking with one of the military leaders over a secret direct telephone line I heard the following conversation with General Postovsky talking to unknown persons in Voronezh:

'Yeremeyev will be shot by my own hand in front of all those who have suffered from his traitorous hand.'

Your Excellency: Gordon, Komarov and Chayduchenko are not commissars, but former officers who have been conscripted. Every day squads of reinforcements are sent off towards the railway line along the Don. The windows of the headquarters of the Fortified District are blacked out. We shall bring up on lorries from there a heavy three inch gun. Chayduchenko and Gordon are one and the same person.

I extend to you a fraternal handshake Major-General Postovsky.

f. 17, op. 109, d. 44, I.182

Telephone conversation across siege lines

29 September 1919

I am General Postovsky

I am Yeremeyev, Commander of the Fortified District

I am General Postovsky, Head of the Don Army's Special Detachment. The ring is closed round your town. The town will certainly be taken by my troops, by those of General Mamontov, by the men who have arrived from Kuban, together with the infantry companies from Tula, Tambov, Kozlov and Yelets. As you of course know, your escape routes are cut off. The road to Liski is still open for the time being, but probably that route is not much to your fancy. General Mamontov's detachments – 'hand-picked cut-throats', as Trotsky proclaimed – never back away from any task set them. The men from the Don have already captured Tambov, Kozlov, Lebedyan, Boborykino, Izmalkovo, Yelets, Kastornoye, Zadonsk, Zemlyansk, Gryazi, Usman – and the same fate will befall Voronezh, because your conscripted men do not want to fight us and are surrendering – a thousand at a time. In one battle zone we have taken 61 thousand men prisoner. They are released by us to go home and serve as the best agitators in our favour. If you have any idea of what is to come, of course you know perfectly well that Soviet power is living out its last days. The fall of the Soviets is close at hand. After them the Constituent Assembly will be convened and, freed from your Terror, the Russian people will summon all the main Soviet activists to face their judgement without fear or favour – which can only be terrible for you. In my political views I am a Socialist Revolutionary, and – most of all as someone with a clear all-loving heart – I do not desire bloodshed. I suggest that you should see reason, search out your heart and stop this murderous war. I propose that during the night you should either disband your forces, or give up your arms and surrender to me. By the honour of a Russian, unsullied by any crime against my conscience, I swear to you that in either case I will guarantee, at the price of my own life, your complete freedom, the inviolability of your person, and free passage to go to any town or village in Russia, or anywhere abroad. If you offer no resistance to me, then not a single hair shall fall from the head of all the commissars, commanders, members of the Soviets, leaders of units, headquarters staff, rank and file soldiers, volunteers, Communists, nor in general shall anyone be harmed who has acted for the Soviets, whether in a military or a civilian capacity. If the town and its surroundings surrender of your free will, then in the area occupied by your army not a single Jew or his family shall suffer. You have a lot of regiments, but they are not all reliable, and tomorrow three quarters of them will come over to our side, as happened in Kastornoye. Deserters are coming over every minute from your side. I know precisely where your positions are situated and the defences of your troops, besides their numbers and the state of their morale. Once more as an honest Slav I declare that I am coming to meet you. I am proposing that you do not waste the blood of your soldiers to no good purpose, and that you disperse or surrender. For the third time I declare to you … in the morning strife and woe to the vanquished; those who surrender shall be released immediately. I shall even allow all the commissars and all senior military leaders to retain their arms, while those who for some reason or another do not wish to go into the lands of Soviet power or any other State will be taken under my special protection and the protection of the whole of my detachment.

I have finished.

Remember that we and the Russian people have all your real names – and we also have portraits for many of you. There is nowhere you can save yourselves from us. Even if you manage to hide after losing the battle, that will only be for a little while.

Remember this, and in order to obtain full pardon, either surrender to me, or in God's name disperse wherever you want.

Up to 6 o'clock my guard posts will not touch anyone coming out of the town.

Vladimir Ivanovich Postovsky,
Major-General i/c Kuban and Don Cossacks

I must add that refusal to act on this present proposal will entail the merciless annihilation and plunder of all the main political leaders of Soviet civil power in the town of Voronezh.

26 August from the front line at Voronezh
General Postovsky

Reply by telephone over No. 1743; only warn your units that they should not destroy the lines. If the direct line does not work, then send a written reply with truce messengers across the railway bridge. The envoys need only carry a large white flag.

REPLY
Transmit over direct line 1743:
To: General Postovsky.
From: Commander of the Fortified District, empowered by the All-Russian Central Executive Committee of the Soviets of Workers and Peasants Deputies.
Konstantin Stepanovich Yeremeyev has given orders that your disgusting threats of plunder and complete slaughter shall be answered by a six-inch shell. K. Yeremeyev.

Beloborodov: importance of cavalry

From 1919 the Communists realized that the Whites had derived much advantage from having large numbers of horsemen, and that mounted troops were not just playthings for the gentry. It is curious to note at the end of Beloborodov's report that Red Army units still greatly feared the White cavalry, and this even after Budyonny's first victory over Shkuro.

f. 17, op. 65, d. 155, l.48

Report to Central Committee Russian Communist Party
From: Beloborodov
3 November 1919 Balashov
Dear Comrades,

Evidently we should conclude that the enemy has finished his operation against our army. Over the last two days our divisions have begun to push forward without encountering any resistance. Our men have occupied the stations Samodurovok and Povorino almost without a fight. As far as we can judge by the information at our disposal, the enemy is regrouping his forces in order to make a new thrust on the right flank of the 9th Army and the left flank of the 8th Army (in the area of the stations Koleno and Borisoglebsk). It is quite obvious that Denikin has exhausted his reserves of men for service. While I have been with the 23rd division, half of the prisoners who have come into our hands are old men from 49 to 55 years. The prisoners are not in any official uniform, they are going into action wearing the clothes in which they left home. If our soldiers are badly off for uniform, that is absolutely not because things are lacking, but arises from the scandalous, exasperating disorganization of our supply system. There is as yet no visible intake of active, efficient workers into this branch of our organization (I am taking the 9th Army as an example). For this same reason our soldiers go hungry, since in areas where military operations are actually taking place one will never see a single food supply commission, charged with buying food. Cavalry units suffer especially from this, being frequently moved about: the supply commissions are completely unable to attend to their needs. Our cavalry have a miserable time through the fault of another body, the so-called 'purchasing commission'. They too, stay far back in the rear and work slowly, at a snail's pace. The cavalry units get no remounts and the men (horsemen with no horses) are left hanging around in the baggage trains.

The army's sanitary and medical services are still in a disgusting state. The typhus epidemic has stopped, and cases of typhus are now quite rare; but, on the other hand, care for our wounded is terribly badly organized, particularly any form of first aid to be given during a battle. I spent two days near our advanced positions ; men who came out of the line had to drag themselves along for several versts before they could get a first dressing for their wounds. This was happening during very fierce fighting in the 23rd Division's sector (in the area of the station Budarino).

There is no reading matter in the front lines. I had to cover about 200 versts in the course of a week, and I did not see a single newspaper, even in the rear areas. Neither the Red Army men, nor the command staff, nor the commissars have any idea at all of what is going on in the world. Even the Revolutionary Military Council has been without a newspaper for more than a week. It naturally is impossible to carry out any political work in such conditions. The radio station is taken up with operational work and thus the whole army finds itself cut off from the world outside. We are setting to work all that collection of people who are hanging about in the rear with nothing to do. If we can get some intake of Party workers from the centre it will allow us to brush up our complement of commissars, who are mainly an exceedingly uninspiring and inactive bunch. A certain lull at the front will now give us the chance to get some reinforcements into the divisions. In the 9th Army there are really two divisions left, the 22nd and 23rd. In the 14th Division and in each of the brigades of Divisions 36 and 21 there are only a handful of men.

The 56th Division (formerly 4th Ukrainian Division) has been completely disbanded, in view of its absolute collapse under the enemy's blows, and thereafter. The final break up of the Division was brought about by the commanders, who were thoroughly rotten, and by its useless political workers. To crown it all, the remnants of the Division arranged a meeting yesterday, and discussed the order to advance. They sent a delegation to the Revolutionary Military Council. The delegation has been placed under arrest and will be shot; the Red Army men are being disarmed today and every tenth one will be shot. The Division was made up of Ukrainian peasants. Our chief affliction, as before, remains enemy's cavalry. Our infantry have never ceased to fear it, in spite of the greater fire power on our side.

Besides their special cavalry strike units, on the flank of each infantry unit the enemy places a squadron of cavalry (100–200 strong), and by passing round our flanks these force our infantry to fall back. Our own special commissions to deal with cavalry will not be much use, because they are too small in number. The specialists who are meant to give training to the infantry are a completely incompetent lot, less experienced than our average front line troops, and have much to learn themselves before they start teaching others. The only thing the commissions can do is to concentrate the active service commanders' attention on working out methods to combat cavalry. They will do a certain amount of good in this way.

At the present moment Army HQ is moving back to Serdobsk. Here in Balashov there remain only the Revolutionary Military Council and the Army Commander with his operations section.
If the enemy relaxes his pressure the other parts of headquarters will be brought back to Balashov.
With comradely greetings   A. Beloborodov

PS The Army has absolutely no paper. If there was paper it would be possible to work up a strong leaflet campaign among the enemy's units. Our air force is working splendidly. I cannot praise the pilots' conduct too highly. The aircraft may get up to 20 holes when they are carrying out reconnaissance and literature drops. Pressure must be brought to bear on the Head of Paper Supply to stop printing all unnecessary material, concentrating only on what is essential for our defence.
True signature
Beloborodov

After virtually two years of war White cavalry were still considered such a threat that the Red Army even proposed running a course for their men on how to resist them.

f. 17, op. 109, d. 44, I.185

To: Commanders of 8th, 13th, and 14th Armies
From: Chief of Staff Southern Army Group
1 October 1919

Our failures arise principally from the low morale of our forces. Our cavalry is outnumbered by the enemy's, and their energetic spirit of initiative has struck fear into our people. The Revolutionary Military Council of the Republic orders that a campaign of 2–3 weeks instruction shall be announced at company level on how to fight against cavalry. If we can achieve at least some modest success against small detachments of the enemy's cavalry, then the hypnosis of fear will be dispersed.

Chief of Staff, Southern Front, Palevsky
Political Commissar, K. Mazalov

5
Sergeant Budyonny

Fact and myth

In Soviet propaganda, Semyon Mikhaylovich Budyonny played a leading part. Exalted to be an icon of the Revolution and civil war, in some respects he rivalled Trotsky, less as a strategist than as a man of action, and above all as a key defender of the Revolution. Budyonny's role as a strategist was made all the more significant because Trotsky tended to play down his own achievements, presenting himself as someone who merely listened to expert opinion and then passed on appropriate orders (see Serge and Sedova, 1975, pp. 92–3).

The First Cavalry Army became the most famous unit of the Red Army. As its commander, Budyonny developed a persona which approached that of Stalin, and certainly eclipsed Trotsky after the latter was driven into the shadows. Whereas Stalin's image was grafted onto many scenes of the revolutionary struggle, Budyonny's merged with the front line, and represented action that was decisive and central to the turning of the tide in November 1919. Like Stalin, Budyonny developed a fatherly image; Soviet sources emphasized his closeness to schoolchildren and aspiring defenders of the motherland. Unlike Stalin, whose status as supreme leader was held in awe by the Soviet populace, Budyonny was treated by old and young alike as one of their own – a comrade-in-arms to the rank and file, a warm-hearted comrade in the full sense of the word. This was a role that was played over and over again in the Soviet media.

Budyonny had formed the Platov Revolutionary Detachment in February 1918. In June 1919 he was promoted at Tsaritsyn to command his own Cavalry Corps. By September the Corps was already making its reputation, whereas Mironov at this point was still reforming his unit after dissolution in August. Soviet commanders had by now realized the advantage the Whites derived from their large forces of cavalry. In September, Red Headquarters issued the proclamation, *Proletarians to horse!*

Budyonny was not able to catch Mamontov when the raid was in progress. In October, however, he heard that Shkuro and Mamontov were operating in the vicinity of Voronezh, and set off determined to bring them to battle. This was the first action in which a large force of White cavalry was defeated by Budyonny, and marked a turning-point in the whole campaign in the south. The Volunteer Army had reached their most northerly point on 14 October with the capture of Oryol, but could not hold out on this extended front since Budyonny's corps posed a real threat to their left flank and their lines of communication. On 24 October Budyonny took Voronezh, and on 15 November the important rail station at Kastornoye. Budyonny says that General Postovsky was in charge of the White defenders at that point, and affirms that he was cut down by Budyonny's Cavalry Corps, but that is plainly untrue.

White morale collapsed. The Red Army swept south to take Novocherkassk on 7 January 1920 and entered Rostov on 8 January. April 1920 marked the end of the civil war in the Kuban, when the Communists forced the Whites to evacuate their forces from Novorossiysk.

Budyonny was vainglorious as the most famous cavalry commander in the Red Army. It is hardly surprising that he was eager to condemn Mironov's breach of discipline. In August 1919 he issued an order to his Corps that Mironov had been declared an outlaw, and should be shot. At the same time he accused Mironov's commissar and Chief of Staff of not taking decisive measures against their commander.

Stalin later forced the Soviet Union to regard Trotsky as an arch-fiend, whose name was still beyond any hope of redemption when Budyonny published the first book of his memoirs in 1958. It was only natural that, as Stalin's creature, Budyonny should try to link Trotsky with what he regarded as treachery: 'Trotsky came to Filonovo station and ordered that no action should be taken about Mironov' (Budyonny, 1957–83, *Proydenny put*, vol. 1, p. 241). This hardly seems credible, since Trotsky initially wanted to deal severely with Mironov as a deterrent to other commanders who might be tempted to step out of line. When Trotsky ordered Budyonny to send Mironov's commissar and Chief of Staff to Moscow, Budyonny protested that it would seriously affect the fighting strength of his Corps to detach a brigade as escort for the prisoners.

Budyonny claims it was reported to him that Trotsky had said: 'Budyonny's Corps is just a gang, and Budyonny is a Cossack ataman – as a leader he is a sort of Razin of our times' (ibid., p. 245). Budyonny and his men were notorious for their unruly conduct. In an unguarded moment Trotsky may perhaps have been tempted to give vent to his feelings by uttering some sentiment of this sort; many of his senior commanders must have tried his patience sorely at times.

Voroshilov and RVS defend 1st Cavalry

Budyonny's First Cavalry Army was notoriously undisciplined, and this indiscipline was never held in check by their Revolutionary Military Council. Theoretically they should have controlled Budyonny's wild misbehaviour, but far from exercising a moderating influence they backed him throughout. Prominent among them was Voroshilov. Before coming to RVS 1st Cavalry he had been putting down Grigorev's revolt in Ukraine, and in May–June 1919 commanded the 14th Army there. We may get a glimpse of his disrespect for Party Control from his attitude to one group of political workers who were sent to inculcate Party policy among the men. The following report by a half-literate comrade shows how reluctant Voroshilov was to take in 47 Communists, sent by the Party's Central Committee. His offhand attitude to Party workers is in marked contrast to other Red Army officials, who were always appealing for more Communists to be attached to their Political Section to stiffen their men's adherence to Party doctrine.

> Units which numbered 5% or less Communists were considered ineffectual as regards fighting ability; 6–8% was considered satisfactorily; and units with 12–15% of Communists on their strength were considered shock troops.
>
> (Meijer, 1962–64, vol. 1, footnote p. 682)

Most of Shamtsev's report relates to Ukraine. Sinelnikovo is a railway junction at the point where the line Donetsk-Dnepropetrovsk crosses that from Kharkov to Zaporozhe. Vyatka, mentioned as his destination in the last sentence, is to the south-east of Petersburg (renamed Kirov for a number of years from 1934).

f. 17, op. 109, d. 73, l.122

To: Ye. Yaroslavsky, Secretariat of Central Committee of Russian Communist
Party (Bolshevik).
From: Shamtsev and Rezon.
3 June 1919 (entered 30 July in Party records as item 7540)

Highly esteemed comrade Ye. Yaroslavsky, firstly I must send you my comradely greeting, and pass on greetings to all our comrades, and personal greetings to our proletarian leaders Vladimir Ilich Lenin, Trotsky and to everyone at all.

Comrade Yaroslavsky, I am terribly sorry for not submitting this short report as promised concerning the situation of our fellow Communists. A contingent of those mobilized on 5 June was sent on 10 June to be at the disposal of the Political Section of 14th Army of Southern Army Group, but all the same I shall give an explanation in this letter, since I missed seeing you then in the Province Committee. I was late with my report for some reason or other. When I arrived the following day they said you had already left.

A short report. We arrived at Headquarters of Political Section of 14th Army on 15 June in the town of Aleksandrovsk. To meet our first obligation, our elected representatives from the Koluzhen detachment, comrades Rykov, Frumkin, Shults, went into Headquarters of the Political Section with a nominal roll of our people, and requested that we should be speedily posted to units of the Political Section. We were really given a promise that next day, as soon as we had filled in our personal details, they would look at them and immediately take us to our posts. Within two hours we had indeed filled in our questionnaires, and took them to Headquarters for them to look at and assign us to various units. Acting on the promise that had been made by them, those same elected persons went to get the situation clarified and to get themselves appointed. There they were told that their forms had not yet been scrutinized, so that they could not yet be appointed, and they were asked to come back at 7 o'clock that evening. When they returned at 7 o'clock they were faced with the same situation and ordered to wait till the next day, so that apparently the examination lasted three days, but finally, without having looked at the forms, they gave us orders to proceed to place ourselves at the disposal of Army Commander comrade Voroshilov, i. e. to move from Aleksandrovsk station to Sinelnikovo station where comrade Voroshilov's train was.

It was a good 18 or 19 hours after they got there they presented themselves to Comrade Voroshilov. He began to divide out several of them according to his system. They were not appointed – and there also, they left us for the first day, while the second day they took, it seemed, only 10 Communists out of 47, and these 10 were put under the command of one of the divisions, while the remainder of us were simply left waiting for orders. Instead of sending us to front line units they placed us at the disposal of a certain sailor, comrade Alyoshin, with whom we set out to catch deserters at Bolshoye Sinelnikovo station. When once we'd got there, that was the end of it again, with them not directing us on anywhere. It was not simply that they held us there like idle parasites, they fed us per person 2 pounds of bread, and one pound of meat, and also sugar. We would eat and drink a bit, lie down to sleep on our plank-beds, swear and curse between ourselves, argue, accuse one another, not being able to make out what was happening, as though we were layabouts who were making no contribution – while we were quivering with anxiety to get to the front line, and the lads suffered even more keenly when a gang of White Guards began to approach Sinelnikovo, with our side putting up absolutely no resistance. There were hardly any infantry, and men were retreating in panic, while at the same time comrade Voroshilov was right in the front line with his armoured train, and was himself taking part in the battle, as we learned from comrade Alyoshin, who kept us informed. When those White guard swine began to come near Melnikov, then, instead of sending us into action to support and raise the morale of our retreating comrades, they loaded us into wagons and ran us 80 versts to the rear, to the town of Yekaterinoslavl.

And here also we have been parasites right up to the present, i. e. till 22 June, and probably the comrades who have remained there right up to now are fruitlessly sharpening their ?zdeb. Because of this all the comrades without anything to do see their existence as useless, they curse each other, feel quite strung up, almost go out of their mind, and lay all the blame for what has happened on the Political Section – which, frankly, is sleeping even now, and has still not awakened.

Goodbye for the time being, with a comradely greeting to you

Comrade Shamtsev

At the moment I am going to Vyatka Province making towards Chermisi, Urzhumisi and Yaransk Districts, but firstly I shall call into the town of Vyatka, to the Province Committee of the Party and Army Headquarters.

Comrade Rezon

I shall make monthly reports to you in the centre about my further work.

1919: Budyonny attacked commissar Chernov

Chernov's report which follows deals with misbehaviour by Budyonny himself during the Red Army's advance across the Don territory as winter set in at the end of 1919. However we may look at it, a cavalry unit inevitably imposed a double burden on the people of the area, since the men had to feed not only themselves, but also their horses – and the proverbial love the Cossacks had for their horses is shown again and again in Babel's (1929) *Red Cavalry*. The reference to stealing geese has an uncanny echo of one of the most striking episodes in that fictional work of literature. The 'low level of political development' which Chernov refers to was general among the mass of population in Russia, where only a tiny handful understood the first thing about Marxism, or even what distinguished Communists from other political parties.

Underlining shows words underlined in blue pencil in Chernov's typescript.

f. 17, op. 109, d. 73, l.2

To: Central Committee, Russian Communist Party.
From: V. Chernov, Party Membership Card No. 168, Military Political Commissar, 42nd Division, 3rd Army, Ivanovka station, Kupyank.
13 December 1919 (dated with Chernov's signature at the end 20 December, accompanying a telegram to Trotsky dated 11 January 1920)

(I) I consider it essential to draw the attention of the Central Committee to the behaviour of units of the Budyonny Cavalry Corps, and to evidence of the dangerous political state of some of them, which raises the question of measures to combat the resurgence of military–political adventurism in the form of 'mad Budyonnism' [Budyonnovshchina].

The routes followed by our Division and the Cavalry Corps came together in the region of Kostroma, and have not yet diverged (Stary and Novy Oskol and 60 versts further south toward Kupyansk). There is not a single populated place within a distance of 20 to 35 versts along this section of the front in which the presence of Budyonny's men has not provoked unanimous complaints from the inhabitants. The displacement of the Whites by Budyonny troops has been followed by widespread looting, violence and rape. With no attempt to discriminate between *kulaks* and peasants, units of Cavalry Army have robbed the inhabitants of clothing, boots, forage (sometimes not sparing even a pood of oats), and provisions (chickens, geese etc.) – and without paying them a single kopeck.

They have broken into chests and stolen women's underwear, money, clocks, crockery, etc. There have been instances of rape and torture. Horses have been quartered in houses. The cooperatives in Stary Oskol and Chernyanka have had tens of thousands of roubles worth of goods taken from them, but in Stary Oskol not a single kopeck was paid, and in Chernyanka only seven thousand roubles instead of 50 000. The peasants are asking 'What is the difference – first we were robbed by the Whites and now we are being robbed by the Reds!' The hatred of the populace for the Budyonny forces contrasts sharply with their warm, almost affectionate, attitude to the infantry units. I have attached documentary material to my report to Southern Army Group command via Revolutionary Military Council 13th Army. When I spoke to them, the Head of Political Section, 6th Division, Cavalry Corps and his two assistants did not dispute the above-mentioned facts, but attributed them to the unsatisfactory supply of uniforms and provisions to the Cavalry Corps. It must, however, be said that such an explanation is insufficient and that there are also other factors in play – the extremely low level of political consciousness in the cavalry units, the personal conduct of the command staff of the Corps, and the halo of 'Saviour' which surrounds the name of Budyonny. The consequence is a totally un-Marxist treatment of facts and the attribution of all achievements and successes of the Cavalry Corps to <u>Budyonny</u> personally.

Dispatches have been reporting the daring exploits of Budyonny's Cavalry Corps, and the Communist press has been writing how 'Comrade Budyonny smashed...', Budyonny defeated...', and so on. Flattery and glorification of Budyonny (the sole content, for example, of the pronouncements of Communist speakers at the meeting held in Stary Oskol by the Political Section of the Cavalry Corps) could not fail to turn the head of a man with the personal attributes and characteristics of Budyonny, reinforcing his belief that 'I can do anything I like! I can permit anything!' The Head of the Political Section of Cavalry Corps 6th Division told me that Budyonny permitted the cavalrymen to loot, provided that they avoided being caught or arrested – and that only one had in fact been found guilty of looting and shot. It is not difficult to imagine how this is interpreted in the minds of the troops.

On the day when 42nd Division Staff transferred to Stary Oskol, comrade Budyonny, who was extremely drunk, struck Divisional Head of Communications, comrade Valsky, with his swagger stick, and drove all the operators out of the telephone exchange. When comrade G. Pyatakov (who by personal request had just been appointed Political Commissar, 42nd Division) and I went to headquarters to request an explanation of the circumstances of the attack and presented ourselves to comrade Budyonny as senior commander, he abused us in the foulest language. And when comrade Pyatakov stated that he would have to report this behavior to 13th Army Revolutionary Military Council, he received a rapid blow to the head with the same swagger stick, which broke in two. A second blow was aimed in my direction, but I was hastily shoved to the other side of the room by the two persons accompanying Budyonny, who were also drunk. Rushing back, I saw Budyonny aiming his pistol point blank at comrade Pyatakov, but thanks, apparently, to a fault in the mechanism, the gun did not fire. Still determined to vent his rage on comrade Pyatakov, Budyonny yelled: 'I am the man who destroyed Shkuro, Mamontov and Ulagay, and you dare to criticize me!' He threatened to shoot us both, as well as the Divisional Commander and the Divisional Chief of Staff, then to have us flogged, and then to arrest us and send us to central headquarters. The message of his drunken outbursts was clear: 'I can do anything I like!'

Later this was independently reported to 13th Army Revolutionary Military Council by the Divisional Commander, Divisional Chief of Staff, and myself. The Head of Political Section of 6th Cavalry Corps, whom I have already mentioned, told me that there had been an occasion when the Political Commissar had been attacked in the same way.

All this together constitutes the primary or basic reason why what is now being created is a 'private' army, the Budyonny, not a Republican Red Cavalry.

(II) After the incident with Comrade Pyatakov, the Divisional Chief of Staff went to headquarters to report Budyonny, and discovered that in the rooms next to the telephone exchange at Corps Staff headquarters a drunken orgy was taking place, complete with women and an orchestra. Toasts were ringing out: 'Long live the dictatorship of the proletariat and our leader, Budyonny!' That same evening our telegraphist received an amendment to Corps Staff operations communiqué, claiming that a single squadron had captured Novy Oskol, although in the circumstances this was impossible, and in fact Novy Oskol was taken by units of 42nd Division, together with mounted units of the Cavalry Corps, some two days later.

Drunkenness is an everyday ocurrence in units of the Corps. The Head of Supplies is referred to simply as 'Grishka'. Drunken fraternizing and the 'benevolence' of the commanders toward their subordinates explains the absence of discipline in the units of the Cavalry Corps. Further conclusions from the above are clear. This is the second reason, closely allied with the first, why what is now being created is a 'private' army, the Budyonny Corps, not a Republican Red Cavalry.

list 3

(III) The acute shortage of political workers, which the Head of Political Section 6th Cavalry Division had told me about, and the poor quality of their work, which I have to some extent been able to observe for myself, have resulted in a very low level of political development in the ranks of the Cavalry Corps, and in this the question of personality has played by no means the least important role.

The Head of the Political Section of 6th Cavalry Corps told me that in one brigade, in which the cavalrymen had not been distinguished by the warmth of their reception of Communists, the Brigade Commander had joined the Party, after which nearly all the men had become Communists out of regard for their commander and a desire to emulate him – so much so that the Head of the Political Section was now striving to 'convert' another Brigade Commander to the 'Communist faith' in order to bring about a mass conversion of his men to Communism. Leaving aside the question of the Communist 'maturity' of the Head of the Political Section, I must comment that in such a mass enlisting of cavalrymen into the Party their 'Communism' springs not from an onset of class consciousness but from a subjective allegiance and respect for an individual person, and from a desire to emulate him. There is therefore a danger that this mass 'emulation' might produce unexpected results. If the Brigade Commander decides, for example, to kill the Communists, the entire brigade will kill them – and so on. This fear has a sound basis: not one but many Commissars, Commanders, and Red Army men of the 14th Division have reported hearing from the lips of Budyonny's trops: 'Let's kill the Whites first, and then we can start killing the Communists!' The cavalrymen are for Soviet power, but so were Makhno's men – for Soviet power but without the 'Yids' and Communists.

Budyonny's forces have no feeling of unity, ties or comradely solidarity with other units of the Red Army. There have been various instances of hostile attitudes to units of our division, as the following example shows. At the village of Melovoye, No. 373 Regiment of 2nd Brigade, 42nd Division was forced to remain outside in the frost for three hours. Budyonny's men threatened to massacre the Red Army soldiers unless they left the village, and only after three hours did they 'have pity' on them and allow them to take shelter in the houses. The poor quality of the commissars, and the weak nature and insufficient numbers of political workers are the causes of the very low level of political awareness of the men in the Cavalry Corps, and this is the third reason why what is being now created is a 'private' army, the <u>Budyonny</u> Corps, not a <u>Republican</u> Red Cavalry.

All this leads to one general conclusion: there is a growing threat of a new adventurism, <u>Budyonnovshchina</u>, in the style of Mironov, or even of Makhno. From the political point of view the attitude of units of the Cavalry Corps presents a real threat. Soviet power must be maintained as a mighty military force by inundating the Cavalry Corps with reliable and responsible political workers and Commissars, and by changing the command of the Cavalry Corps, including the removal of Budyonny and of others like him. This would be a logical corollary of the process of reorganizing the Cavalry Corps into the first Cavalry Army, and the formation of its Revolutionary Military Council.

1920: Red Army take Rostov

In his memoirs, Budyonny gives 8 January as the date on which his cavalry were approaching Rostov. He claims that some of the Whites were celebrating the Orthodox Christmas when they were surprised by the Cavalry Army's 6th Division breaking into the town. Rostov was completely cleared of Whites by 10 January (Budyonny, 1957–83, *Proydenny put'*, pp. 377–82).

f. 17, op. 109, d. 73, l.6

To: Comrade Chicherin.
From: Secretary to Chairman Revolutionary Military Council, Glazman.
Telephonogram
Received: Sentorovich, 10 January 1920, 15. 00 hours

On the instructions of comrade Trotsky I am sending on open line a message from comrade Stalin which is to be broadcast by radio 'placing special emphasis on the capture of tanks'.

'On the night of 7–8, after bloody battles, units of the Budyonny cavalry fought their way into Rostov and Nakhichevan. In taking Rostov they captured 11 000 prisoners, 7 tanks, 33 guns, and 170 machine-guns. Street fighting took place on the 8th in the environs of Rostov. Captured material is still being counted.'   Stalin

f. 17, op. 109, d. 73, I.7

Revolutionary Military Council Southern Army Group, Kursk
To: comrades Stalin, Yegorov, Serebryakov; copies to comrades Lenin and
Trotsky, Moscow.
From: *Cavalry Army Commander, Budyonny; RVS member Voroshilov*
[No heading. Taganrog secretariat].

At 20.00 hours on 8 January the Red Army cavalry took Rostov and
Nakhichevan. Our brave cavalry annihilated every living enemy protecting
this wasps' nest of aristocratic-bourgeois counter-revolution. More than
10 000 White soldiers and nine Regimental Commanders were taken prisoner, with 32 guns, about 200 machine-guns, a large number of rifles, and
a colossal quantity of baggage. These trophies were won through fierce
fighting.

The opposition was so thoroughly beaten that the enemy did not even
observe our entry into the town, and during the night of the 8th we liquidated various White headquarters and military establishments. On the
morning of 9 January street fighting began in Rostov and Nakhichevan and
continued throughout the day. By 10 January the town was completely
cleared, and the enemy was driven back beyond Bataysk and the Aksaysk
River branch. It was only the dreadful mist and rain that prevented us pursuing the enemy further, and enabled him to destroy small crossings over
the River Kavsam at Bokaism and across the Don at Aksayskaya. The
bridges and railway in Rostov are undamaged. In Rostov the Revolutionary
Military Council has formed a Revolutionary Committee and appointed a
Garrison Commander and a Commandant. Inside the town a mass of com-
missariats and other storehouses stuffed with all sorts of goods have been
inventoried and are being held.

On 11 January a review of the two cavalry divisions took place, attended
by large numbers of workers from Rostov and Nakhichevan and led by
Communists of the underground movement. Greetings were proclaimed
to the Red Army, to the Soviet Republic, and to the great leaders of the
Communist Revolution. In the name of the Cavalry Army, the
Revolutionary Military Council congratulates you on a splendid victory and
raises a rousing, hearty cheer for our leaders. Long may they live!

Cheka report on South Russia

All Cossacks were notorious for looting any place they occupied, and
this habit may well have led to Budyonny's men fighting on the streets

of Rostov with soldiers of Sokolnikov's 8th Army. In his quarrel with the Commander of 8th Army Budyonny attempted to defend the behavior of his men: Sokolnikov came to Rostov on 13 January, and called his divisional commanders to meet Budyonny and Voroshilov.

At the outset of the operation, on 3 January Southern Army Group had directed the Cavalry Army to advance along a line further to the west, to reach the Sea of Azov by taking Taganrog. If this had been followed Rostov would have been to the east of Budyonny's main line of advance. In Sokolnikov's phrase, the Cavalry Army ought to have had 'the courtesy to knock before entering someone else's house'. Budyonny claimed that Southern Army Group's directive had never been communicated to him.

After the capture of Rostov, Budyonny felt that his Army was being misused. The Army Group commander, Shorin, wanted them to cross the Don and make a frontal attack on the town of Bataysk. In January 1920 there was a thaw, which meant they could not trust the ice on the river. The south bank of the Don turned into a boggy morass, quite unsuitable for cavalry manoœuvres. 8th, 9th and 10th Armies were still regrouping their forces, and could not lend their support. The Whites turned all their strength against the Cavalry Army. Their shells broke the ice on the Don, and at one moment commissar Voroshilov was plunged into the water. After suffering heavy losses the Red Army men were forced back to the north bank of the river. Budyonny and Voroshilov appealed to Shorin to call off the frontal attack on Bataysk, and refused to engage their Army further in what they regarded as a disastrous operation.

1st Cavalry Army was transferred from Rostov to outflank the depleted White forces in the area of Tikhorestskaya. On 19 February the 1st Cavalry Army crossed the River Manych. The Whites suffered severe losses in the open steppes in a snowstorm, and this presaged their retreat through the Kuban.

After the Red Army took Rostov on 10 January the White forces on the south bank of the Don were protected by the wide waters of the great river, where to their good fortune the ice had melted. The Whites regrouped on their shorter front. On 2 February when the ice reformed on the Don they crossed back to the north bank of the river to break into Rostov, causing no little panic to the Communists in the city. *List* 91 emanates from Rostov before the Whites returned.

Being a report to Cheka headquarters the following communication would be highly confidential, and to be seen only by a small inner circle of those who sought to gain a true appreciation of the public mood and the real situation in South Russian areas recently retaken from the Whites. Peters expresses his fear of White strength threatening Rostov, and thinks the enemy were given time to regroup by the indiscipline of Budyonny's men. The Red Army command must have felt in the heat of the campaign that it would be impracticable to replace one of their most successful commanders. If such an extreme measure were adopted any possible benefit would probably have been nullified by leaving Voroshilov in post as commissar. Budyonny and Voroshilov were obviously as thick as thieves.

f. 17, op. 109, d. 73, l.91

To: Comrade Dzerzhinsky.
From: Peters.
after 15 January 1920

I arrived in Rostov yesterday, together with Savinov, whom we attached to our train at Kharkov. The situation in Rostov is one of apprehension. The military authorities say that abandonment of the city cannot be excluded. The enemy has managed to build and coordinate significant forces. The Army anticipates an enemy attack. The situation has been worsened by disagreements between the two armies, Budyonny's Army and 8th Army, mainly because of the disposition of Budyonny's Army.

According to local comrades, after the occupation of Rostov the Whites panicked and fled beyond Bataysk, but instead of pursuing the fleeing army Budyonny's Army preferred to spend its time in looting and drunkenness in Rostov. Local comrades have spoken of atrocities in the pogroms carried out by Budyonny's men.

But even this is less important than the behaviour of Budyonny himself. He will speak to no one and seems to be suffering from delusions of grandeur. It is imperative that the flattery should stop and that the Revolutionary Military Council should appoint others to replace him, possibly leaving Voroshilov temporarily in place. No doubt much has been written to the Centre about this by comrades Sokolov and Aleksandrov, whom Budyonny called counter-revolutionaries in the presence of his own military specialists.

Moreover, despite comrade Trotsky's order strictly prohibiting the presence of women in the front line zone, it is a fact that various women, including some straight from the streets – possibly with Denikin spies amongst them – are continually being brought into Army headquarters. Details of this will be conveyed to you by comrade Lander.

Along the Kursk road there is dreadful indiscipline, chiefly because the posts of responsibility have been seized by Communists who are quite unable to deal with the disorder, thus reducing all progress to nil. Moreover, much of the blame lies with the local Supply Organs, since the workers are receiving no supplies at all.

The stocking of provisions is also prohibited, so that willy-nilly the men have to fill up their bags with whatever they can get hold of, and the effect of all this together is to reduce progress to zero.

Further south the situation is different. The discipline of the workers is exemplary. They work hard, but once again they have no provisions. Workers' pay is much lower than in Moscow and no rations are issued, so that everything has to be bought at speculator's prices, for which of course, the wages are insufficient. But even these wages are not being paid; under Denikin some workshops received no money for several months – and, despite all the good work they have done in the period of Soviet power, they are still not being paid. In Belgorod, for example, when Denikin was evacuating the town, the workers themselves hid their machine belts and lathes from the Whites in order to preserve them for Soviet power, but now they are left without wages. Obviously, the workers are not all affected to the same extent, but production is falling.

Further south there is widespread indiscipline among the troops. The commissars travel in private trains, for which they seize fuel, and this indisciplined behaviour disrupts rail trafic. Particularly badly behaved is 13th Army.

In Ukraine hooliganism and banditry are inceasing daily in the villages. The Donets Basin will undoubtedly become the heart from which the movement of rail traffic will circulate. There is coal and grain, discipline in the workshops is good, and essential order was not particularly disrupted by the Whites. A firm guiding hand...

I enclose a report from the Communists working in the Special Section, but must add that I cannot completely endorse it. I have already taken steps to initiate work in the Section, and shall be taking further measures. I urgently request you to send amended instructions by hand, and urge you also to send workers to put the Special Section in order and set up the Cheka in the oblasts we have occupied. This must be done with all possible speed. Greetings to all!   signed

Cavalry take transport: Sokolnikov and Mironov cannot control

Budyonny wanted to get substantial numbers of infantry allocated to the Cavalry Army, to be placed under his direct command. This is

what Sokolnikov has in mind when he complains of Budyonny's
unauthorized appropriation of 2300 men and 6000 prisoners of war.

f. 17, op. 109, d. 73, I.91

*To: Comrade Skylansky, Central Committee Russian Communist Party; copies
to Soviet Defence Chairman, Lenin; Chairman Revolutionary Military Council,
Trotsky.*
From: Commander 8th Army, Sokolnikov.
5 February 1920, Lugansk

The task of preserving revolutionary order in Rostov, entrusted to me by 8th
Army Group Commander, is proving impossible because of the behaviour of
Budyonny. On his orders, units of the Cavalry Army have been carrying out
armed attacks on our outposts. Budyonny has also threatened to use force to
destroy 8th Army Field Headquarters. Despite the Army Group Commander's
orders to leave Rostov, Budyonny refuses to move his units. Also contrary to
Army Group Commander's orders, Budyonny has transferred from Rostov to
Taganrog 2300 men of the Rostov Regiment, intended by Army Group
Commander for use as reinforcements for 8th Army. Cavalry Army Staff have
refused to accept orders from Shorin because of his counter-revolutionary
attitude, and have announced their decision to carry out an armed struggle
against Shorin and his counter-revolutionaries, i. e. against 8th Army.

Budyonny's failure even to make proper dispositions at the front has
created a state of total anarchy. In such conditions I cannot take the responsibility for restraining a part of the army. To the weakening of our forces
through losses in battle and illness must be added a fall in morale, due to
increasing antipathy within the ranks, which are riddled with disruptive
rumours about a counter-revolutionary plot, with 8th Army as an unwitting
agent. A direct role in this monstrous provocation is being played by the
Cavalry's Revolutionary Military Council, in particular Voroshilov and
Shchadenko. Voroshilov has announced that he will not acknowledge any
external authority over the Cavalry. The discontent within the Cavalry
Revolutionary Military Council which has manifested itself in such an un-
acceptable form was because Shorin had blocked Budyonny's plan to form
two infantry divisions. This is hardly the moment to propose new divisions,
since in fact there are too many such divisions in existence already – and
their complement is dwindling every day. From a military point of view,
Budyonny transferred about 6000 prisoners of war, won over from the
Whites to the Red Army, from Rostov to Taganrog in order to form new

divisions, instead of using them to reinforce divisions already at the front. His actions are criminal and cannot be supported. Budyonny's plan for reorganization is a scheme to cover up the looting and plundering which is being perpetrated by his men in Rostov, despite our efforts and those of the Don Revolutionary Committee with whom we are working in complete harmony.

Numerous measures are being taken to avoid conflict, but in view of the danger of the current position I request categorical insistence on removing from Rostov all Cavalry Army units and establishments, and a categorical command to Cavalry Revolutionary Military Council to carry out all orders issued by Shorin, unless countermanded by you.

No one seriously supposed that Shorin had counter-revolutionary tendencies. The term 'counter-revolutionary' obviously carried dire implications, but was used pointedly as a way of discrediting someone with whom one disagreed – a failing which Budyonny was specially prone to indulge.

Coming to Rostov, Shorin stayed in his train at the station, where on 23 January he interviewed the command staff of 8th Army, and then Budyonny, Voroshilov and Shchadenko. Budyonny's quarrel with Shorin dated back to October 1919, but he now renewed his plea for some other plan of attack. He claims that at this point Shorin leapt to his feet to accuse the Cavalry Army of drunk and disorderly conduct. Budyonny said that he wished to be relieved of his command if Shorin was going to persist in his order to cross the Don directly opposite Bataysk. Red Army command realized that now their task would be to drive the Whites out of the Kuban. To match this objective, in January 1920 South-Eastern Front was renamed as 'Caucasus Front'.

f. 17, op. 109, d. 73, l.9

To: *Lenin, Trotsky, Central Committee Russian Communist party; Krasin
(Moscow).*
From: *Peters and Lomonosov.*
Telegram   coded, copy of copy

It is essential to put an immediate end to the discord between 8th Army and the Cavalry Army, which is now threatening to become armed conflict. The behaviour of Budyonny's Army is deteriorating daily: looting, drunkenness, and the frequent presence of women of suspicious character in the auxiliary services at headquarters have resulted in the murder of our most politically aware comrades. Budyonny no longer pays attention to anyone.

His disreputable behaviour on the railways is quite incredible, with constant seizures of fuel, locomotives, wagons and special trains, and plundering of material taken in battle. Every unit has its own line of wagons packed with women and stolen goods. According to comrade Mironov, the number of such wagons has now reached approximately 120 for each division.

f. 17, op. 109, d. 73, l.17

> To: *Military Commissar for Military Communications of the Republic.*
> From: *Mironov, Assistant to Chief of Military Communications, Political Section, Caucasus Front.*
> *18 February 1920*

I wish to report the irregular situation in the Cavalry Army, which has rendered impossible the fulfilment of any proper work on the movement of troops in the sector entrusted to the Army.

Since I came to the Rostov region I have several times had to appeal to the Chief of Staff and the Cavalry Army to cease taking independent action... but up to now 1st Cavalry Army has refused to conform to my regulations. It continues to seize locomotives for various private trains, and holds in its divisional bases more than 100 wagons, instead of the 12 divisional and 50 army wagons allocated to them under the regulations.

The following example will illustrate the attitudes shown to legitimate orders for transfers. At the beginning of this month the Cavalry Army was ordered to transport 1st Infantry Regiment from Rostov to Taganrog. The order was transmitted according to proper military procedure. Transport was made available, and the train left in good time. But when it was already on the way, a telegram arrived from the Army Group Commander ordering the handover of 1st Infantry Regiment and Cavalry to 8th Army, and I later received an order from Deputy Commander 8th Army, comrade Aleksandrov, ordering me to return the regiment to Rostov. Acting on Army Group Commander's order, I instructed Chief of Military Communications of 1st Cavalry Army to turn back the regiment immediately and to report the Army Group Commander's order to 1st Cavalry Revolutionary Military Council. I then received a telephone call from Commander of 1st Cavalry Army, comrade Budyonny. I report below the conversation that followed:

Budyonny: Who am I speaking to?
Mironov: I represent the Chief of Communications of Army Group.
B: You gave an order to turn back 1st Rostov Regiment?
M: Yes, I did.

B: On whose authority?

M: On the authority of 8th Army Revolutionary Military Council, acting on orders of Army Group Commander.

B: To hell with 8th Army Revolutionary Military Council (*foul language*) and Army Group Commander too. I'll send you and that traitor to the Revolution to (*foul language*). Or perhaps you would prefer me to have you shot ...

M: You may shoot me, and you can send whoever you like to wherever you like, but my duty is to carry out the order of the Army Group Commander. I am now going to call the Deputy Commander of 8th Army, comrade Aleksandrov, to the phone, and I suggest you speak to him. I cannot prolong this conversation.

B: Very well, call him.

There followed a stormy exchange between Budyonny and Aleksandrov, and then between Aleksandrov and Voroshilov. While this was going on, 1st Cavalry Chief of Communications, Koltsov, told me that his Revolutionary Military Council had said that if 1st Rostov Regiment did not proceed to Taganrog, he would immediately be shot. On my insistence, a meeting was arranged between 8th Army Revolutionary Military Council and 1st Cavalry Revolutionary Military Council, after which 8th Army Deputy Commander Aleksandrov announced that an agreement had been reached (in his words, forced upon him) allowing 1st Rostov Regiment through to Taganrog – and in fact the regiment did proceed to Taganrog without hindrance.

There has been a whole series of instances of seizure of locomotives and wagons by units of 1st Cavalry Army, and of commandeering of freight wagons and engines, and 1st Cavalry Chief of Transport says that every time he receives an order it is accompanied by a threat to shoot him.

If necessary, I request the setting up of an enquiry.

Checked: Secretary

Stalin and Ordzhonokidze protect Budyonny

The Cavalry Army's Revolutionary Military Council sent a telegram to Trotsky and Stalin, explaining that the thaw had made it impossible for their horsemen to operate on the south bank of the Don, and that Shorin's stubbornness would lead to the destruction of the Republic's best cavalry.

The Commander-in-Chief ordered the frontal assault to be called off, and on 26 January the Cavalry Army was transferred east, to cross the River Manych. Here they were supported by 3300 Cossacks under the command of Dumenko.

Budyonny had originally served under Dumenko when 1st Socialist Regiment was formed in 1918. Budyonny claims that in 1920 he now suspected his former leader of planning to take his Corps over to the enemy. Dumenko was actually arrested in February, and shot in May, but the charges against him were later shown to be groundless. In his account of the fighting on the Manych, Budyonny slights Dumenko's efforts to support him, which he says were fragmentary and half-hearted. This accusation may be attributed also to Budyonny's overweening vanity which would allow him to brook no rivals.

f. 17, op. 109, d. 73, I.13

To: Revolutionary Military Council of the Republic.
From: Revolutionary Military Council member, Shchadenko; Army Chief of Staff, Shcholokov; Military Commissar Army Staff, Belyakov.
Received 10 March 1920; decoded 10 March 1920 Secretariat of Deputy Chairman Revolutionary Military Council of the Republic.
Telegram

9th Division has sustained considerable losses and fallen back from the position on the Rostov–Taganrog railway line which had been assigned to it. The Military Commander 9th Division went to Taganrog with a request to the Cavalry Army Chief of Staff for assistance, because if the enemy went over to the offensive, the 9th Division units and 8th Army in general would not be able to hold, and would have to fall back. Comrade Voyskov based his statement on the exhaustion and depleted numbers of the 8th Army units. Military operations in the 8th Army sector over the past month have assumed the character of a dance of death. In one sector they have usually begun an attack in the morning, and by the evening they have retreated back to their start line. Heavy losses in men have led to a fall in morale. 8th Army has been operating in a thin, sparsely stretched line along a front of 50–60 versts. The enemy has been attacking on the flanks and gradually occupying a line from Azov through Bataysk and Khoputov.

The recapture of Rostov and Nakhichevan in an attack on the night of 2 February was carried out by two Markov infantry regiments, comprising

1500–2000 men each, plus two light batteries and 250 cavalry armed with sabres. The infantry was partly made up with conscripted Taganrog workers, who came over to us in batches at Rostov station, but in the face of such a small group our entire army fell back. When it became known that units of 8th Army were fighting in the region of Temernik station of the Vladikavkaz railway, then it was decided to withdraw the headquarters of the Cavalry Army from Rostov in marching order. The headquarters left, going towards Aleksandrov-Grushevitsky, where the Operations Section also arrived, on 23 February. On 25 February the Operations Section and Chief of Staff left for Rostov and set about their work.

While these military operations were in progress comrade Shchadenko, a member of the Revolutionary Military Council, was away at Caucasus Army Group Field Headquarters in Millerovo. In the fighting around Rostov on 20–22 February the Cavalry Army lost two armoured trains: 'Red Cavalryman' *Krasny kavalerist* and 'Free Russia' *Svobodnaya Rossiya*. Their loss can be explained by many more passenger coaches having being included in the trains than are allowed for under the proper establishment. So it was that the armoured trains had been turned into scandalous harems of female employees for the Red Army men. When fighting began in the area of the station all this dissolute horde rushed to rescue their concubines, and did not think about saving the armoured trains. Cavalry Army Revolutionary Military Council is strongly opposed to such breaches of regulations and is making the armoured trains more mobile, stronger and more military in character. Revolutionary Military Council requests that the number of passenger coaches in armoured trains should be reduced, making a general restriction to allow only one passenger coach in every five coaches, and four goods wagons for provisions and men.

A further factor leading to the loss of the trains was that when the first shots were fired the railway workers ran away, and someone had closed the points in the tracks out of the station, making it impossible to move the trains about. The case of the surrender of the two trains has been referred to 1st Cavalry Army Revolutionary Tribunal.

Stalin responded to Budyonny's telegram by arranging for Shorin to be replaced, and also for Ordzhonokidze to be appointed to the Revolutionary Military Council of the Army Group. Stalin expressly notes for Budyonny's benefit that Ordzhonokidze is well disposed towards his Cavalry Army. In March 1920 Budyonny's men were accused of looting in Novocherkassk. Ordzhonokidze showed Budyonny the letter he had sent to Lenin to counter this accusation and explain the difficulties of supply faced by First Cavalry:

Not a single unit of the Cavalry Army entered Novocherkassk. Right from the time it took Voronezh the Cavalry have had no pay and no proper body to provide their supplies. That is why they had to do their own foraging. As the troops were densely disposed over a small area their attempts to get provisions inevitably led to hardship for the local population. (Budyonny, 1957–83, *Proydenny put*, vol. 2, p. 13)

With all his great powers Ordzhonokidze seems to have been blind to the excesses of the First Cavalry Army – or if not blind then deliberately determined to overlook their flagrant breaches of discipline.

f. 17, op. 109, d. 73, I.18

To: Chairman Council of People's Commissars, Lenin; Chairman of Revolutionary Military Council, Trotsky; (in black ink) sent to comrade Lenin.
From: Revolutionary Military Council Caucasus Army Group, Tukhachevsky; Ordzhonokidze, Rostov.
20 March 1920 Received and decoded in Secretariat of Deputy Chairman Revolutionary Military Council.
Cypher telegram   Top secret
21 March 1920

From visits to Cavalry Army we have verified that from the point of view of military strength and preparedness the active service troops are of a high standard and have a significant number of good horses. The artillery and special troops are in good condition. Cavalry Army has an assured supply of materials and other necessities. There is an acute shortage of uniforms, greatcoats, boots and saddles. Political work is insufficient because of the lack of Party workers. There are 2000 Communists in the Cavalry Army. Anti-Communist sentiment has completely disappeared and Red Army men *en masse* are on the side of the Party. There is an urgent need to reinforce the Army as soon as possible with not less than 1000 political workers and the same number of Red commanders. The requirements of Cavalry Army were set out in more detail in our telegram 592 Op. of 9 March to Commander-in-Chief. Hooligan and drunken elements are being very strictly weeded out from units of Cavalry Army, and put on trial. Two men were sentenced to death today. The troops of

Cavalry Army are favourably disposed to the possibility of being transferred to Western Front.

f. 17, op. 109, d. 73, I.19

To: *Chairman of Soviet Defence Council, Lenin; Chairman Revolutionary Military Council, Trotsky; Commander-in-Chief, Kamenev; copy to Smilga; [in red ink] sent to Lenin.*
From: *Revolutionary Military Council Caucasus Army group, Tukhachevsky, Ordzhonokidze.*
Telegram 423   Top secret
25 March 1920, Rostov

From what comrade Lebedev has said we have learned that, because of the false information he had received, Revolutionary Military Council of the Republic has gained a mistaken impression of Cavalry Army and in particular its commander, Budyonny. We therefore consider it our duty to bring to your notice the following facts:

(1) With regard to prowess in battle Cavalry Army is beyond praise. It excels by its discipline in action and extraordinary daring, acting always in cavalry formation, using cold steel or revolvers. Not one of the enemy's cavalry units can withstand a head-on attack by units of the Cavalry Army. The divisional commanders are very bold and able leaders.

(2) Army Commander Budyonny is gifted with exceptional natural talent, both in operational and other respects. None of the other commanders, except comrade Uborevich, can come up him. Regarding the brilliant manœuvre and victory, when the enemy had moved into our rear in the area of Sredne-Gorlyksoye, credit must be given to Budyonny rather than to 10th Army Commander Pavlov, since the latter was a long way from the troops and had lost touch with them, so that units of 10th Army were in fact being led by the cavalry commander. Politically, comrade Budyonny is an unsophisticated Communist, but he is absolutely devoted to the cause of Soviet power.

(3) It is totally untrue that 13th Cavalry Division wreaked havoc in Novocherkassk. Not a single unit of the Cavalry Army entered Novocherkassk. The town was occupied by Dumenko's Cavalry Corps. In the looting in Rostov, 8th Army played no less a part than Cavalry

Army, as is shown in the inventory of the stores. 8th Army units were exculpated only through the political authority of comrade Sokolnikov.

(4) Since the time it was at Voronezh, Cavalry Army has received no pay and has had no proper system of supply. It has therefore had to fend for itself, and as the men were concentrated in a small area, their attempts to get provisions inevitably led to hardship for the local population.

(5) Because of the total absence of political workers, and due also to 1st Cavalry being constantly in action, political work has been weak. Nevertheless anti-Communist feeling in the Army has disappeared, and there are now more than 2000 Communists. We declare that if not less than 1000 Communists were immediately directed to us, with a similar number of commanders, and efficient political workers to strengthen its staff – then 1st Cavalry Army would become Soviet cavalry in the full sense of the word.

Ordzhonokidze must have written paragraph 5 of the above with his tongue in his cheek. Every Red Army commander was crying out for more political workers to give his troops some inkling of the principles they were fighting for. Educated Communists were in extremely short supply, and some of those who were most zealous had only a short experience of civil war conditions. Situations must have often arisen when some raw young Komsomol member might find himself preaching the elements of Marxism to men who were older than him and with a tough experience of several years fighting behind them. Time would have to be set aside from the exigencies of constant combat, and even with good will conditions for political education might be hard to find. Even if that were possible, would Voroshilov create conditions in which political workers could have calm conditions for educating the rank and file?

f. 17, op. 65, d. 323, l.23

To: Lenin (only for Lenin).
From: Ordzhonokidze, Rostov on Don.
28 March 1920

Yesterday I came back with the Cavalry Army from Yekaterinodar. Things are not bad in the Cavalry Army. They need political workers and commanders. A full report will be made by Smilga, who is leaving in an hour's time. We are expecting to hear any minute reports that Yekaterinodar has fallen.

May: campaign against the Poles

In *list* 20 Beloborodov seeks clarification of his being moved to the Urals. According to Danilov he remained a member of Revolutionary Military Council of 9th Army till June 1920, though, once posted to the Urals he can hardly have taken much part in operations in the Kuban. In November 1919 Admiral Kolchak had been defeated and he was executed in January 1920. Since the Red Army had overcome the main danger on its Eastern Front, priority now had to be given to restoring Russia's ruined economy. The Urals Bureau of Central Committee was created on 8 April to deal with shortages of food, fuel and other necessities, and to take charge of Party organizations. Prominent among Trotsky's objectives was to convert the 3rd Army into the 1st Revolutionary Army of Labour (see Swain *et al.* 1996, *The Russian Civil War*, ch. 4).

f. 17, op. 109, d. 73, l.20

To: Deputy Chairman Revolutionary Military Council, comrade Sklyansky;
copy to Central Committee of Communists.
From: A. Beloborodov, member of Revolutionary Military Council of Cavalry
Army.
23 April 1920, Rostov

The day before yesterday you informed me that I had been appointed a member of the Urals Bureau, and obviously this decision plus the order to appoint comrade Shchadenko finally determine my leaving the Cavalry Army. I find myself in a very ambiguous position for the lack of any official order relieving me of my duties as a member of the Military Council of the Cavalry Army. I do ask you most strongly to expedite the issuing of the appropriate order by official telegraph. I request Central Committee of the Party to make a definitive clarification of my position and to give me precise orders.

As Germany lost the war in 1918 the Poles declared that their nation once more existed as an independent sovereign state. Without major geographical features the eastern boundary of Poland has long been a matter of dispute. In April 1920 the Polish Army entered Ukraine, and took Kiev on 6 May.

The Bolshevik High Command was already preparing its counterstroke. It was decided to move the First Cavalry Army west to form

the spearhead of their attack. They left Rostov on 23 April and proceeded across country to reach Uman on 25 May. It was hoped in
May that a visit by Kalinin might have a steadying influence on 1st
Cavalry Army and restrain the men from some of their worst
excesses.

Places mentioned here and in Zhilinsky's report are in Ukraine
(Zvenigorod, Uman, Novograd-Volynsky, Rovno, Zhitomir, Berdichev).

f. 17, op. 109, d. 73, l.23

To: Central Committee Russian Communist Party.
From: Revolutionary Military Council 1st Cavalry Army: Voroshilov,
Budyonny, Minin; Vasilev, Secretary, Revolutionary Military Council,
South-West Front.
Message by direct line Cypher; Top secret 0943 107 11 17 46

Extract from telegram is transmitted herewith: 'About 25 May our Cavalry
Army will come out into the Zvenigorod-Uman area. This will be approximately the start line for the Cavalry Army. It is desirable for this event that
comrades Kalinin and Rakovsky should arrive by this time as heads of the
Soviet Republic, for they are greatly liked and popular with Cavalry Army.
Do not fail to inform Revolutionary Military Council of Cavalry Army
whether you can meet our wish.'

Nr. 2665/VII

f. 17, op. 109, d. 73, l.2

To: Revolutionary Military Council of Caucasus Army Group; copies to
Secretariat of comrade Sklyansky, Central Committee Russian Communist
Party.
From: Deputy Head, revolutionary Military Council Political Directorate,
Aleksandrov Head of Political Section.
Telegram
2 May 1920 (received 14 May)

In view of severe shortage speed up return to 1st Cavalry Army of its
political workers, held back in Rostov or temporarily seconded.

list 24

To: comrades Trotsky, Lenin, Commander-in-Chief.
From: Rakovsky.
Transmitted by Telegraphist-in charge, Plan; received by Sofonova

In the neighbourhood of Mezhdurechiye, half-way between Novograd-Volynsky and Rovno, Cavalry Army has taken 1000 Polish prisoners, with 60 killed. Four artillery pieces, 40 machine-guns, and 1000 shells were captured.

f. 17, op. 109, d. 73, l.53

To: South-West Army Group Political section, Kharkov; copies to Central Committee of Communist Party, Kharkov; Central Committee, Moscow.
From: Head of Cavalry Army Political Section, Vardin: Head of Cavalry Army Propaganda Section, Belochkin.
23 July 1920

In the recent bloody battles, in which all divisions of Cavalry Army, without exception, took part, an extraordinarily high number of political workers, commissars and political soldiers were killed. Entire units lost more than half their Communists. Precise data are being collected and will be presented to you soon. Send us political workers, commissars and political soldiers urgently. Also send us infantry for 45th Division and 24th Division.

August: Zhilinsky criticizes 1st Cavalry

On 12 June the Red Army retook Kiev. North of the Pripet Marshes Tukhachevsky advanced rapidly towards Warsaw, but in August the Reds were forced back to conclude a peace, which gave Poland the territory it would hold until 1939. Zhilinsky's report which follows lays great emphasis on the social make up of 1st Cavalry Army. According to Marx, revolutions would be led by members of the urban proletariat – as the most class conscious element in society – though of course those who knew about the 'class struggle' were enjoined to spread Communist ideology among the rural masses.

Anti-Semitism had long been rife in South Russia, Ukraine and Poland, and had obviously been encouraged by the Tsarist regime. Communist principles proclaimed internationalism and the brotherhood of all peoples; but from many other sources besides Zhilinsky one can see how much enlightenment was still needed to further that ideal. Commenting on 11th and 14th Divisions, Zhilinsky talks of men 'deserting from Denikin'. We need to remember that in the spring of 1920 there was virtually open warfare between Kuban nationalists and the Whites, who insisted on retaining their slogan 'Russia one and indivisible'. Some disillusioned Kuban Cossacks came over to the Red Army during Denikin's last campaign. Many more could not get onto the ships evacuating the Whites from Novorossysk. If they wanted their lives to be spared their best hope was to join the Red Army.

f. 17, op. 109, d. 73, II. 25–49

To: N. N. Krestinsky.
From: Zhilinsky, Deputy Head Political Section of 1st Cavalry Army; Head of Information Section, Avanesov; True copy attested by Secretary of Information Section.
Printed Booklet   Top secret
Field press of Political Section of 1st Cavalry Army

Political state of 1st Cavalry Red Army:
15 June–15 August 1920

1st Cavalry Army consists of four Cavalry Divisions (4th, 6th, 11th, and 14th) and a Special Duties Brigade. For a limited period 45th Soviet Rifle Division was on temporary attachment.

The social composition of the Cavalry Army consists of peasants and Cossacks from the Don, Stavropol, and some from the Kuban. 11th Division comprises mainly mobilized peasants, together with some workers from the central provinces. The great majority of the Red Army men are volunteers. A significant number of them have been in the ranks from the very beginning of the civil war. The Army contains few from the working class, an insignificant group of workers have only recently been brought in as 'politically conscious soldiers'. In the political sphere the second half of June marked a watershed for the Cavalry Army. Firstly, 200 political workers came in from Political Section of South West Army Group. Secondly, the entire leadership of the Army's Political Section was replaced.

List 49

Political Data No. 2767
Political Section of Cavalry Army

4th Division
Communists 675, Communist cells 38, Education Workers 23, School of Literacy 21. No political work is carried out because the Division is always on the move. During periods when they are stationary discussions are held on the themes of anti-Semitism and chauvinist attitudes towards the Poles. Banditry is widespread: prisoners are stripped of all their clothes, and anti-Semitic agitation is practised almost openly. Most of the commanders and political workers are failing in their duty, and make no serious attempt to counter the above-mentioned phenomena. Supplies are not reaching the Division, and the Red Army men have had no bread for two days. Not enough horses are allocated to them; many of the men, and almost all the political workers, travel in carts.

6th Division
Communists 90, most of whom have only recently joined the Party, and hardly understand anything about politics. No political work is done because they have no experienced and politically conscious workers. Educational work nil: there is no money to pay teachers, no schools are organized. We must bring in some new political workers.

A harmful new element has come into the Division, and under its influence there has been a notable increase in Jew-baiting, while banditry and violence against the civilian population have increased. Prisoners of war are stripped; 150 prisoners taken at Novograd-Volynsky were massacred. When the Division was passing through Zhitomir and Berdichev people were robbed of everything they possessed. The supply organs are not functioning, which forces the troops to fend for themselves, and that is the main reason for the lawlessness and banditry of the units. Punitive organs – the Tribunal and Special Duties Brigade – are extremely weak, and give a poor account of themselves in the struggle with the Division's negative features.

11th Division
This consists largely of workers and peasants from Central Russia, supplemented by Kuban Cossacks, captured or deserting from Denikin, who are given to looting and plundering, and have had a disruptive effect on the other Red Army men of the Division. The political workers are making great

efforts to stop marauding and violence against the populace, but they are not always successful. They frequently come up against opposition from the commanders, who themselves indulge in looting personal possessions and requisitioning food from the peasants. The main body of political workers must be changed and most of the commanders replaced.

14th Division
This Division consists mainly of men who have deserted from Denikin, politically immature, given to looting and requisitioning food from the local peasantry. The supply organizations are doing nothing – there are no uniforms, soldiers help themselves. There is a great shortage of horses, which leads to the requisitioning of mounts from the peasants. The requisitioning is done in a haphazard way – and basically is just downright theft. In view of the absence or incompetence of supply organs these irregularities are difficult to deal with – while the commanders not only fail to put a stop to all this, they themselves behave in the same way. They drink and steal along with the men, telling their orderlies to get them chickens, geese, clothes, sometimes even gold and other valuables.

It is essential to replace the commanders, and in the first place the Divisional Commander. The number of political workers must be increased, and a proper system of supply must be set up. The Tribunal simply does not live up to its name, and completely misunderstands its purpose. There have been instances of openly criminal behaviour on the part of the Tribunal, as for example sentencing prisoners to be shot.

1st Cavalry Reserve Brigade
The Brigade does not have a satisfactory supply of provisions and forage. There is a great shortfall in the number of horses, and a shortage of uniforms and weapons, all of which makes the Red Army men very discontented. The commanders are satisfactory, though the squadron commanders are inexperienced and most of them are not up to their task.

In general the Red Army men are confident and keen to be sent to the front.

Special Duties Brigade
Discipline is satisfactory, but most of the men are politically immature. A new commissar has been appointed and has straight away launched a stronger campaign against anti-Semitism and banditry.

On 30 June a meeting on the current situation in international relations was attended by about 300 Red Army men and 50 civilians. On the same day there was a meeting of Communist cells, attended by 36 persons.

General information
On 30 June there was a meeting of divisional political officers, military commissars of all units, and representatives of Communist cells. Reports revealed an accelerating deterioration in the Army, and the growth of banditry, robbery and drunkenness. Overall the banditry stems to a great extent from the encouragement and connivance of the commanders.

The front-line zone
Most of the populace are cowed and frightened by the raiding and debauchery of our cavalry. They distrust the Red Army, and occasionally react with fury against the incessant requisitioning of horses, carts and various other goods. No political work is being carried out among the population, and the areas we have occupied with the Red Army's advance still do not have any structure of administration. The Political Section cannot meet the needs of the populace, because we have no political workers. They are absolutely no Polish political workers within the Political Section, a shortcoming which makes itself most painfully felt. Because there is no political work of any sort and because the Red Army carries out requisitioning and robberies as it moves through, our rear areas are very unstable and are a real danger for the Army. We need large numbers of political workers to work among the civilian populace.

August: 1st Cavalry versus Zhilinsky

The next letter is an indignant rebuttal of Zhilinsky by commanders of the 1st Cavalry Army. One of their comments has been inserted into Zhilinsky's report: 'There was not a single soldier from 6th Division in either Zhitomir or Berdichev.'

Minin was an old crony from Budyonny's time in Tsaritsyn in 1918–19. Stalin was allied with him to form the 'military opposition', which declared itself against Trotsky's plan of creating a professional Army, staffed largely with ex-Tsarist officers. Voroshilov also fought in the defence of Tsaritsyn and always worked hand in glove with Budyonny. Anfilov finds him completely lacking in military expertise (see Shukman, 1997, *Stalin's Generals*, pp. 313–4). We may guess that he was probably the main author of the letter to Trotsky and the Central Committee.

Looking back over the century it is not easy for us to strike a balance between Zhilinsky and the 1st Cavalry Army. Several features of their behaviour were prominent in many other units of the Red Army. After six years of war Red Army men had scanty or non-existent supplies of food or clothing. It was common practice to strip prisoners or dead soldiers of all they were wearing, and their boots were specially prized. There may be some truth in Voroshilov's assertion that the fast-moving Cavalry Army was even worse off than infantry units, since supply organs had difficulty keeping up with them.

The 1st Cavalry commanders do not flatly deny the charges of anti-Semitism, but ask whether a Jew could survive among the Cossacks, so strongly prejudiced against them. Isaak Babel's personal experience may go some way towards answering that question. He served through the Polish campaign as a journalist for Budyonny's paper *Red Cavalryman (Krasny kavalerist)*. A Communist from his early youth he did not practice religion, but his writings reflect his affection and respect for Jewish traditions of scholarship, culture, and close-knit supportive family life. Babel was a Jew and an intellectual, both of which features made the soldiers react with their usual hostility.

He wrote a series of sketches about the Cavalry Army, the collection being brought together under the title *Red Cavalry (Konarmiya)*. Several of these pieces give a frank account of the problems he faced in living among his crude companions in arms. *Red Cavalry* is a work of fiction, transposing or touching up incidents which befell the author during the war against the Poles. Fictional as some of the details may be, it has remained one of the best sources for understanding the mentality of the Cossacks. Tough and recklessly courageous, they suffered heavy casualties. Furthermore there was some justification for 1st Cavalry commanders to claim: 'The Cavalry Army finds provisions as best it can. It is frequently hungry and undergoes the most dreadful hardships – and then it fights like few of our armies fight.'

With regard to plundering, the Cavalry Army was probably one of the worst offenders, but their staff make the point that few units in the Red Army were completely blameless. We have to remember that the Whites also had a bad reputation in this respect. Peasants mocked the 'Volunteer Army' by renaming them 'the Looting Army' *(Grabarmiya)*, formed from the word *grabezh*, as applied by Zhilinsky to the 1st Cavalry.

Babel shows all too clearly how primitive was the Cossack understanding of politics, and derives much humour from their attempts to use the slogans of the Revolution. The men's minds were concentrated on the daily problems of survival, and on winning the war. Faced with these pressing concerns they appeared heartless and indifferent to the sufferings of the civilians around them. There is furthermore no doubt that anti-Semitic pogroms took place on a large scale, both in Ukraine, and in other areas along the route of 1st Cavalry Army.

At the end of this letter to Trotsky we have to approach the plea for more *politrabotniki* with a certain scepticism. We may bear in mind Shamtsev's report of 3 June 1919 (f. 17, op. 109, d. 73, 1. 50 above). In June 1919 Voroshilov was commanding the 14th Army in Ukraine. One gets the impression from Shamtsev that he simply found political workers an awkward inconvenience, coming between the commander and his men. There was probably much hypocrisy in the staff appealing for more of them to be assigned to 1st Cavalry. They must have known that the supply of experienced and effective *politrabotniki* was severely limited. They were quite safe to clamour for more of them, parading their 'correct' attitude but knowing full well their request could not be met.

'Political education' was probably needed for all ranks in the Red Army, and the cavalry commanders are simply stating the obvious when they say that the decline in units' behaviour was due to the shortfall in food and other necessities. They recognize that the lack of supplies could only be remedied by rebuilding the Soviet economy after the war was won.

Nevertheless, whatever excuses Voroshilov may try to find, Zhilinsky's report gives some warning of the unbridled savagery which broke out as 1st Cavalry Army traversed Ukraine on their way to the front against Vrangel.

f. 17, op. 109, d. 73, I.50

To: *Central Committee, Russian Communist Party; [written in blue crayon] to comrade Trotsky.*
From: *Members of Revolutionary Military Council of 1st Cavalry Army: Voroshilov; Budyonny; S. Minin; Head of Political Section, Vardin (Mgeladze). Intercepted letter with report on Political Section of 1st Cavalry Army*

Dear Comrades,
In late June senior Party worker, Zhilinsky, whom you know, arrived at 1st Cavalry Army to take up duties as Head of the Political Section.

Comrade Zhilinsky became Deputy Head of the Political Section – but after a few days he had to leave, since we considered it impossible for him to continue in that post. The incident with comrade Zhilinsky prompts us to raise with Central Committee of our Party <u>the general question of the attitude to 1st Cavalry Army of *politrabotniki* and organizations in the rear areas.</u>

Comrade Zhilinsky had to go because, holding the post of Deputy Head of the Political Section, in the absence of the Head of the Political Section, he signed a <u>political report</u> on Cavalry Army Political Section, which is compounded of lies, common poisonous gossip, and libel. But the report presented Cavalry Army <u>just as it is seen by the mass of political workers in the rear,</u> but not as it actually is.

We are aware, and doubtless it is no secret for Central Committee, that in the rear it is officially 'fashionable' to heap unlimited praise on the Cavalry Army in the Press and at meetings – though in the privacy of the home it is called 'bandit', 'hooligan', 'anti-Semitic'. A significant proportion, perhaps even the majority of our comrades, sincerely believe, for example, that it is impossible for a Jew to exist in the Cavalry Army, that Communists and commissars are killed, and that when the Army is not actually engaged in battle it inevitably turns to plunder, rape, torture, and so on and so forth...

Central Committee knows well that no one 'formed' the Cavalry Army, that it came together not through some 'official decision', but came into being 'spontaneously', by men joining as volunteers. The strength of the Cavalry Army lies in the fact that it embodies <u>the elemental spirit of the peasantry, who rose against the alliance of Russian landowners and rich Cossacks from the Don and the Kuban.</u> This spirit has been channelled by the government of the proletariat in a politically conscious direction, but nothing, or virtually nothing, has been done to develop its elemental force.

First of all: Has our Army received even one tenth of what is needed by any regular official army? Has it received supplies, uniforms, or food? Have they put a lot of political workers into its ranks? Has the Party done even one tenth of what it should have done to re-educate the peasant element – raw, politically unaware, riddled with superstition?

The Army has been <u>forced</u> to get its own supplies, forced to do the necessary 'plundering'. It cannot observe all the rules of commercial transactions.

The men understand this. The vast majority are peasants themselves. They realize it is wrong to take away the peasants' corn, their livestock, and often even their horses and carts. But they also know that the Soviet government is a government of the poor and cannot provide all the things they need, and they sympathize with the difficulties of our authorities ... But then they are called 'bandits'.

<u>The soldiers know that in the rear people call them 'bandits'</u> – and this offends them to the depths of their souls. But what would happen if one fine day all the Red Army men suddenly announced: 'We don't want to be plunderers, we want to be honourable Red Army soldiers, so give us everything the regulations lay down'? What would the moralists in the rear have to say then? The Cavalry Army finds provisions as best it can. It is frequently hungry, and undergoes the most dreadful hardships – and then it fights like few of our armies fight.

Along with the unavoidable plundering, which the Army cannot do without, there is, of course, some plundering done by the Army which is 'not essential' to its needs. <u>But what army is without such goings on?</u> There can be no doubt that the White Poles behave disgracefully – raping, plundering, and pillaging so much more fiercely than some of our most 'bandit' elements.

Some of our infantry regiments would certainly score more points than our most 'bandit' cavalry units. But no one makes a fuss about the infantry misbehaving. They tell tall stories about our cavalry, and isolated instances of banditry are exaggerated and attributed to our Cavalry Army as a whole. Why is this? It is because a certain amount is known about the infantry units, whereas about us they know nothing – because any infantry army has many threads that link it to the rear, while we feel completely cut off from it.

It is as a consequence of this isolation, this lack of knowledge – and from the frivolously scurrilous attitude to our Army – that comrade Zhilinsky's 'political report' appeared. We append that 'report' to our submission – and we ask Central Committee to decide: If our Army were really as Zhilinsky's document presents it, do you think it would still be able to fight? Would it not immediately disintegrate? Would it not have taken up with Makhno, who tried so hard to get it to do so? Would it not have dispersed throughout Ukraine, so full of bandits?

In our opinion there is yet another circumstance which builds up the ill will displayed in the rear towards the Cavalry Army, namely that fate has decreed that the Cavalry Army has become the most visible expression of the power and might of Soviet Russia. It is natural that it has attracted the hatred of the bourgeois, middle-class intellectual elements. These elements influence a significant proportion of our comrades in a thousand ways, especially those who come from petty-bourgeois and intellectual backgrounds. They succumb to the influence of elements hostile to our revolution, and as a result they join their voices to those who disparage the Cavalry Army. Cavalry Army is predominantly a peasant army, which requires a <u>sympathetic, attentive, caring attitude, not one of prejudice and neglect.</u> The Cavalry Army wishes to become, and could become <u>a politically aware Communist army.</u>

The Army therefore needs political workers who, before they begin to teach, will take the trouble to study it, get to know it and understand it. <u>The authority of our Party and regime stands unusually high in the army.</u> Communists are regarded almost as saints. If an 'unsuitable' type of person signs on to join a cell the Red army men often protest that the Party has admitted someone 'unworthy' of it. Recently one of our brigades held a solemn celebration when the Brigade Commander joined the Party. The soldiers have a great desire to study and enlighten themselves about politics, but our Army's Political Section has such insignificant resources. It is only two months since South-West Army Group sent us the first political workers. Having 'digested' the first batch the Cavalry Army is openly now defining the real extent of its appetite. We need more political workers.

Our requests are as follows:

(1) To explain to the broad Party membership the real nature of our Cavalry Army and to dispel prejudice against it.
(2) To achieve a definite increase in the flow of serious, experienced, and qualified political workers – wherever possible workers from the industrial centres.
(3) To take measures to strengthen links between the Army and the rear; to organize a collection of gifts for the Army, to send us delegations of workers, and to regularize the supply of literature etc.

We should emphasize that if the rear does not particularly like the Cavalry Army, then neither is the Army universally enamoured of the rear. 'Our Communists', the soldiers sometimes say, 'are fine fellows, but back there in the rear they need a purge'... Of course they understand the term 'purge' rather more simply than the Secretaries of Party Committees.

We respectfully request, dear comrades, that you strengthen the ranks of Party workers in the Cavalry Army to make it an invincible, consciously Communist force.

With comradely greetings, members of the Revolutionary Military Council [4 signatures in crayon]

f. 17, op. 109, d. 73, l.53

Russian Communist Party (Bolshevik) Central Committee
To: comrade Trotsky
17 August 1920

Dear Lev Davydovich,
I enclose, for you to read and return to me, a letter from Revolutionary Military Council 1st Cavalry Army, containing a complaint against comrade Zhilinsky, who signed the attached political report (which was held back by 1st Cavalry Revolutionary Military Council). The report is accompanied by a protest against comrade Zhilinsky.

I have read the political report very carefully. Nowhere does Zhilinsky attack the Red Army soldiers themselves; he always points out that they are obliged to plunder because there are not enough supplies. He attacks only the supply organs, the commanders, and to some extent the political workers. If one also takes into account the fact that the report was compiled not for publication but for the information of Army Group Revolutionary Military Council and for RVS of the Republic, so that measures could be taken to set right things which are wrong, then I cannot find any blame attaching to Zhilinsky. Indeed the tone adopted by 1st Cavalry Revolutionary Military Council seems to me too hysterical and not appropriate to official correspondence.

I recommend that no decision be taken, that we should lodge in the archive the papers containing this exchange of insults, and that Cavalry Army be strengthened with good and independent political workers.

With comradely greetings [not signed but stamped and initialled]

f. 17, op. 109, d. 73, I.55

To: Special Section Caucasus Army Group; Military Commander Caucasus, comrade Gittis; copy to comrade Trotsky. Herewith a copy of telegram Nz TK318 to Revolutionary Military Council South-West Army Group.
From: Berzin, Member of Revolutionary Military Council of South-West Army Group, Kharkov; 918 No. 850 RVS [of 1st Cavalry] Voroshilov; Budyonny; Secretary Orlinsky.
No heading
13 August 1920

Revolutionary Military Council 1st Cavalry Army requests immediate measures to punish traitors to Soviet Power through relatives remaining behind; and also commanders of Kuban Cossack Regiment of Cavalry Group of comrade Osadchiy who went over to Polish side on 20 July: Deputy Commander of 1st Reserve, comrade Rovensky, a Cossack from Uman stanitsa of Kuban Oblast ... 2) Regimental commander comrade Lashtaber, Andrey Mikhaylovich of Kushevskaya stanitsa, of same Oblast ... 4) commander Ost 1, Sutint, Mikhail, a Cossack from that same stanitsa and Oblast. 5) Head of Supplies, Shevchenko, Ivan, a Cossack from stanitsa Atamanskaya of that same Oblast; Chief Clerk Agayenko, Akim, a Cossack from stanitsa Uman of that same Oblast. (I request that you take all measures to act on the same telegram)
Berzin, member of RVS of South-West Army Group

Stiffen political reliability

f. 17, op. 109, d. 73, l.57

To: Central Committee, Russian Communist Party, Mokhovaya 7, Moscow;
Secretariat of RVS South-West Army Group, Stalin – to all addresses.
From: Minin, Berdichev.
received 26 August 1920

In recent operations in Lvov region 1st Cavalry Army suffered heavy losses among political workers and commissars, who fell, fighting heroically side by side with commanders and non-Party soldiers. Revolutionary Military Council 1st Cavalry requests that when political workers are mobilized and assigned, the Cavalry Army will not be neglected, and that the maintenance of its strength will continue to be developed.
[In black ink under telegram] Secret archive
On the instructions of Commander-in-Chief, comrade Melnichansky and several hundred mobilized comrades are proceeding there on Sunday 29 August.
Note (30 August)
On the instructions of Commander-in-Chief 100 Red commanders are assigned to 1st Cavalry Army, to be drawn from those who complete the Moscow cavalry courses on 1 September.

Signature attested

September: Makhno's influence; commissar murdered

It is not surprising that the Soviet command feared their men might go over to Makhno. The anarchist leader had considerable military ability, and enjoyed widespread support in the Ukrainian countryside, preaching on themes which had mass popular appeal – and anti-Semitism was one slogan which attracted many poorly educated peasants. Makhno had a fixed dislike and distrust of the upper classes, and to this extent he found common ground with the October Revolution and supported the idea of 'free Soviets'. He fought vigorously against Denikin, and during three separate periods joined forces with the Red Army. His last alliance with the Soviets began on 29 September 1920, when he signed an agreement with Southern Army Group to cooperate in driving Vrangel back into the Crimea, and eventually expelling all the White forces from their last stronghold.

At first glance it may seem strange that Budyonny's unruly soldiers should advocate killing 'Communists and commissars'. We have to remember that back in 1917 many people of all classes had been enthusiastic for the idea of 'Soviets', by which they understood widely-based elected 'councils' mandated to carry out the will of the 'people'. With the threat of military pressure and considerable political skill, the Bolsheviks managed to dominate the Soviets, gradually excluding all other parties from having a voice in important decisions. The population at large had only the crudest notions of what was happening in politics. They were seeking someone to blame for the shortages of food and consumer goods: the foreign word 'Communist' seemed a useful label to apply to politicians who had brought these misfortunes down on Russia. At meetings one could even find misguided simple people shouting for the 'Bolsheviks' against the 'Communists', not realizing that by 1919 the two terms were virtually synonymous. In 1919 also we find Cossacks in favour of the 'Soviets', but against the harsh regime brought in by 'Communists'. Commissars were obviously regarded as existing to ensure that Red Army units would serve the purposes of the Moscow government, and that society did not slip back into the slack and easy ways which the Communist Revolution had swept away.

In his memoirs, (1957–83) Budyonny made some attempt to find excuses for the conduct of his men. In the areas through which 1st Cavalry had to pass on their way to operate against Vrangel he claims there were many enemy agents, who provoked the men into behaving badly and breaking all the bounds of military discipline. In *Proydenny put'*, vol. 3, p. 32, he specifically mentions the disorders in Lyubar and Priluki. On p. 33 he claims that local inhabitants wishing to operate as bandits were advertising to barter items of food for arms and equipment: '15 poods of sugar for a rifle, 4 poods for a military style greatcoat, 10 poods of salt for boots, 60 poods of salt for a horse.'

f. 17, op. 109, d. 73, l.58

To: *Revolutionary Military Council of 1st Cavalry Army.*
From: *Commission Investigating case of killing of comrade Shepelev, Military Commissar of 6th Division, by soldiers of 31st and 32nd Regiments of 1st Brigade 6th Division.*

Commission acted to carry out the task assigned to it on 1 September, in village of Glinsk, this being where Headquarters of 6th Division is located.

Members of Commission – Chairman: comrade Melnichansky; Commission member: comrade Belyakov; member and Secretary of Commission: Stepanenko.

We called in for interrogation those who had actually witnessed the murder, and comrades who had been with Shepelev all day from the morning. Interrogation of the victim's secretary established that the circumstances of the murder were closely related to the general mood of the units, demoralized by counter-revolutionary elements, who had insinuated themselves into the Division, and whose work had been very effective, because commanders and commissars were completely inactive.

Since the earliest days when the units started to move, in certain groups within 6th Division a feeling started: 'Let us purge the rear of Jews – Let's go and join up with old man Makhno – Let's live without commissars and Communists'. From the very beginning commanders and commissars took no action to restrain this mood. Throughout the night before Shepelev's murder there were pogroms, looting, murder and rape.

When Shepelev arrived in the morning the looting was still going on. As Shepelev was dispersing the bandits he came across a medical attendant of 33 Regiment and a nurse, Maria Chumakova, from the same regiment, who were robbing the bodies of murdered Jews. The medical attendant tried to run away, but Shepelev shot him with his revolver, then arrested the nurse and sent her back to the unit. On her way back the nurse managed to tell some soldiers that he had killed a soldier, and this inflamed their anger: 'The Military Commissar is protecting Jews. He deserves to be killed ...' and so on.

From witnesses' testimony it is clear that no attempt was made to suppress this mounting rage by commanders of 31st and 32nd Regiments – except for two or three military commissars and squadron commanders of 31st Regiment, Cherkasov and his assistant, Sedelnikov, Kniga, and military commissar Romanov. Even when Shepelev was first wounded no effective protection was offered, which could have been done by the commanders themselves, if there was no one they could rely on for that. After killing Shepelev the soldiers went back into the ranks, as though hiding and waiting to see what would happen. When Kniga and the commanders were interrogated and asked to point out those who had carried out the shooting and murders – since the squadron and troop commanders had undoubtedly been present and knew their men's names by heart, there was a blank refusal. There was more talk, people were shuffled about – and we could not pin the blame on any individual. After the incident neither the brigade commander nor any commander took any action to find those who had done the shooting and the murder. Further investigations of units in the place called Lyubar disclosed that an organized pogrom had taken place, in which, we were told, about 60 Jews were killed; but once again the commanders had taken no steps to bring the pogrom to an end or to arrest those who had taken part in it. Then when we were with 6th Cavalry Division, there were raids on wine factories and cellars in Priluki and Vokhnovka. At Priluki 21 people were killed and 12 wounded, and many women and children were raped. According to the locals, women were being raped in the street in full public view, many of the prettiest girls taken off into the transport wagons. In Volkhnovka 20 were killed, no one knows how many were wounded or raped, and 18 houses were burnt.

In the pogrom in Priluki our whole commission witnessed with our own eyes the depravity of the units of 6th Cavalry Division, and the complete inaction, not to say approval, of the commanders.

The pogrom was started by billeting staff of 2nd Brigade before the eyes of a troop from 6th Division Staff Squadron, who had been stationed here to give protection, but who failed to protect anyone, since they just stood aside in confusion – while some of their individual soldiers even took part in the looting themselves. The military commissar of the squadron did personally try to persuade the mob to stop, but without success. Our whole commission rushed to the scene of the pogrom, dispersed the bandits, and arrested two of them, who were subsequently handed over to the squadron military commissar – and then, apparently, rescued and set free by the other soldiers.

The present pogrom broke out towards nightfall. When we arrived at the place where divisional headquarters is located we sent a note to Head of 6th Division, pointing out that it was his responsibility to send units to put a stop to the pogrom. However, although he did issue an order to the Commandant to dispatch some units for that purpose, it became obvious during our enquiries that the order had remained a dead letter. From interrogating the Head of 47th Division, who were occupying Priluki, it emerged that Head of 6th Division had told him in advance that if the cavalry were to get up to mischief then 47 Division should not touch them 'in order to avoid conflict'. When the pogrom flared up individual soldiers of 8th Special Division and 47th Division took part in it. In our opinion Head of 47th Division did not take the necessary measures to put an end to the pogrom, and in fact made no serious attempt to do so. That is obvious from his report.

The participants in the pogroms were mainly soldiers of 2nd Brigade, with some individual soldiers from 1st and 3rd Brigades.

Having encountered such a situation at the Division, we realized that the Commission could not establish who was directly responsible for the murder, and therefore would not be able to make an arrest.

The Commission is convinced that there must be a radical reorganization of the unit, that the commanders must be replaced and brought to book for their failure to take action and the way they allowed hooliganism to happen. As a matter of urgency 6th Division must be purged of its commanders and hooligan elements.

In the case of the murder of Shepelev responsibility must be laid on all the commanders of Regiments 31 and 32, except Cherkasov and Sedelnikov. In Regiment 33 Nurse Chumakova and medical attendant Nekhayev must be arrested immediately. As for the demoralization of the units, the inaction of the authorities in failing to take measures to protect the populace and consequently allowing the pogroms to happen, then responsibility must be laid on Apanasenko, on the commanders of 1 and 2 Brigades, Kniga and Pogrebov, and on all the commanders of 33rd Regiment. 3 Squadron of 33rd Regiment must be liquidated down to the last man. Only by such measures can the hooligan element be removed and the units restored to order.

Together with the appointment of new commanders it is essential to examine and replace a whole lot of military commissars who are not up to their jobs and to regularize their relations with each other, so that military commissars should have more authority in the eyes of the masses.

f. 17, op. 109, d. 73, 1. 5

To: *Chairman of Revolutionary Military Council of the Republic, comrade Trotsky VX No. 10003.*
From: *RVS 1st Cavalry: Voroshilov, Budyonny, Secretary Orlovsky.*
10 September 1920

Revolutionary Military Council Cavalry Army requests you to approve dispatch to Cavalry Army soldiers – extra to all regular supplies – of any rubber capes or felt coats which you may have in the Republic's stores. These are specially needed because the soldiers are spending some 20 hours a day in the saddle, and also because due to the bad weather and onset of the cold, the incidence of illness in the army is on the increase. Do not fail to inform Cavalry Army Revolutionary Military Council of any orders you may give.

October: moving to fight Vrangel; pogroms in Ukraine

In the summer of 1920, while the Red Army was driving the Poles back to Warsaw, the Soviet government hoped that the common people would rise to support them against the Polish gentry. Nationalism proved stronger than any remote hope of a class-based revolution. By September, as the Russians retreated in some disorder, Polish forces regained most of the territory they had lost in July. The campaign on the Red Army's western front was now winding down. On 21 September the Soviets started to negotiate peace terms with the Poles.

They had recognized that they must transfer forces from the west to deal with the last large body of Whites still operating against their regime. General Vrangel had advanced out of his base in the Crimea and overrun Southern Ukraine. From 8 to 17 October he even held a bridgehead on the west bank of the Dnieper.

On 21 September the armies massing against Vrangel were given the title of Southern Army Group, and on 27 September Frunze was appointed to take charge of them. The Army Group headquarters was established at Kharkov, and 1st Cavalry Army was ordered to proceed from its operations near Lvov to join Southern Army Group. Frunze was impatient for them to arrive, so that he could start Red Army's advance to drive Vrangel from the Crimea. Lenin tried to hasten their march by exhorting 1st Cavalry to 'heroic' efforts to proceed faster (Meijer, II, p. 326). It was during their march across Ukraine that the disorders occurred which form the main theme of this section. Bat'ko, Ukrainian for 'Father', with a hint of affection, might almost be translated as 'old Daddy Makhno'. There must also be a certain irony in thus describing one of the most redoutable and ruthless Civil War leaders whose name could strike terror into the heart of whoever he was warring with at the time. In 1918, when Soviet forces were in disarray, he won much popular sympathy by daring to come out against the German occupation of Ukraine. In the spring of 1919 he helped the Red Army against Denikin, but from 29 May broke with the Soviet government. He was briefly allied with the Reds as they pushed Vrangel into the Crimea in November 1920. In 1921 the Soviets finally forced Makhno to seek refuge in Romania.

f. 17, op. 109, d. 73, l.60

Series G for immediate dispatch. Secret archive of Central Committee Russian Communist Party (Bolsheviks).
To: Revolutionary Military Council of 1st Cavalry Army: copy to Commander South-West Army Group.
From: Chairman of Revolutionary Military Council, Trotsky; Commander-in-Chief, Kamenev; member of Revolutionary Military Council of the Republic, Danishevsky.
Telegram   Copy.
Telegraphist on duty for series G. Popov
3 October 1920

I am passing on the following message which I have received: By order of Commander South-West Army Group I forward copy of report of 2 October from comrade Primakov, Head of 8th Cavalry Division:

'I must report that today and yesterday 6th Division of 1st Cavalry Army went across the positions where my Division was stationed. As they passed through they carried out mass robbery, killings and pogroms. Yesterday more than 30 men were killed. At Salnischcha they killed the chairman of the Revolutionary Committee and his family, at Lyubar more than 50 men. Their commanders and commissars do nothing to put a stop to this. Now a pogrom is still happening in Ulanov with 3 squadrons of 2nd Brigade, 6th Division, 1st Cavalry Army. What are your instructions? Are we to use armed force against those who are involved in the pogrom? Considering that the commanders also are taking part, when we confront those who are organizing the pogrom an armed clash will obviously result between my Cossacks and Budyonny's men. I spoke yesterday with head of 6th Division, who told me that a few days ago the Military Commissar and several commanders were killed by their own soldiers because they had executed some bandits. The rank and file soldiers do not obey their commanders, and according to Commander of 6th Division they will not take orders from him either. 6th Division is proceeding to the rear areas with the slogan "Kill the Jews, Communists and Commissars and save Russia" – and the soldiers quote Makhno as the leader who gave them that slogan. There is no sign of commanders trying to control the troops. Chief-of-Staff of 33rd Regiment and Commander of 2nd Squadron of that Regiment themselves joined in the pogrom.'

Signatures.

Measures to restore order

Instructions from Commander South-West Army Group are transmitted to you in copy of telegram G series No. 1079/section/5883 ops
Chief-of-Staff South-West, Petin; Military Commissar Iordansky

I hereby order that one member of Revolutionary Military Council of the Army shall go immediately and place himself at the disposal of 8th Cavalry Division to check the truth of the above report. If the report is correct he must immediately restore order in 6th Cavalry Division, and if necessary use armed force, relying on 8th Cavalry Division. Report on this being carried out.

To: comrade Krestinsky.
From: Manager, Political Section, Officer of Chairman, Revolutionary
Military Council of the Republic.
3 October 1920

On the instructions of comrade Trotsky I am sending you a copy of the above-mentioned telegram for information.
Central Committee of Russian Communist Party (Bolshevik)
To: comrade Krestinsky.   Secret
Printed form
18 November 1920

For your information we are sending you herewith an extract from report by agent 'Kope' concerning new pogroms carried out by 1st Cavalry Army.

f. 17, op. 109, d. 73, l.62

To: Trotsky, Chairman Revolutionary Military Council, Central Committee
Russian Communist Party, Moscow.
From: Commander Southern Army Group, Frunze: Malinovsky, for member
of Revolutionary Military Council.
Telegram
Received 6 October 1920, 21.00 hrs. Decoded Office of Deputy Chairman
Revolutionary Military Council, 7 October 01.05 hrs.

New evidence has confirmed information previously reported concerning the counter-Revolutionary mood in parts of Budyonny's army. Although that information was undoubtedly exaggerated there is nevertheless a good deal of truth in it. Since Makhno is in the area of the front, and there is inevitably some contact between his units and ours, the above-mentioned information about Budyonny's army assumes special significance. This must be taken into account, even though there can be no doubt about Budyonny's own position and devotion to Soviet power. Revolutionary Military Council Southern Army Group proposes:

(1) An immediate visit to 1st Cavalry Army by one of the Party's most out-standing political activists in order to check the state of the political work and to mount a broad propaganda campaign.
(2) To settle as soon as possible the question of transferring 1st Cavalry Army to Southern Army Group, since the training of units under front-line leadership will produce better results than in the current interim situation.

> *To: Krestinsky, Central Committee Russian Communist Party; copy to Trotsky.*
> *From: Rakovsky.*
> *Telegram*
> *Received: 6 October, 23.59 hrs; decoded 7 October, 23.59 hrs in office of J. Stalin, Deputy Chairman Revolutionary Military Council of the Republic.*

Together with other measures to re-establish discipline and good order in 1st Cavalry Army, I think it would be wise to arrange a visit by Kalinin. He enjoys a certain respect to authority there.

f. 17, op. 109, d. 73, I.63

> *To: comrade Frunze.*
> *From: Chairman Revolutionary Military Council, Trotsky.*
> *Postal telephonograph*
> *9 October 1920*

Following this morning's discussion I consider that 51st Division should be placed under special care of the Moscow Soviet. L. B. Kamenev should be asked to proceed to the area of 51st Division to conduct propaganda work, transfer political workers, gifts etc. As for Kalinin, Lunacharsky, Kursky and Preobrazhensky, it would be best if they were immediately sent to join 1st Cavalry Army, and remain with it until it goes into action.

Budyonny (1957–83) says that the area through which his men had to pass was 'swarming' with White agents. Several were found by the Special Section. He claims that 'hostile elements' remained undetected, and that it was they who incited his men against the local inhabitants (*Proydenny put'*, 3, p. 12)

f. 17, op. 109, d. 73, l.65
[Sections of this handwritten document are difficult to read]

To: Chairman Sovnarkom, Rakovsky.
From: Chairman Provincial Revolutionary Military Council, Vetoshkin et al.,
Kiev.
14 October 1920; received 15 October; decoded 18 October

Recently there has been a continual deluge of complaints about the lawless behaviour of units of 1st Cavalry Army on the move. In Taraytsank the entire populace, including Soviet workers and even Soviet institutions, were robbed by units of 1st Cavalry Army as they went through. A general estimate is 150 killed. On 10 October they brought about a Jewish pogrom, a massacre of Communists. The jail was broken open, four houses were burned, 30 people were killed and 4 wounded. The Chairman of the Revolutionary Committee and his colleague were killed, all the political workers were disarmed. At Belaya Tserkov Monastery 1st Cavalry units moving through are robbing villagers and forcing the militia to do the same. They take horses even from commandants, who therefore cannot travel to Provincial or All-Ukrainian Congresses. There is a report that after units of 1st Cavalry had passed through only five of the sixteen local (*volost'*) military commissars remained; all the rest had disappeared without trace. Khodarkov Furniture Factory was plundered and many peaceful villagers slaughtered. Berdichev telegraphs that passing 1st Cavalry units are robbing the Jews; we live in fear of a pogrom. Kiev Province Military Committee reports that at Borodyansk station passing units of 1st Cavalry Army executed the staff of the Commission for Purchasing Horses, together with seven Red Army men.

The work of the Commission on Desertion has come to a halt. Budyonny's men are hunting its members in order to shoot them, and several local military commissars have been shot. Reporting this, Provincial Revolutionary Committee requests urgent action against commanders of 1st Cavalry Army to bring the lawlessness to a halt. We cannot do this with our own forces. The Punishment Squad detachments are afraid, and lack the strength to cope. Immediate orders must be given to commanders of 1st Cavalry Army, and other measures must be implemented without delay.

f. 17, op. 109, d. 73, l.64

To: Central Committee, Russian Communist Party; [note in pencil] sent also
to comrades Lenin and Sklyansky.
From: Chairman Revolutionary Military Council of the Republic, Trotsky (on
his train).
Message by direct line
13 October 1920

Since the whole Southern Army Group has been engaged in battle, a propaganda excursion into their area would not be very appropriate. Therefore, with the agreement of Revolutionary Military Council South-West Army Group, all the political workers who have arrived from Moscow have been sent without exception to 1st Cavalry Army to provide back-up in the change-over and expedite movement.

f. 17, op. 109, d. 73, l.67

To: Central Committee, Russian Communist Party, Moscow; Chairman of
the Republic, Lenin; Trotsky; copies to RVS South-West; RVS South; Avganov,
Deputy member RVS.
From: Minin, member of Cavalry Army RVS.
Telegram   Coded. Top secret
Received 16 October 1920

(1) Following the operation of 11 October, in 6th Division the rooting out of bandits and purging of the units is continuing. A total of 387 men from the criminal elements have been arrested, almost all of them from 6th Cavalry Division. To investigate this case, the Army Special Section has been called in, together with a mobile session of the Army Tribunal. The Army Tribunal should arrive today to expedite and back up the work with a complete staff.

(2) Political workers who arrived from the Centre have been divided into groups, headed by Kamenev, Kalinin, and Lunacharsky, together with Budyonny, and Head of the Army's Political Section, Vardin. They left early in the morning to join 4th, 11th and 14th Cavalry Divisions, who

have a rest today. It is intended to hold meetings by brigade, and the themes for discussion are:

(a) Reading Order No. 89 of 11 October, and the general struggle with reactionary elements and negative features in the Army.
(b) General political and special reports, related to the present moment in the internal struggle, and complete reform.

Budyonny argues against Frunze's plan

The Soviet chain of command went approximately as follows:

1. Revolutionary Military Council of the Republic (RVSR) with Trotsky as its Chairman (pred RVSR);
2. Commander-in-Chief (*Glavkom*), from 1919 to 1924 the post held by Sergey Sergeyevich Kamenev. (The letter following of 20 October is addressed to Lev Borisovich Kamenev, a member of the Political Bureau, with Lenin, Krestinsky, Stalin and Trotsky);
3. Each Army Group (front). (In 1920 Frunze commanded Southern Army Group);
4. Each Army within the Army Group;
5. Divisions;
6. Brigades;
7. Regiments.

The 1st Cavalry Army's suggestion that they should report directly to the Commander-in-Chief would have effectively promoted them from being one of several Armies within the Southern Army Group to bypassing the proper order of subordination, and elevating 1st Cavalry to be on a par with the Army Group itself.

Trotsky: Budyonny to obey Frunze

f. 17, op. 109, d. 73, l.69

To: *Comrade Kamenev, L. B.; copies to comrades Lenin and Krestinsky.*
From: Trotsky.
Direct line message coded
20 October 1920

Revolutionary Military Council of 1st Cavalry Army has again raised the question about subordinating 1st Cavalry in all respects directly to the

Commander-in-Chief. From a military point of view this demand is plainly ridiculous, and has been brought about by the extreme separatism of RVS 1st Cavalry. It was precisely to counter this attachment that I proposed attaching Gorbunov to them. You have blocked his being brought in, which I consider not right. I shall raise the question tomorrow in the Politburo. In any case I ask you to make clear to RVS 1st Cavalry that its separatism has already caused the gravest difficulties. In the coming campaign it is essential for 1st Cavalry Army to be absolutely obedient to comrade Frunze in all operational matters.

f. 17, op. 109, d. 73, l.70

To: *Comrade Kamenev L. B.*
From: *Trotsky.*
Direct line message   coded
22 October 1920

The Politburo has confirmed the attachment of Gorbunov to Revolutionary Military Council 1st Cavalry. The separatism of RVS 1st Cavalry has again manifested itself in their request to come directly under the Commander-in-Chief, which is plainly absurd from an operational point of view. It is possible that comrade Voroshilov will be transferred to an independent command, so strengthening the Revolutionary Military Council will improve the whole situation.

Frunze's plan was for 1st Cavalry to strike eastwards from Kakhovka towards Melitopol, thus cutting the routes along which the Whites would withdraw their forces from South Ukraine into the comparative security of the Crimea. Budyonny proposes that the cavalry should firstly destroy the western group of Whites near the isthmus at Perekop, and then move quickly to cut the more easterly escape route at Sivash.

For the defence of the Crimea itself Vrangel might eventually hope to defend the two narrow strips of land leading into it – at Perekop, and further east at Chongar.

f. 17, op. 109, d. 73, I.71

To: Commander Southern Army Group, Frunze; copies to Commander-in-Chief; Chairman RVSR, Trotsky; Central Committee Russian Communist Party, Lenin.

From: Commander 1st Cavalry Army, Budyonny; member of Revolutionary Military Council, Voroshilov (at Znamenka).

Telegram   coded. Top secret

21 October. Received 22 October, decoded in Field Headquarters (by Tsirit).

With regard to preliminary directive No. 0163, section 157, op 192, I should point out:

(1) Our Army cannot start its operation on 27–28 October, because, as a result of the radical purge and re-establishment of order, 6th Cavalry Division is four-days march behind schedule, and will reach the Belousovok region only on 27 October. Among those arrested were the divisional commander and two brigade commanders from 6th Cavalry Division, and, with the shortage of command staff in 8th Army, they have not yet been replaced by anyone. 11th Division is still being brought up to strength, because reinforcements from the Centre have arrived late. The Army is concentrating on achieving full battle readiness to move off on 30 October.

(2) The directive does not include an assessment and evaluation of the enemy's strengths and intentions.

(3) The directive does not cover all operations on this front, and completely omits to say anything about operations on the peninsula itself.

(4) The staggered nature of our Armies' attacks gives the enemy the chance to strike at our forces piecemeal.

(5) The separation of 2nd Cavalry Army from our main forces on the flanks deprives those units of 2nd Cavalry's support, and risks 2nd Cavalry either remaining inactive, or being overwhelmed.

(6) The enemy is undoubtedly massing his main forces as shock troops in the area of Melitopol, with the larger force at Perekop.

(7) The enemy certainly has strong reserves in the Crimea to ensure the defence of the fortified neck of land, and, if he is successful, he can reinforce the essential sector and bring the operation to an end.

For my part I would propose:

(1) Start the operation on 31 October at 20.00 hours, and time it to begin at the same moment along the whole front, keeping a strong Army Group reserve free to act.
(2) Before starting the attack, 2nd Cavalry Army should be concentrated in the area of Berislav, to combine its operations with 1st and 6th Armies.
(3) To achieve greater mobility it is absolutely essential to unite 1st and 2nd Cavalry Armies under one and the same command.
(4) Our right-hand group would have as its objective to deliver a combined blow to destroy the enemy between Perekop and the River Dnieper. 6th Army would leave two divisions in the area of Kolonchaka, Oskal and Yanov, while its other forces would break into the peninsula on the enemy's heels. If 6th Army is successful two cavalry divisions would speed behind to back them up.

   After annihilating the enemy's Perekop group, all remaining cavalry forces would be directed at Melitopol. Their objective would be to cut off the enemy's escape route towards Sivash and destroy his forces. Our right hand group would deliver a swift concentrated blow, heading towards Melitopol in support of the left-hand group.
(5) Above are the ideas which my Revolutionary conscience prompts me to lay before you.

f. 17, op. 109, d. 73, l.73

To: Trotsky, Moscow; copies to Lenin and Enukidze, All-Russian Central Executive Committee.
From: Kalinin, from his train October Revolution at Aleksandriya.
Telegram [typed in red]   Nr 1607
21 October 1920. Received 23 October. High priority to all addressees.

I have completed work with 1st [Cavalry] Army. With Frunze's agreement am proceeding by train to 2nd Cavalry Army.

f. 17, op. 109, d. 73, l.74

To: Revolutionary Military Council, 1st Cavalry; copies to Commander Southern Army Group, Commander-in-Chief; copy to mail to Chairman Soviet Defence Council, Lenin.
From: Chairman Revolutionary Military Council of the Republic, Trotsky.
23 October 12.00 hours. Decoded 23 October

In reply to your telegram 1711. In the name of RVSR I order you:

(1) To bear in mind that your responsibility is for 1st Cavalry Army, not for the entire Army Group, and to pay more attention to your own Army in order to avoid any repetition of the breakdown of order or the lawlessness the Soviet Republic has witnessed.

(2) To align your forces with the rest of the front and not to expect the front to align itself with you.

(3) To carry out in detail the directive from the Army Group Commander No. 0163, sec. 5407, op. 92. Fulfilling these orders is the personal responsibility of comrades Budyonny, Minin, and of Chief-of-Staff, comrade Klyuyev.

(4) Report to those in charge within 6 hours of receiving this order.

f. 17, op. 109, d. 73, l.75

To: comrade Kamenev, Lev Borisovich.
From: Trotsky.
By direct line   cypher
23 October 1920

Contrary to your assertions, Revolutionary Military Council, First Cavalry, has been unforgivably wayward and tardy. If possible go and put some real pressure on them. In future avoid serious confrontations which may badly affect our aims, but make Budyonny and Voroshilov realize that Revolutionary Military Council of the Republic and Central Committee of the Party will not put up with any disruptive or independent behaviour.

November: 1st Cavalry refuse to receive delegations

The Revolutionary Military Council of the Republic, with Trotsky at its head, had the ultimate voice in matters concerning the Red Army. RVS of 1st Cavalry should by rights report not directly to the RVSR, but only through the RVS of the Army Group. The refusal to accept any delegation would be gross insubordination whichever channel was used. Headquarters obviously considered it significant that Trotsky took 'no action' in this case.

f. 17, op. 109, d. 73, I.76

To: *Revolutionary Military Council of the Republic; copies to RVS Caucasus Army Group; Field Headquarters of Chief of Staff.*
From: *Member of Revolutionary Military Council, Minin for Secretary RVS, Okunov.*
Telegram   coded. Top secret
2 November 1920

(1) A delegation to investigate the situation in the rear, under direction of Berlov, has been admitted by RVS in view of the peculiar juncture of circumstances.

(2) There have been no other delegates or delegations for this purpose, and there will be none. On this occasion RVS 1st Cavalry has resolved to turn back the delegation headed by Berlov coming to report on 1st Cavalry's rear areas.

(3) RVS 1st Cavalry requests you to detail all members of delegations guilty of disrupting work in the rear, or to arrest them and hand them over to local tribunals, acting with great care and with due regard to the tactical situation.

(4) We request you to pass immediately to Revolutionary Military Council 1st Cavalry Army material evidence or basic reasons for accusations against participants in such delegations.

Decoded in Field Headquarters of Revolutionary Military Council of the Republic. Given to comrade Trotsky. No action taken.

December: reinvigorate the Communist Party

From 1918, the Communists made strenuous efforts to recruit suitable activists into the Party, and it is claimed that some quarter of a million Party members were sent to the front. Even if we do not accept this figure fully there is no question that membership expanded at a tremendous pace. Efforts to increase Party membership continued, and at the end of 1919 it was claimed that a 'Week for the Party' brought in 14 000 new recruits from Moscow alone. Naturally it was found that some of those who subscribed had joined to further their careers, and were not over-enthusiastic for the lofty aims of constructing Socialism. Trying to get rid of these undesirables, the local Party organizations would often resort to 're-registration' of members. It may be apposite here to quote a brief extract from the Kupan' earlier in 1920:

4 April 1920 The local re-registration of Party members has been completed. The results of the re-registration are still not clear, but there are grounds for thinking that there will be very few members of the Yekaterinodar organization, for we are making stringent demands on Party members, since local conditions make it essential to exercise particular care in admitting them, and there must be a thorough purge of the organization in general.

Vitolin reports the wilder spirits in the 1st Cavalry as picking up the current jargon when they claim they want to 'purge the rear'. I have retained the conventional translation 'purge' for the Russian verb *chistit'*. As the 1920s went by, political confrontations within the Party were often resolved by so-called 'purges'. In the 1930s expulsion from the Party was seen as the first step in the disgrace and ruin of any Communist, and huge numbers were then condemned to be shot or sent to labour camps, where the chances of survival were weighted against them.

f. 17, op. 109, d. 73, l.92

To: *Central Committee, Russian Communist Party, Moscow.*
From: *P. Vitolin (Party ticket 759.151), Southern Army Group Political Section.*
17 December 1920

In issue 772 of *Poverty (Bednota)* of 5 November there was an article by comrade Vardin, Head of Army Political Section, in which it is stated literally: 'The mood of our troops is excellent'. The idea that all is well, everything is going fine was emphasized by elections to the All-Ukrainian Conference, which turned out to have chosen no one but selected Directors of Political Work, Heads of Army Political Sections, members of Revolutionary Military Councils, and Military Commissars of Divisions. Having worked in 1st Cavalry Army for two months as a member of South-West Army Political Section with full powers for Party conference, although it was impossible to develop that work properly – which I told comrade Preobrazhensky about at the first opportunity – I am forced to conclude that all these confronting political reports are just a way of glossing over the real state of affairs.

Despite the large number of Communist Party members in the ranks of 1st Cavalry Army (about 20–25%), no Party work is being carried out. Bureaucracy has spun its own cosy little nests, both in the Army Political Section and also in the political cells. All independent activity by the masses has been stifled. Party cells have become empty names or, at best rooms in the Military Commissar's office. (Before the All-Ukrainian Conference a secret order came round, saying that 'for political reasons' it was proposed to elect Vardin, Minin, and Voroshilov to attend the conference.) Preparation for the conference has been non-existent. There is no centre giving political direction. There is, of course, the Army Political Section – indeed there are no less than five of them – but in practice they amount to nothing. They all leave things to each other, so that in the end they all do nothing and prevent each other from working. There is no connection between Army and Divisional Political Sections. In late October all the Divisional Political Sections and Field Army Political Section were in Berislav, but the latter did not know where the former were, nor what they consisted of. At Nikolayev I had to check the work of 10–12 cells, and not one of them had any contact with Army Political Section, nor had they received any directives or instructions for the past 2–3 months. Very often political institutions are headed by people who are totally politically illiterate. (The Head of 4th Division is a former Guards officer, and when the political workers make their reports they have to deliver them standing to attention and saluting.) When such political workers are appointed, no one asks to what extent this one or that one may be able to take charge of the work, but only how subservient or obedient they may be. There are experienced and able Party workers occupying minor posts. I met one nationally qualified teacher, who had graduated from the University of Sverdlovsk, and was working in the Field Political Section as a messenger. 'The horse's head symbol has replaced the Red Star', so say the political workers. This phrase aptly defines the state of all political work in 1st Cavalry Army. One can meet Communists who refuse to answer this or that question which a soldier may put, or even to discuss them. Because there is no Party setting, young Communists – and quite often older ones – submit to the atmosphere around them.

The units are, as one Party worker put it, in a 'fighting' mood: 'Kill the Jews and the Communists, and save Russia'. Frequently one could hear: 'We'll finish off Vrangel, we'll go and fight the Commune, we'll go to "purge" the rear'. The period of pogroms, rape and looting has for the moment subsided, or, more correctly they have been subsumed in military activities, and become less prominent. If there is another long period of quiet all these anti-Soviet, anti-Communist forces will show up again. Amassing personal possessions is common. In the Party cells there have appeared a whole series of senior comrades who go about with carts in tow, with winter coats of fox fur and other clobber. Treasure hunters are a common sight. People in areas traversed by units of 1st Cavalry have been literally terrorized. I myself witnessed the following scene: a peasant who was going along with a pair of horses pulling his cart was being chased by a Red Army man on horseback who was firing at him. The soldier wanted to exchange horses. (Horse trading has become almost a recognized occupation.) Pursuer and pursued raced towards our detachment with Chief-of-Field-Staff and the Military Commissar riding at its head. The peasant went off home with his own horses, and the Red Army man was told to return to his unit – and that was all. He was not even reprimanded. And there are many such instances.

On the basis of a wealth of material collected in all Divisional and Army Political Sections, the Political Inspectorate has decided to propose to South-West Army Group Political Section the following measures which should be implemented in full:

(1) Establish a close link between the Centre and the Army with regular visits by the Political Inspectorate. The personnel to be selected from people, who have not only theoretical knowledge, but also organizational skills.

(2) Organize a single political centre, in which the instructors can be brought together.

(3) It is essential to replace Head of Political Section, Vardin; Deputy Head of Political Section, Shulgin; Secretary of Field Army Political Section, Kleymenov; Head of Soviet Department, Vishnek; Head of Political Education Section, Plotnikov. The individuals replacing them should be sent from the Centre.

(4) A whole series of Party workers at less responsible levels must be removed and replaced by those in the ranks of the Army.

(5) Reassign political workers to different jobs.

(6) Instead of being selected from people who are dumbly obedient to their leaders, conferences should spend their time examining Party work.

(7) We must get rid of all those ways to stifle grievances and cancel all orders made 'for political reasons'. A healthy Party climate must be created, with a unified Agitation and Propaganda Section, and an end to all pogroms, all hoarding up personal possessions, and anti-Semitism. The dreadful events that took place in 6th Division came about because there had been no political education, and the blame lies not only with the 141 Red Army men who were shot but with the Political Section itself.

(8) For administrative work cadres should be chosen from those already in the Army.

(9) Form a body of lecturers (mounted).

(10) Put a stop to the unconstrained behaviour of 1st Cavalry Army.

(11) Introduce into 1st Cavalry Army a group of comrades who have full powers and are fully determined to use them.

One copy will be submitted to Southern Army Group Political Section, another copy as a report to Central Committee of Russian Communist Party.

The visit to Central Committee did not take place because of misunderstandings which occurred between colleagues in the Political Inspectorate on the one hand and Inspector of Southern Army Group Political Section on the other, who during his time in 1st Cavalry took on the post of Deputy Head of Political Section of the Army.

Central Committee may at any time demand to see any papers, and may call anyone it wishes to see to make a personal report.

Unless measures of some sort are urgently taken in order to get Party work properly done, then you may expect to hear from 1st Cavalry Army not a few surprises – like firing on the train of Revolutionary Military Council, attacks on Cheka, pogroms against the populace.

My address: P. Vitolin, Southern Army Group Political Section, editor of newspaper *Red Donets Basin (Krasny Donbas)*.

Appendix I: Glossary and Abbreviations

(D) refers to terms used by the Don Army.

Accounts Clerk (D)	Schotnyy chinovnik
Almighty Voysko of the Don (D)	Vsevelikoye Voysko Donskoye (White Cossacks under Krasnov, Bogayevsky)
All-Russian Central Executive Committee of the Soviets	Vserossiysky Tsentralnyy Ispolnitelnyy Komitet (VtsIK) Sovetov
All-Russian Cheka	Vserossiyskaya Chrezvychaynaya komissiya po borbe s kontrrevolyutsiyey i sabotazhem
All-Russian Chief of Staff	Vserossiysky glava shtaba (Vseroglavshtaba)
All-Russian Constituent Assembly	Vserossiyskoye uchreditellnoye sobraniye
All-Russian Council of the National Economy	Vserossiysky sovet narodnogo khozyaystva (VSNKh)
All-Russian General Staff	Vserossiysky glavnyy shtab
All-Union	vsesoyuznyy
Almighty Voysko of the Don (D)	Vsevelikoye Voysko Donskoye (White Cossacks under Kaledin, Krasnov, Bogayevsky)
anti-profiteer detachment	zagraditelny otryad (formed in January 1918 to protect food stocks and prevent illegal trading)
area	(1) volost' (subdivision of okrug) (2) rayon
Armed Forces of South Russia	Vooruzhonyye Sily Yuzhnoy Rossii, name given to the joint White forces in January 1919. Denikin was placed in overall command of: (1) Volunteer Army (May-Mayevsky), (2) Almighty Voysko of the Don (Don Cossacks under Krasnov, succeeded in February 1919 by Afrikan Bogayevsky), (3) Kiev District (Dragomirov), (4) Caucasus Army (Vrangel)
Armoured Car Section (D)	Bronevoy divizion
Armoured Car Squad (D)	Bronevoy vzvod
Army Group	front
army in the field (D)	deystvuyushchaya armiya
Army Technical Branch	armeysky tekhnichesky kontingent (armtekont)

239

arshin	pre-revolution measure of length, 0.71 metres approx.
Assistant	Pomoshchnik
attested	utverzhdayu (*lit.* 'I confirm')
audit commission	khozyaystvennaya komissiya
Auditor (D)	Kontrol'
authorized representative	upolnomochennyy (upol-)
Base Food Shop	Bazprodmagazin
Black Hundreds	Chornyye Sotni (extremist right wing Russian nationalists, noted for their anti-Semitism)
Board of Criminal Investigation	Upravleniye Ugolovnogo Rozyska
Caucasus Front	Kavkazskiy front (as the South-Eastern Front was renamed from January 1920)
Cavalry Sergeant (D)	vakhmistr
Central Committee	Tsentral' nyy komitet (TsK)
Central Management of Coal Industry	Tsential'noye prsmyshlennosti
Central School of Soviet and Party Construction	Tsentral' naya Shkola Sovetskogo i Partiynogo Stroitel' stva
Central Supply Administration	Tsentral'noye upravleniye snabzheniy (TsUS)
chain of command	armeyskiye apparaty
Cheká (counter intelligence service)	Chrezvychaynaya komissiya po bor'- bes kontrrevolyutsiyey i sabotazhem
Chief Clerk	Deloproizvoditel'
Chief Instructor	voyennyy rukovoditel' (voyenruk)
C. -in-C. (Commander-in-Chief)	Glavnokomanduyushchiy
Chief of Staff	Nachal'nik shtaba (Nashtab)
Civil Authority	Grazhdanskoye upravleniye (Grazhdupr)
command staff	komandsostav (i.e. Red Army officers, called 'komandir' in Soviet terms to avoid connotations of the word 'ofitser' from the pre-revolutionary Tsarist army)
Commission in charge of Stores	kontrekhozkomissiya
Committee for Supplies (D)	Komitet Snabzheniya
Communications Section	Otdel putey soobshcheniya
communiqué	soobshcheniye/informatsionnyy byulleten
Communist cell	kommunisticheskaya yacheyka
Comrades Court	tovarishcheski sud
Cossack ranks	*see* Ranks in White forces
Cossack Section of All-Russian Central Executive Committee	Kazachiy otdel VTsIKa
Council of Executive Heads (D)	Sovet Upravlyaushchikh Otdelami

	(administered the Voysko between sessions of the Krug)
Council for the National Economy	sovet narodnogo khozyaystvo (sovnarkhoz)
Council of People's Commissars	sovet narodnykh komissarov (Sovnarkom)
Counter-insurgency Forces	Ekspeditsionnyye voyska
creameries	maslodel' nyye arteli
Daredevil Team	komanda smel' chakov
dear	as a salutation Russians start a letter with the word *dorogoy* only if writing to family members or close friends. As documents in this selection are official communications they are prefaced with 'Esteemed' or 'Highly esteemed' (*mnogo/uvazhayemy*. Adapting to the English equivalent I have translated both these terms as 'Dear...'
de-Cossackification	raskazachivaniye
Defence Council	Sovet oborony
Department of Finance (D)	Otdel Finansov
Department of Food Supply (D)	Otdel Prodovol' stviya
Department of Information and Communications (D)	Otdeleniye Informatsii i svyazi
Department of Internal Affairs (D)	Otdel Vnutrennikh Del
Department of Public Education (D)	Otdel Narodnogo Prosveshcheniya
Director (D)	upravlyayushchiy
District	(1) uyezd, from 1929 rayon (administrative division of oblast') (2) in Cossack territory okrug (D), administrative division of Voysko (3) In 1918 the territory of the Soviet Republic was divided into 11 Military Districts
division of artillery	divizion (usually consisted of 2–3 batteries, each battery containing 8, sometimes 6 guns)
doctor	vrach
Donbass	Donetsky kamennougolny basseyn
Don Army	Voysko Donskoye, White Cossack force under (1) Kaledin November 1917 to February 1918, (2) May 1918 P. N. Krasnov; (3) February 1919 A. P. Bogayevsky. Ataman Krasnov resuscitated the old name Vsevelikoye in 1918. Allied to the Volunteer Army. Subordinated to Denikin's overall command from December 1918

Donburo	Donskoye Buro of the RKP (b)
Emergency Committee for Supplies	Chrezkomsnab
Empowered to act	upolnomochenny
ensign	praporshchik
Entente	the *Entente Cordiale*, 1904, which allied Britain and France against Germany in the First World War
Evening Times	*Vecherneye vremya*
Executive Committee	Ispolnitel' ny komitet (ispolkom)
Extraordinary Supply Commission	Chrezkomsnab
field controller	polevoy kontrolyor
field hospital	lazaret
field station	okolodka
file	delo, subdivision of opis' (the alternative form yedineniye sokhraneniya has also been abbreviated to d. in our headings)
First Cavalry Army	Pervaya Konnaya Armiya (Konarmiya)
folio	list (page in delo)
Food Supply Administration	Uprodkom
Food Supply Army	Prodovol'stvenno-rekvisitsionnaya armiya Narkomproda RSFSR (Prodarmiya)
Food Supply Section	Prodov. [ol' stvennyy] Otdel
food requisitioning	prodrazvyorstka
food supply commission	prodovol' stvennaya komisiya
Fortified District	ukreplyonny rayon (ukreprayon)
Front (Army Group)	front (exercising control over several Armies)
GARO	State archive of Rostov Oblast' (Gosudarstvenny arkhiv Rostovskoy oblasti)
GHQ (General Headquarters)	general' nyy shtab
Green Army	zelyonaya armiya
Ground forces	Sukhoputnyy otdel
harness-maker	shornik (saddler)
Head of Military Administration (D)	Nachal' nik Voyennogo Upravleniya
Head of Paper Supply	glavbum
Head of Political Section	Zavpolitdel
Head of Staff for All-Russia	Vseroglavshtab
Head of Supply Administration	Glavkhozupra
Head of Supply of Equipment	glavny nachal'nik snabzheniya prinadlezhnosti
Headquarters (HQ)	shtab
Higher Council of the National Economy	Vysovnarkhoz

Higher Military Council	Vysshiy Voyennyy Sovet
Higher rank officer (major, colonel) (D)	shtab-ofitser
Industry Board	promburo
Information input	vkhodnaya informatsiya
Information Unit	informatsionnaya chast'
inogorodniye	non-Cossack inhabitants in Voysko areas
inventory, headings of contents	opis' (subdivision of fond)
isolation hospital	barak
Junior officer	ober-ofitser
Junior NCO (D)	mladshiy uryadnik
Komsomol	League of Youth
Krug (D)	Assembly of Cossack delegates
kulaks	better off peasants, usually employing some hired labour
Labour conscription	trudovaya povinnost'
Labour Section	Otdel truda
lieutenant	podkhorunzhy
Lieutenant-Colonel, Lt. -Col (D)	Voyskovoy starshina (in Cossack regiments)
Main Commander-in-Chief	Verkhovny glavnokomanduyushchiy (Glavkoverkh)
Major (D)	(In Cossack ranks) yesaul, (theoretically equivalent to *kapitan* in Tsarist army)
Managerial Unit	Komendantskaya chast'
martial law	voyennoye polozheniye
Mayor	Gorodskaya golova
medical attendant	fel' dsher (doctor's assistant, medical practitioner lacking graduate qualification)
medical orderly	sanitar
middling Cossacks (or peasants)	serednyaki
Military Commissariat	voyenyy kommissariat (voyenkom)
Military Director	voyennyy rukoviditel' (voyenruk)
military hospital	gospital'
Military Procurements Department	otdel voyennykh zagotovok (Voyenzag)
Ministry of Food	Ministerstvo prodovol' stviya
National Economy	Narodnoye khozyaystvo
New times	Novoye vremya
Note of Report	Dokladnaya zapiska
nurse	medsestra
oblast'	sub-division of republic. The oblast' of the Donskoye voysko was divided into 9 Districts (okruga)
operations section	operativnyy otdel (operod)

Organizational Bureau of Central Committee — Organizatsionnoye Buro TsK (Orgburo)

'outsiders' — non-Cossack inhabitants in Voysko territory (inogorodniye)

Parliament (of Voysko) (D) — Krug

Party Court — Partiynyy sud

Party worker — politrabotnik

People's Commissar for — Narodny komissar

Internal Affairs — vnutrennikh del (Narkomvnudel)

Labour — Narkom truda

Land — zemli (Narkomzem)

Military Affairs — Narkomvoyen

Social Services — Narkom sotsialnogo obespecheniya

State Supervision — gosudarstvennogo kontrolya

Supplies — Narkomprod

Transport Communications — Narkomput (putey soobshcheniya)

People's police force — militsiya (in Soviet terms to avoid connotations of the word 'politsiya' from the pre-revolutionary imperial police)

Petrograd — later Leningrad, St Petersburg

Platov Revolutionary Mounted Detachment — Platovsky Revolyutsionny konnyy otryad

Plenopotentiary — upolnomochennyy

Policeman — zhandarm (gendarme). The former imperial police were thus named by those who opposed the Tsarist regime

Politburo — Politicheskoye buro (decision making organ of various bodies)

political authority — politicheskoye upravleniye

Political Education Commission — kult'prosvetkomissiya

Political Education Section — Kul'turno-Prosvetitel' nyy Otdel

political worker — politrabotnik (see also workers) Principally to undertake 'Political Education' in the ranks of the armed forces, and also among the civilian population

Political Section — politotdel

pood — pre-revolution measure of weight 16.38 kilograms approx

POW (prisoners of war) — voyennoplennyye

Principal Military Engineering Administration — Glavnoye voyenno-inzhenernoye upravleniye (GVIU)

Principal Head of Supplies — Glavnyy Nachal' nik Snabzheniy (Glavnachsnab)

Prisoner of War Section — Otd. [el] Voyenno-plen[nykh] otdel Obobshchestvlecheniya

Property Nationalization Board —

province — guberniya, replaced later by oblast'

Provincial Military Commissariat	gubernskiy voyenyy komissariat (gubvoyenkom)
pud	*see* pood
punishment squad	karatel'nyy otryad
Purchasing Bureau (D)	Zakupochnoye Byuro
Purchasing Commission (D)	zakupochnaya komisiya
quartermaster	dovol' stvennik
Rabocheye delo (newspaper)	*The Workers' Cause*
Rada	Elected Assembly in Ukraine and the Kuban'

Ranks in White forces:

From 1884, Cossack ranks had been brought roughly into line with those in the regular army:

Cossacks	*Volunteer Army*	*Approximate English equivalent*
Voyskovóy starshiná	podpolkóvnik	lieutenant-colonel
yesaúl	kapitán	captain
podesaúl	shtabs-kapitan	staff-captain
sótnik	porúchik	squadron commander
khorúnzhiy	podporúchnik	second lieutenant
podkhorúnzhiy	podpráporshchik	junior ensign (a temporary wartime rank)
vákhmistr	fel'dfébel'	sergeant-major
uryádnik	únter-ofitsér	sergeant
prikáznyy	yefréytor	corporal
kazák	ryadovóy	private

rayon	sub-division of oblast'
Red Army man	krasnoarmeyets
regimental commander (D)	polkovoy komandir
Report on political situation	Politicheskaya svodka
Revolutionary Committee	Revkom
Revolutionary Labour Army	Revolyutsionnaya armiya truda (Revtrudarm)
Revolutionary Military Council	Revolyutsionnnyy voyennyy sovet (Revvoyensovet or RVS). The body with ultimate authority over each Army Group (Front) or smaller unit. Until September 1918 the Supreme Military Council was headed by Bonch-Bruyevich. It was then renamed Revolutionary Military Council of the Republic, and Vatsetis

246 Appendix I: Glossary

RGVA (Rossiysky Gosudarstvenny
Voyenny Arkhiv)
Rifle Division
RKP (b)

RSFSR

RTsKhIDNI

Russian Communist Party

RVS
RVSR

secretariat
SEER
Senior Medical Assistant
Senior NCO (D)
shares
Signature attested
Source
South-Eastern Front

Southern Front
South-Western Front

Soviet Labour Army
Soviet regime
Soviet of People's Commissars
   (Russian Communist Government)
Special Council

Special Section

Special Service Detachments

became its Chairman until July 1919,
when he was replaced by Trotsky.
Throughout the rest of the Civil War
Trotsky held the title of
Predrevvoyensovet Respubliki
Russian State Military Archive

strelkovaya diviziya
Rossíyskaya Kommunissstícheskaya
pártiya (bol'shevikóv)
Russian Soviet Federative Socialist
Republic (Rossiyskaya Sovetskaya
Federativnaya Sotsialisticheskaya
Respublika)
Rossiysky tsentr dlya khraneniya i
izucheniya dokumentov noveyshey
istorii (former Central Party Archive,
Moscow)
Rossiyskaya kommunisticheskaya
partiya (bolshevikov), RKP (b)
Revolutionary Military Council
Revolutionary Military Council of the
Republic (the supreme body in charge
of all military strategy)
kantselyariya
Slavonic and East European Review
fel'dsher
starshiy uryadnik
aktsii
S podlinnym verno
Spravka
Yugo-vostochnyy front (Shorin's
Special Strike Force took this name
from 30 September 1919)
yuzhfront
Southern Front renamed January 1920
as Yugo-zapadnyy front
Sovtrudarmiya
Sovetskaya vlast' (Soviet power)
Sovet narodnykh komissarov
(Sovnarkom)
Osboye Soveshchaniye, established in
Yekaterinodar in August 1918. This
was intended to serve as a sort of
'government' under Denikin and
consisted of a few conservative
officials headed by General Lukomsky
Osobyy otdel (osobotdel)
(Counter-intelligence)
chasti osobogo naznacheniya (ChON)

Special Staff	Chrezvychayny shtab
squadron of Cossack cavalry (D)	sotnya
stanitsa (D)	large Cossack village, administrative centre within territory of voysko. Stanitsa names end in -aya.
State Archive of Rostov oblast'	Gosudarstvennyy arkhiv Rostovskoy oblasti (GARO)
Sub-district	subdivision of uyezd
Summary of operations	operativnaya svodka
Superintendent of Section	Zav[eduyushchiy] otd[elom]
Supply Commission (D)	prodovol'stvennaya komissiya
Supreme Commander	Verkhovnyy glavnokomanduyushchiy
Supreme Council of the National Economy	Vysovnarkhoz
Supreme Military Council	Vysshyy voyennyy sovet (superseded September 1918 by Revolutionary Military Council of the Republic) In October 1918 RVS of the Republic decreed that Red Army infantry units were to be named Strelkovaya diviziya, brigada etc. As units were seldom up to strength, divisions contained for the most part some 7 to 15 000 effectives
sympathizer	sochuvstvuyushchiy
Tax Receipt Department	Otdel povinnosti
Temporary Executive Head	Vremenno ispolnyayushchi dela (Vrid)
Temporarily carrying out the duties (D)	Vremenno ispolnyayushchiy obyazannosti
Territory	kray
To find at current address	Po mestu nakhozhdeniya
Top secret	S(overshenno) sekr(etno)
Trade union	prof[ional' nyy] soyuz
Troop Movement Section	Otd. [el] Peredv. [izheniya] Voysk
Troops for the Internal Security of the Republic	Voyska vnutrenney okhrany Respubliki (VOKhR)
Tsaritsyn	later Stalingrad, Volgograd
Ukraine Council of People's Commissars	Ukrsovnarkom
Union of Czechoslovak Associations in Russia	Soyuz Chzeckoslovatskikh Obshchestv v Rossii
uyezd	district (subdivision of guberniya)
verst (a)	pre-revolutionary measure, approximately 1.07 kilometres
Volunteer Army	Dobrovol'cheskaya Armiya, title taken from January 1918 by the White units, consisting largely of former

Voysko

War Department
Whites

with highest priority
workers

Workers' and Peasants' Defence
  Council
Workers' Settlement
working class

working-class Cossacks
yesaul

officers, coming originally under
General Alekseyev, and later headed
by Denikin
(1) One of 11 areas in the Russian
Empire settled by Cossacks. (2) Cossack
armed forces serving under the
Voysko ataman. (Voysko Donskoye
see Don Army)
voyennoye vedomstvo
Occasionally translating 'Cadets'
(Constitutional Democrats), liberal
party in Tsarist Duma. During the
Civil War the appellation 'Cadets' was
loosely applied to denote the Whites
in general
vne vsyakoy ocheredi
The term had two distinct meanings,
expressed by different Russian words:
(1) *rabochiy* someone doing physical
work, and consequently a member of
the 'working class'. (2) *rabotnik*,
generally a 'Party worker' (an official)
or a 'political worker', who was to
instil Party doctrine into the minds of
the unenlightened
Sovet rabochey i krestyanskoy
oborony
sloboda
The term 'working-class' was normally
applied to city dwellers rather than
the rural poor. Industrial workers were
regarded as unfailingly loyal to the
Socialist Revolution. It was, however,
essential for the Communists to keep
the peasants on their side, since they
comprised the overwhelming mass of
the population.
Hence the concept of:
trudovyye kazaki
see 'ranks in White forces'

Appendix II: Some Persons Mentioned

Alekséyev, Mikhail Nikolayevich (1857–1918). 1917 Commander-in-Chief of Imperial Army, Chief of Staff under Kerensky's Provisional Government; after October Revolution organized opposition to Bolsheviks in South Russia; first commander of Volunteer Army.

Antónov-Ovséyenko, Vladimir Aleksandrovich (1883–1939). December 1917 Commander of forces acting against Kaledin; March–May 1918 Commander-in-Chief of Soviet forces in South Russia.

Arálov, Semyon Ivanovich (1880–1969), November 1918 Head of Intelligence Department of Field Headquarters. June 1919 member of Revolutionary Military Council of 12th Army. In 1960s helped in campaign to rehabilitate Mironov.

Avtonómov, Aleksey Ivanovich (1890–1919). April–May 1918 Commander-in-Chief Armed Forces of Kuban' Soviet Republic, defended Yekaterinodar against Volunteer Army; 28 May removed from post for insubordination, and transferred to command armoured train in Caucasus. February 1919 died of typhus.

Baránov, Pyotr Ionovich (1892–1933). January 1918 Chairman of Military Revolutionary Committee of 8th Army; April 1918 Commander of Donets Army; June-September 1918 Chief of Staff of Commander-in-Chief, South Russia; 1919–1920 RVS 1st Army.

Barýshnikov, Vladimir Arkhipovich (1889–1919). From November 1918 to June 1919 Head of 9th Army's Political Section; from June 1919 member of Revolutionary Military Council of 8th Army. September 1919 captured by Mamontov and hanged.

Beloboródov, Aleksandr Georgiyevich (1891–1938). Head of Ural Oblast' Committee 1918, signed Nicholas II's death warrant in July. From April 1919 plenipotentiary of Workers' and Peasants' Defence Council for suppressing the Don Rebellion.

Bogayévsky, Afrikan Petrovich (1872–1934). February 1919 succeeded Krasnov as Ataman of Don Army; November 1920 emigrated from Russia.

Bogayévsky, Mitrofan Petrovich, brother of Afrikan. Supported Kaledin. Antonov-Ovseyenko executed Mitrofan 14 April 1918.

Bonch-Bruyévich V. D. (1873–1955). Head of Supreme Military Council till September 1918.

Budyónny, Semyon Mikhaylovich (1883–1973). February 1918 commanded cavalry detachment; March 1919 division; June 1919 corps; November 1919 1st Cavalry Army.

Bykadórov, Isaak Fyodorovich (1882–1957). In First World War lost sight of one eye, 1917 regimental delegate to first session of Don Voysko Krug, 1918 chosen to lead local stanitsas against Reds. 1920 emigrated.

Chichérin, Georgy Vasilevich (1872–1936). From May 1918 succeeded Trotsky as Minister for Foreign Affairs (Narkomindel). This was virtually equivalent to Foreign Secretary, and in the early 1920s Chicherin established the Soviet foreign service on a sound basis. His best-known achievement was the Rapallo Treaty with Germany in 1922, which ended the Soviet Union's isolation from world politics.

Danishévsky, Karl Yuli Khristianovich (1884–1938). 1919 Chairman of Revolutionary Soviet for Latvia; 1919–1920 Military Commissar at headquarters.

Degtyárev, ex-officer, from April 1918 appointed Chief of Staff for Don Soviet Republic. Degtyarev was one of the many former officers recruited as 'military specialists'. This policy was successfully pushed forward by Trotsky, and in the course of the civil war no less than 48 000 ex-officers were serving in the Red Army.

Deníkin, Anton Ivanovich (1872–1947). Lieutenant-General, from April 1918 commanded Volunteer Army till succeeded by Vrangel April 1920.

Drozdóvsky, Mikhail Gordeyevich (1881–1919). 1918 Colonel Drozdovky led his regiment across Ukraine to Novocherkassk. Distrusted Romanovsky and Denikin. Died 1 January 1919 from sepsis.

Duménko, Boris Mokeyevich (1888–1920). 1918 commanded Don Cossack Cavalry Division in defence of Tsaritsyn; September 1919 to February 1920 Cavalry Corps. Falsely accused of killing his political commissar; executed May 1920.

Dúndich, Tomo (1897–1920), Yugoslav. 1918 partisan leader; in International battalion defending Tsaritsyn, served under Duménko and Budyonny.

Dútov, Aleksandr Ilich (1875–1920). Ataman of Orenburg Cossacks; March 1918 sent as regimental representative to All-Cossack Congress in Petrograd. When Kolchak took power Dutov was promoted to General and nominated Campaign Ataman of All Siberian Cossack Voyska.

Dyógot, Vladimir Aleksandrovich (1889–1944). 1918 Chairman of Odessa Soviet; March 1918 retreated from Germans with 3rd Socialist Army.

Dzerzhínsky, Felix Edmundovich (1877–1926). Of Polish gentry family. Party activist from 1895. December 1917 Lenin appointed him as head of secret police (Cheka); September 1918 Dzerzhinsky started Red Terror.

Eremeev etc. (for surnames with initial 'e' *see* Ye).

Frénkel', A. A. Donburo delegate to 8th Party Congress. Wrote a day by day account of Podtyolkov's march from Rostov towards the north in May 1918, and this was published as *Eagles of the Revolution (Orly revolyutsii)* (1920). Frenkel' managed to leave Podtyolkov's expedition before other members of the detachment were arrested and executed by the Whites.

Frúnze, Mikhail Vasil'evich (1885–1925). After successes on the Eastern Front was appointed from 27 September 1920 to command the Southern Army Group, which drove Vrangel's forces from the Crimea.

Gay, Gaya Dmitriyevich (1887–1937). 1918 fought Czechs and Dutov's Cossacks; 1919–1920 commanded cavalry corps.

Gíttis, Vladimir Mikhaylovich (1881–1938). December 1918–January 1919 commanded 8th Army, January–July 1919 Southern Army Group, July 1919–April 1920 Western Army Group.

Gólubov, lieutenant-colonel. 1918 fought against Kaledin's partisans, wanted to become ataman of independent Cossack state, killed at Zaplavskaya by a student.

Grigór'ev, Nikolay Aleksandrovich (1878–1919). Supported Ukrainian Rada, Petlyura, Skoropadsky. 2 February 1919 helped Red Army against French and British. 7 May 1919 led Ukrainian units against Red Army, helped Denikin, tried to join Makhno but killed by him 27 July 1919.

Kalédin, Aleksey Maksimovich (1861–1918). Army commander in war against Germany. 30 June 1917 Ataman of Don Army (first ataman to be freely elected by all Don Cossacks). Realizing that Novocherkassk had to be surrendered to the Reds Kaledin committed suicide 11 February 1918.

Kalínin, Mikhail Ivanovich (1875–1946). From 1919 to 1938 Chairman of All-Russian Central Executive Committee; 1919–1921 headed propaganda train, making many visits to fronts.

Kámenev, Lev Borisovich (1883–1936). Chairman of Moscow Soviet. From 1920 to 1925 member of Politburo.

Kámenev, Sergey Sergeyevich (1881–1936). September 1918 Commander Eastern Front; in July 1919 against Trotsky's wishes Central Committee appointed S. S. Kamenev to replace Vatsetis as Commander-in-Chief.

Kamínsky, Grigory Naumovich (1895–1938). Chairman of Tula Provincial Committee, member of Revolutionary Military Council of Tula Fortified District.

Khodoróvsky, Iosif Isayevich (1885–1940). From January to July 1919 was a member of the Revolutionary Military Council of Southern Army Group.

Kikvídze, Vasily Isidorovich (1895–1919). Left Socialist Revolutionary; December 1917 Chairman of RVS of South-western Army Group; March 1918 defended Khar'kov. In May 1918 formed a division, which he commanded till mortally wounded in January 1919 at the village of Zubrilov.

Knórin, V. G. (1890–1938). 1917 Secretary of Minsk Executive Committee; August 1919–June 1920 Military Commissar of Smolensk District; July–September 1920 member of Minsk Provincial Military Revolutionary Committee.

Knyagnítsky P. E. Commander of 9th Army, December 1918–June 1919.

Kolchák, Aleksandr Vasil'evich (1873–1920) Admiral. Led main White movement in Siberia. November 1919 defeated, January 1920 executed at Irkutsk.

Kolegáyev, Andrey Lukich (1888–1937). February 1919 Head of Extraordinary Supply Commission for Southern Front and subsequently member of RVS of Southern Front.

Kovalyóv, Viktor Semyonovich (1883–1919). Organized Cossack section of All-Russian Central Executive Committee; 1918 Chief of Special Headquarters under Podtyolkov; 22 April Commander of Counter-revolutionary Forces in Don Soviet Republic. On Bolshevik attitude to Kovalyov *see* Murphy (1993) *The Don Rebellion*, pp. 323–4.

Krasnóv, Pyotr Nikolayevich (1869–1947). Ataman of Almighty Voysko of the Don (Vsevelikoye Voysko Donskoye), May 1918–Feb 1919.

Krestínsky, Nikolay Nikolayevich (1883–1938). 1918 People's Commissar for Finance; November 1919 to March 1921 Secretary to Central Committee.

Krivoshéin, Aleksandr Vasilevich (1857–1951). Helped Stolypin with agricultural reform; March 1919 fled to join monarchists in Kiev; from end of 1919 in charge of supplies for Armed Forces of South Russia. 1920 Vrangel' invited Krivoshein from Constantinople to be his most trusted adviser.

Krivoshlýkov, Mikhail Vasil'evich 1894–1918. Ensign in First World War; 1917 elected Chairman of Committee of 28th Don Regiment; January 1918 Secretary of Cossack Military Revolutionary Council; March 1918 member of

Central Executive Committee of Don Soviet Republic; 11 May hanged by White Cossacks.

Kropótkin, Prince Pyotr Alekseyevich (1842–1921). Anarchist. From 1876 in Western Europe. Supported Provisional Government after his return to Russia in 1917. Criticized, firstly excesses of Bolsheviks and, secondly, foreign intervention in civil war.

Kudínov, Pavel Nazarovich (1891–1967). Junior officer in 28th Regiment of Don Army. March–June 1919 leader of Upper Don rebellion.

Lánder, Karl Ivanovich (1883–1937). Plenipotentiary representative of Cheka in Don and North Caucasus.

Lunachársky, Anatoliy Vasil'evich (1875–1933). 1917–30 People's Commissar for Education.

Makhnó, Nestor Ivanovich (1889–1935). Anarchist. 1918 fought Germans in Ukraine. 1919 allied with Reds against Denikin; 29 May against Reds; September led army of 30 000 against Whites. 1920 spring and summer against Soviets; October agreed to act with Red Army against Vrangel'. 1921 raids on Soviets in Ukraine and Don territory, August forced to cross Dnestr and surrender to Romanians.

Mámontov (Mamantov), Konstantin Konstantinovich (1869–1920). 1918 commanded White partisans. 1919 appointed to command of 4th Cavalry Corps. August–September 1919 led raid deep in rear of Reds, almost to Oryol. December 1919 protested against Vrangel being given authority over Don Cossacks. Died February 1920.

Márkov, Sergey Leonidovich (1978–1918). Lieutenant-General. Commanded 1st Officers Regiment and 1st Infantry Division in Volunteer Army. Died of wounds in North Caucasus. 1st Officers Regiment renamed Markov Regiment, and subsequently infantry division also named after Markov.

Mekhonóshin, Konstantin Aleksandrovich (1889–1938). 1918 One of those entrusted with forming the Red Army. 1918–19 Member of Revolutionary Military Council of the Republic and of Revolutionary Military Council of Southern Army Group.

Mezhláuk, Valery Ivanovich (1893–1938). January–June 1919 Deputy People's Commissar for Military Affairs of Ukrainian Soviet Socialist Republic. Valery's elder brother Ivan was Head of Supplies for the Red Army.

Mínin, Sergey Konstantinovich (1882–1962). Studied in Vienna; September 1917 to June 1918 Mayor of Tsaritsyn; December 1917 to June 1918 Chief of Staff of Council for Defence of Tsaritsyn; March 1919 delegate to 8th Party Congress, joined the 'Military Opposition'; July-September 1919 member of Revolutionary Military Council of 10th Army.

Mirónov, Filip Kuz'mich (1872–1921). Lieutenant-Colonel in war against Germany. December 1917 elected Commander of 32nd Don Cossack Regiment. 1919 Condemned for insubordination, but reprieved on eve of execution. After leading his 2nd Cavalry Army against Vrangel', Mironov returned home to the Don, but local Cheka sent him to Moscow. April 1921 shot in the back while exercising in prison yard. 1960 Supreme Court cleared Mironov of all accusations made against him. The Trifonov brothers had a good opinion of Mironov, and Valentin's son Yuri wrote a fictionalized acount of his career in his novel *The Old Man* (Starik).

Ordzhonikídze, Sergo (1886–1937). Extraordinary Commissar of South Russia. Defended Tsaritsyn. Member of Central Executive Committee of Don Soviet Republic; member of Revolutionary Military Council of 16th Army; member of Revolutionary Military Council of Caucasus Front; 1920 Chairman of Bureau for Re-establishing Soviet Power in North Caucasus.

Petróv, Grigory Konstantinovich (1892–1918). Commander of 1st Southern Revolutionary Army, fought against Kaledin; from May 1918 in Ukraine; September 1918 shot as one of 26 Baku Commissars.

Podbélsky, Vadim Nikolayevich (1879–1920). Member of All-Russian Central Executive Committee; May–August 1919 granted special powers on Tambov sector of Southern Army Group.

Podtyólkov, Fyodor Grigorevich (1886–1918. 1894–1918). Lieutenant in First World War; 1918 January Chairman of Cossack Military Revolutionary Council; March Chairman of Don Soviet Republic; 11 May 1918 hanged by White Cossacks.

Polyakóv, K. S. Chief of Staff of Don Army in 1918.

Postóvsky, Vladimir Ivanovich. Major-General commanding Kuban, and Don Cossacks; October 1919 threatened Voronezh; November headed defence of Kastornoye, 15 November defeated by Budyonny's Cavalry Corps.

Rakóvsky, Khristian Georgiyevich (1873–1941). Born in Bulgaria., From 1905 active in promoting revolution in the Balkans. From January 1919 Lenin named as head of Ukrainian Soviet Government.

Rodzyánko, Mikhail Vladimirovich (1859–1924). From March 1911 President of the Duma. August 1917 supported Kornilov against Provisional Government. 1920 emigrated to Yugoslavia.

Ryabolov, Nikolay Stepanovich (1883–1919), engineer; President of Kuban Rada. Against Denikin's wishes Ryabolov wanted Kuban' Army to be independent. He was assassinated in Rostov 27 June 1919.

Rýkov, Aleksey Ivanovich (1881–1938). Plenipotentiary for Supplies for Army and Navy, People's Commissar for the Interior; after Lenin's death Chairman of Council of People's Commissars; 1938 executed by Stalin.

Serebryakóv, Leonid Petrovich (1888–1937). Follower of Trotsky condemned to death in 1937.

Shchadénko, Yefim Afanasevich (1885–1951). November 1918 member of Revolutionary Military Council of 10th Army, defended Tsaritsyn; January 1919 Deputy Military Commissar of Ukraine; November 1919 member of Revolutionary Military Council of 1st Cavalry Army (Budyonny), July 1920 of 2nd Cavalry Army (Mironov).

Shkuró, Andrey Grigorevich (1887–1947). In First World War led raids behind German lines. 1918 formed White cavalry 'Wolf pack', dressed in caps of wolf skin. Kuban' Cossacks regarded Shkuro as their hero; 1919 leader of 3rd Kuban' Cavalry Corps; October 1919 defeated at Voronezh by Budyonny; 1947 executed by Soviet Government.

Shórin, Vasily Ivanovich (1870–1938). September 1918 commanded 2nd Army on Eastern Front; July 1919 appointed to Southern Front to command so-called 'Special Group', the strike force assembled to roll back Denikin's offensive. From 30 September Shorin's 'Special Group' was renamed as the 'South-Eastern Front'.

Shulgín Vasily Vitalevich (1878–1976). Russian nationalist in Duma; March 1917 sent to demand abdication of Nicholas; after the revolution Shulgin was strongly monarchist; opposed Ukrainian independence.

Sívers, Rudolf Ferdinandovich (1892–1918). January–February 1918 in Taganrog against Kaledin; March 1918 commanded Red forces in area of Tikhoretskaya; summer 1918 commanded brigade in Ukraine; December died of wounds.

Sklyánsky, Yefraim Markovich (1892–1925). Deputy People's Commissar for War, Trotsky's most trusted supporter.

Smílga, Ivar Tenisovich (1892–1938). July 1919 member of Revolutionary Military Council of the Republic (appointed against Trotsky's wishes); 1920 Commissar of Tukhachevsky's Western Army Group.

Sokól'nikov, Grigory Yakovlevich (1888–1939). Lawyer and economist. 1917 returned with Lenin from exile. 1918–20 Member of Central Committee and Member of Revolutionary Military Council of Armies successively 2, 9, 13, 8. 1922–26 People's Commissar for Finance.

Stásova, Yelena Dmitriyevna (1873–1966). 1917–1920 Secretary to Central Committee.

Stopáni, Aleksandr Mitrofanovich (1871–1932). 1918 People's Commissar for Labour; 1920 member of North Caucasus Revolutionary Committee.

Sverdlóv, Yakov Mikhaylovich (1885–1919). Chairman of All-Russian Central Executive Committee, headed the administration of the Central Committee, and was chiefly responsible for implementing its policies.

Syrtsóv, Sergey Ivanovich (1893–1937). 1912–16 student in Petersburg. 1917 Party work in Petrograd and Rostov. 1919 favoured harsh measures against Don Cossacks. In the Soviet period Syrtsov rose to high office, clashed with Stalin and was executed during the purges.

Trífonov, Valentin Andreyevich (1888–1938). June–July 1919 Military Commissar of Counter-Insurgency Corps (father of author Yury Trifonov).

Trífonov, Yevgeni Andreyevich (1885–1937). Elder brother of Valentin. 1918 commanded joint Red Guard forces against Kaledin. Military Commissar of South Russian Oblast's. April 1919 member of Revolutionary Military Council on Kharkov front.

Trótsky (Bronshtein), Lev Davidovich (1879–1940). February 1918, as People's Commissar for Foreign Affairs, declared war with Germany finished. From March 1918 People's Commissar for War, Chairman of Revolutionary Military Council of the Republic. 1928 exiled; 1940 assassinated in Mexico.

Tukhachévsky, Mikhail Nikolayaevich. Commander of 8th Army January–March 1919.

Ulagáy, Sergey Grigorovich (1877–1946). 1919 replaced Mamontov at head of Don Cossacks (White).

Vatsétis, Ioakim Ioakimovich (1873–1938). First World War Colonel i/c Latvian Regiment which he led onto Bolshevik side. July–September commanded Eastern Army Group; September 1918–July 1919 Commander-in-Chief Red Army.

Venedíktov, Yevgeny Mikhaylovich (1895–1918). Commanded 2nd Revolutionary Army; 4 May 1918 captured and killed by Whites at Kazanskaya.

Vlásov, Andrey Andreyevich (1900–1946). 1920 fought Vrangel and Makhno. 1941 defended Moscow. 1942 captured by Germans. Led anti-Soviet Russian Liberation Army. Hanged by Soviets.

Voroshílov, Kliment Yefremovich (1881–1969). March 1918 Commander of First Lugansk Socialist Detachment, fought Germans near Khar'kov. April 1918 Commander of 5th Army. July 1918 defended Tsaritsyn. August–September 1918 member of Military Council of North Caucasus. November 1918 member of Provisional Worker–Peasant Government of Ukraine. May–June 1919 commanded the smashing of Grigorev's movement. November 1919–May 1921 member of Revolutionary Military Council of First Cavalry Army.

Vrángel' (Baron Wrangel), Pyotr Nikolayevich (1878–1928). Led Caucasus Army to capture Tsaritsyn 30 June 1919; 1920 commanded Whites in Crimea and Southern Ukraine.

Yakír, Iona Emmanuilovich (1896–1937); 1914–15 studied in Basle and Khar'kov; December 1917 elected member of Executive Committee of Bessarabian Provincial Soviet; 1918 commanded Red Guards against Romainians and Germans; October 1918 to June 1919 member of Revolutionary Military Council of 8th Army; August–October 1919 led Southern Group of 12th Army from encirclement.

Yegórov, Aleksandr Il'ch (1883–1939). December 1918–May 1919 commanded 10th Army in defence of Tsaritsyn; July–October 1919 14th Army; from October 1919 Commander Southern Army Group.

Yereméyev, Konstantin Stepanovich (1874–1931). Defended Moscow Kremlin in July 1918. July–September 1919 Commander of Voronezh Fortified Region.

Záytsev, Iosif Mikhaylovich (1890–?). 1918 commanded reconnaissance unit under Golubov. Commissar on Eastern Front. From July 1919 commissar of 1st Don Division in Mironov's Cavalry Corps.

Zemlyáchka, Rozaliya Samoylovna, real name Samoylova (1876–1947). January–July 1919 Head of Political Department of 8th Army, October 1919 to November 1920 Head of Political Department of 13th Army.

Známensky, Andrey Aleksandrovich (1886–1943). June 1919 member of Revolutionary Military Council of 10th Army; June 1920 Chairman of Don Oblast' Soviet.

Select Bibliography

Antonov-Ovseyenko, V. A. (1924–33) *Zapiski o grazhdanskoy voyne*, 4 vols (Moscow-Leningrad).

Aten, A. T. and Ormost, A. (1962) *Last Train over Rostov Bridge* (London).

Babel', I. E. (1929) *Red Cavalry* (London: A. A. Knopf)

Berz, L. I. and Khmelevsky, K. A. (eds) (1962) *Yuzhny front may 1918–mart 1919: sbornik dokumentov* (Rostov on Don).

Borokhova, I. M, Bukhanova, L. I. Perelygina, V. N. and Shcherbina, T. M. (eds) (1957) *Za vlast' sovetov na Donu 1917–1920 gg., sbornik dokumentov* (Rostov on Don).

Bradley, J. (1975) *Civil War in Russia* (London: Batsford).

Brinkley, G. A. (1966) *The Volunteer Army and Intervention in South Russia* (Indiana: Notre Dame).

Budyonny, S. M. (1957–83) *Proydenny put'* 3 vols (Moscow).

Bulgakov, M. (1973) *The White Guard* (Harmondsworth: Penguin).

Butt, V. P., Murphy, A. B., Myshov N. A. and Swain G. R. (1996) *The Russian Civil War: Documents from the Soviet Archives* (London: Macmillan).

Danilov, V., Shanin, T. and others (eds) (1997) *Filipp Mironov: Tikhiy Don v 1917–1921 gg.* (Moscow: Demokratiya).

Denikin, A. I. (1921–26) *Ocherki Russkoy Smuty* (Paris).

Frenkel', A. A. (D''aktil) (1920) *Orly revolyutsii* (Rostov on Don).

Golubintsev, S. V. (1975) 'Vsevelikoye Voysko Donskoye', *Rodimy kray*, 119.

Kaklyugin, K. P. (1924) 'Donskoy ataman P. N. Krasnov i yego vremya', *Donskaya letopis'*, 3 (Belgrade) pp. 68–162.

Kakurin, N. (1990) *Kak srazhalas' revolyutsiya*, 2 vols (Moscow: Politizdat).

Kenez, P. (1971) *Civil War in South Russia, 1918* (Berkeley).

Kenez, P. (1977) *The Defeat of the Whites: Civil War in South Russia, 1919–1920* (Berkeley).

Kenez, P. (1985) *The Birth of the Propaganda State* (Cambridge).

Kenez, P. (1984) 'The Ideology of the Don Cossacks in the Civil War', in *Russian and East European History*, ed. R. C. Elwood (Berkeley).

Khromov, S. S. (ed.) (1983) *Grazhdanskaya voyna i voyennaya interventsiya v SSSR: Entsiclopediya* (Moscow).

Kiriyenko, Iu. K. (1988) *Revolyutsiya i donskoye kazachestvo (fevral'–oktyabr' 1917 g.)* (Rostov on Don).

Kislitsyn S. A. (1992) *Variant Syrtsova* (Rostov on Don).

Kislitsyn S. A. (1996) *Gosudarstvo i raskazachivaniye* (Rostov on Don).

Klich bednoty (newspaper), Ispolkom Bogucharskogo uyezdnogo komiteta Sovetov Voronezhskoy gubernii.

Klich kazach' ei bednoty (newspaper), published by Cossack section of All-Russian Central Executive Committee, Moscow.

Klich trudovykh kazakov (newspaper), Moscow.

Krasnov, P. N. (1922) 'Vsevelikoye Voysko Donskoye', *Arkhiv russkoy revolyutsii* vol. 5 (Berlin).

Kudinov, P. (1931) 'Vosstanie verkhne-dontsov v 1919 godu (Istoricheski ocherk), *Vol'noye kazachestvo*, nos. 77–85 (Prague).

Mawdesley, E. (1987) *The Russian Civil War* (London: Allen & Unwin).

Meijer, J. M. (ed.) (1962–64) *The Trotsky Papers*, 2 vols (The Hague).

Milyukov, P. N. (1927) *Rossiya na perelome: bol'shevistsky period russkoy revolyutsii*, 2 vols (Paris).

Mironov, P. K. (1977) Letter (tr. B. Pearce) in Medvedev, R. (ed.) *Voices of the Socialist Opposition in the Soviet Union* (London: Merlin Press).

Mironov, P. K. (1988) 'Letter to Lenin, summer 1919', *Don*, vol. 12.

Murphy A. B. (1989) 'The Don after the White Retreat', *Revolutionary Russia*,

Murphy A. B. (1993) 'The Don Rebellion March–June 1919', *Revolutionary Russia*, vol. 6, no. 2, December.

Nensky, V. (1970) 'O rabote v kazachikh oblastyakh yuga', *Donskaya pravda*, 15 October.

Orlov, A. (1954) *The Secret History of Stalin's Crimes* (London).

Pearce, B. (1987) *How Haig saved Lenin* (London: Macmillan).

Polyakov, I. A. (1962) *Donskiye kazaki v bor'be s bolshevikami* (Munich).

Poole, F. C. (1962) 'Report on Visit of British Military Mission to the Volunteer Army under General Denikin in South Russia November–December 1918 (Public Record Office, WO/106/1191).

Power, R. (1919) *Under Cossack and Bolshevik* (London: Methuen).

Proletarskaya revolutsiya na Donu (*Sborniki* 1, 2 Rostov on Don, 1992; *Sbornik* 4 Moscow-Leningrad, 1924).

Rakovsky, G. V. (1920) *V stane belykh* (Constantinople).

Rodimy kray (Cossack émigré journal), Paris

Serge, and Sedova, (1975) *The Life and Death of Leon Trotsky* (London: Wildwood House).

Sholokhov, M. A., (1996) *Quiet flows the Don*, J. M. Dent, London (translation of *Tikhiy Don*, Moscow 1929–1940).

Shukman, H. (ed.) (1997) *Stalin's Generals* (London: Weidenfeld & Nicolson).

Shukman, H. (ed.) (1994) *The Blackwell Encyclopedia of the Russian Revolution* (Oxford Blackwell).

Sivovolov, G. Ya. (1995) *Mikhail Sholokhov: stranitsy biografii* (Rostov on Don).

Spirin, L. M. (1968) *Klassy i partii v grazhdanskoy voyne v Rossii (1917–1920 gg.)* (Moscow).

Stalin, J. V. (1953) *Collected Works* (Moscow).

Starikov, S. and Medvedev, R. (1978) *Philip Mironov and the Russian Civil War*, tr. Guy Daniels (New York).

Swain G. R. (1995) *The Origins of the Russian Civil War* (London: Longman).

Swain G. R. *et al.* (1996) *The Russian Civil War: Documents from the Soviet Archives* (Basingstoke: Macmillan and New York: St. Martin's Press).

Trifonov, Yevgeni (1932) (pseudonym Ye. Brazhnev), *Kalyonaya tropa* (Moscow).

Trifonov, Yuri (1988) *Otblesk kostra* (Moscow).

Trotsky, L. D. (1923–25) *Kak vooruzhalas' revolyutsiya*, vol. 1, 1923; vol. 2, 1924; vol. 3, 1925 (Moscow).

Trotsky, L. D. (1979–81) *How the Revolution Armed: Military Writings and Speeches* (London: New Park).

Vatsetis, I. I. (1919) 'Borba s Donom', *Izvestiya Narodnogo Komissariata po Voyennym i Morskim Delam* vol. 6, 8 February.

Venkov, A. V. (1988) *Pechat' surovogo iskhoda. K istorii sobytiy 1919 g. na Verkhnem Donu* (Rostov on Don).

Venkov, A. V. (1992) *Donskoye kazachestvo v grazhdanskoy voyne (1918–1920)* (Rostov on Don).

Verkhne-Donskaya Pravda (newspaper) (Vyoshenskaya 1919–20).

Wlliamson, H. N. H. (1970) *Farewell to the Don* (London).

Yegorov, N. D., Pul' chenko N. V. and Chiznova, L. M. (1970) *Putevoditel' po fondam Beloy armii* (Moscow: Russkoye bibliograficheskoye obshchestvo).

Zalesky, M. N. (1970) 'Moralno-dukhovnye sily kazachestva, Vosstaniye Verkhne-donskogo okruga', *Rodimy kray*, vol. 88.

Znamensky, A. (1987) *Krasnyye dni*, 2 vols (Krasnodar).

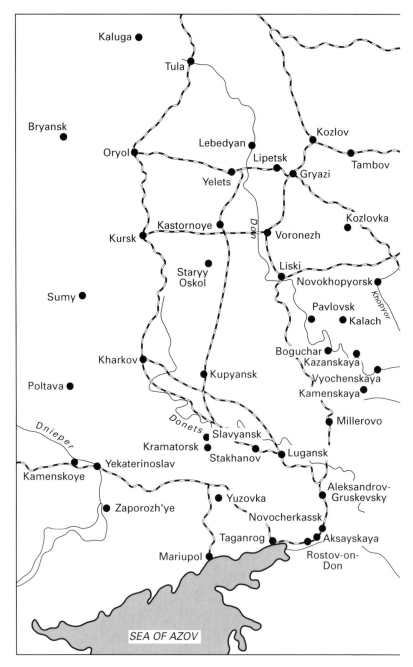

River Don and River Volga

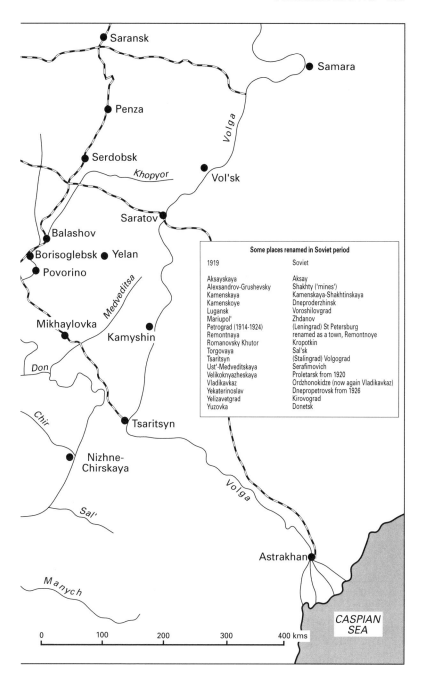

Saransk

Samara

Penza

Volga

Serdobsk

Khopyor

Vol'sk

Saratov

Balashov

Borisoglebsk • Yelan

Povorino

Medveditsa

Mikhaylovka

Kamyshin

Don

Chir

Tsaritsyn

Nizhne-
Chirskaya

Sal'

Volga

Manych

Astrakhan

CASPIAN
SEA

Some places renamed in Soviet period	
1919	Soviet
Aksayskaya	Aksay
Alexsandrov-Grushevsky	Shakhty ('mines')
Kamenskaya	Kamenskaya-Shakhtinskaya
Kamenskoye	Dneproderzhinsk
Lugansk	Voroshilovgrad
Mariupol'	Zhdanov
Petrograd (1914-1924)	(Leningrad) St Petersburg
Remontnaya	renamed as a town, Remontnoye
Romanovsky Khutor	Kropotkin
Torgovaya	Sal'sk
Tsaritsyn	(Stalingrad) Volgograd
Ust'-Medveditskaya	Serafimovich
Velikoknyazheskaya	Proletarsk from 1920
Vladikavkaz	Ordzhonokidze (now again Vladikavkaz)
Yekaterinoslav	Dnepropetrovsk from 1926
Yelizavetgrad	Kirovograd
Yuzovka	Donetsk

0   100   200   300   400 kms

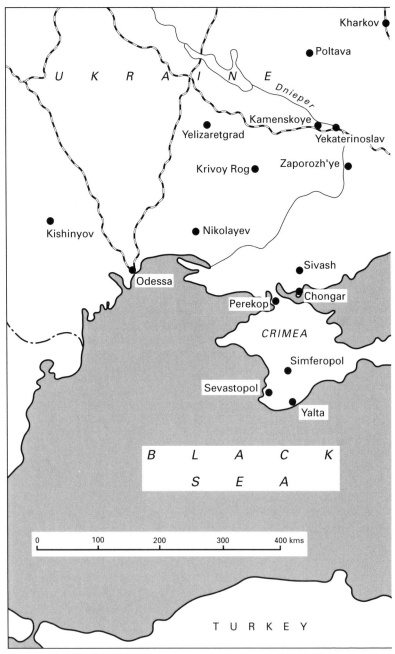

Kuban' and Black Sea

Ukraine to Polish border

Index

Notes: A few items are grouped under general headings, viz. Don, Red Army. Regiments with names are listed alphabetically. Most military reports were addressed to Central Committee, Lenin or Trotsky. Names of addressees are not normally entered in the Index.